PRECIOUS MEANINGS AND ATTAINMENT OF
HOPES FROM THE OUTPOURING OF SIDI ABU
AL-'ABBAS AL-TIJANI

جواهر المعاني
وبلوغ الأماني في فيض
أبي العباس التجاني

*Jawahir al-Ma'ani wa Bulugh al-Amani
fi Fayd Abu al-'Abbas al-Tijani*

Precious Meanings & Attainment of Hopes

From the Outpouring of Sidi Abu
al-'Abbas al-Tijani

VOLUME ONE

Al-Khalifah Ali Harazim b. al-'Arabi
Barradah al-Fasi

translated by
Talut b. Sulaiman Dawood al-Tijani

First published in 2020 by Fayda Books
2690 Campbellton Rd.
Atlanta, Georgia 30311

www.faydabooks.com
Email: info@faydabooks.com

© Copyright Fayda Books 2020
ISBN 978-1-7339631-5-2

English translation by Talut b. Sulaiman Dawood al-Tijani
Edited by Ibrahim Dimson

No part of this book may be reproduced
In any form without prior permission of the publisher. All rights reserved.

Cover design & Typesetting
Etherea Design ♦ enquiries@ethereadesign.com

Printed and bound in the United States of America

Contents

Note From Publishers	I
About the Author	III
Introduction	IX
Prologue	1
Foreword	13

SECTION ONE

1.1 General Information about Him, His Birth, His Parents, His Lineage and His Close Relatives	33
1.1.1 General Information about Him	33
1.1.2 His Birth	34
1.1.3 His Parents	35
1.1.4 His Lineage	37
1.1.5 On His Close Relatives	38
1.2 On His Upbringing, His Setting Out on the Path and His Efforts	41
1.2.1 On His Upbringing	41
1.2.2 On the Description of His Noble Form and His Magnificent Appearance	42
1.2.3 On His Setting Out on the Path	43
1.2.4 On His Effort and Struggle on the Path	45
1.3 On His Taking the Path of Guidance and Direction	53
1.3.1 On the Importance of the Path and of Knowing Allah, and the Importance of a Guide	53

1.3.2 On the Shaykhs That He Met and His Taking the Path of Guidance and Direction	54
1.3.3 On His Meeting the Prophet ﷺ, His Receiving the Illumination and the Tariqah at His Hand and His Benefitting People	62
1.3.4 On the Reason for the Compilation of This Book	64
1.3.5 On Some Good Dreams and Visions That Our Shaykh Had at the Beginning of His Life That Indicated His High Station	64

SECTION TWO — 69

2.1 On His Noble Qualities, His Spiritual States, His Station and His Completeness	71
2.1.1 Introduction	71
2.1.2 On His Ecstatic and Spiritual States	72
2.1.3 On the Station That Was Chosen for Him	75
2.1.4 His Perfection	78
2.1.5 The Reward of the Greatest Name	84
2.2 On His Emulation of the Prophetic Way, and a Description of Some of His High Conduct and His Beautiful Interaction with His Brothers and Loved Ones	95
2.2.1 His Adherence to the Sacred Law and the Sunnah	95
2.2.2 His Keeping and Strengthening of Family Ties	100
2.2.3 His Moderation	101
2.2.4 His Love of the People of the House of the Prophet ﷺ	102
2.2.5 His Excellent Character	104

SECTION THREE — 111

3.1 On His Knowledge, His Generosity, His Munificence, His Nobility, and His Faithfulness	113
3.1.1 His Knowledge	113
3.1.2 His Generosity	115
3.1.2.1 His Home and Family Life	117
3.1.3 His Nobility	120
3.1.3.1 His Forbearance and Pardon	121
3.1.3.2 His Faithfulness	122

3.2 On His Fear of Allah, His Patience, His High Aspirations, His Scrupulousness, His Asceticism, His Spiritual Counsel, and His Independence	125
3.2.1 Introduction	125
3.2.2 His Fear and Patience	1267
3.2.3 His Lofty Aspiration	127
3.2.4 His Scrupulousness and Asceticism	129
3.2.4.1 His Scrupulousness	129
3.2.4.2 His Asceticism	131
3.3 His Guiding to Allah, His Gathering People in His Way, and His Leading People to Him by His Words and Spiritual State	133
3.3.1 His Methods of Guiding	133
3.3.2 His Guiding to Repentance and Avoiding Sin and Sinful Company	140
3.3.3 His Guidance Regarding Hardships and Acceptance of the Divine Decree	143
3.3.4 His Reminding of the Blessings of Allah and Guiding to Gratitude	144
3.3.5 His Guiding People to Rely on Allah Alone	148
3.3.6 His Guidance on Loving Allah and Abandoning Self-Direction	148
SECTION FOUR	153
4.1 On His Litanies and Their Arrangement, His Path, and His Followers	155
4.1.1 Introduction	155
4.1.2 His Litanies and Their Arrangement	156
4.1.3 The Chain of Transmission of His Path	175
4.1.4 The Benefit of Being Among His Followers	176
4.2 On the Benefit of His Litany and the Description and Condition of the True Disciple	177
4.2.1 On the Guarantee for His Disciples and Lovers	177
4.2.2 On the Benefit of His Litany	180
4.2.3 On the Benefit of Seeking Forgiveness of Allah	183
4.2.4 On the Benefit of *Salat al-Fatihi*	184

4.2.5 On the Benefit of the Supplications *al-Sayfi* and *Ya Man Azhar al-Jamil*	185
4.2.6 On the Benefit of *Salat al-Fatihi*	186
4.2.7 On Why the Formula of *Salat al-Fatihi* Does Not Include "Salam"	189
4.2.8 On Various Issues Related to the Transmission from the Prophet ﷺ After His Death and the Superiority of *Salat al-Fatihi*	190
4.2.9 A Beneficial Lesson on the Multiplication of the Rewards of *Salat al-Fatihi*	195
4.2.10 On The Meaning of *Salat al-Fatihi*	196
4.2.11 Another Beneficial Lesson: More on the Multiplication of the Reward of *Salat al-Fatihi*	200
4.2.12 On the Benefit of the Noble Word (la ilaha ill Allah)	201
4.2.13 On the Benefit of His Other Litanies	202
4.2.14 On the Benefit of *Surah al-Fatihah* and *Surah al-Qadr*	202
4.2.15 On the Benefit of Various Other Litanies	204
4.2.16 On the Disciple, His Characteristics and States	206
4.2.17 On What Cuts the Disciple Off From His Shaykh	209
4.3 On the True Shaykh and the Method of the Spiritual Concert and Its People. On His Daily and Nightly Recitations and the Different Supplications That Allah Caused to Flow Upon His Tongue	**215**
4.3.1 On the Importance of Keeping the Company of a Living Shaykh	215
4.3.2 On the True Accomplished Shaykh	217
4.3.3 How to Meet a Shaykh with This Description and How He Is Recognized	218
4.3.4 Testing the Shaykh	221
4.3.5 The Obligation of Seeking a Shaykh	221
4.3.6 On the Rulings of the Spiritual Concert	223
4.3.7 On the Supplications That Allah Caused to Flow from His Tongue	225

Note from Publishers

The translation and publishing of this first volume of the Jawahir al-Ma'ani is indeed a monumental accomplishment for and by the community of Tijani followers of Shaykh Ibrahim Niasse here in the United States. Fayda Books Publishing and Distribution is indebted to Imam Shaykh Tijani Cisse for the permission granted us almost 8 years ago, to translate, publish and distribute the literature of the Muhammadan path best known as Tariqa Tijaniyya-Fayda-Ibrahimiyya. This mission has proven to be a blessing and benefit to the English-speaking world and worldwide Muslim community.

This effort owes a debt of gratitude to our beloved brother Sidi Talut b. Sulaiman Dawood al-Tijani who began translating this work several years ago. The beloved brother deserves immense recognition and praise for his effort and sacrifice. All the brethren who helped bring this book to the people deserve our most ardent prayers as well. Their efforts are greatly appreciated.

We pray this translation brings a better understanding about the life, mission and mandate of the Hidden Seal of Muhammadan Sainthood, Mawlaana Sidi Abu al-Abbas, Shaykh Ahmad at-Tijani as-Sharriff ﷺ.

May Allah give us Allah.

Ibrahim Ahmed Dimson
PUBLISHER, FAYDA BOOKS

About the Author

We have gleaned this short biography from Tijan al-Ghawani of Shaykh Sukayraj and the short biography by Dr. Zachary Wright that is included on www.tijani.org.

He is the Knower of Allah, the famous, great Khalifah, Sidi al-Hajj Ali Harazim b. al-'Arabi Barradah al-Fasi. He was from a noble, majestic family that was related to the ancient families of the city of Fez. Gifted with gnosis and consummate sainthood, Sidi Ali Harazim was known as the greatest inheritor (Khalifah) of Shaykh Ahmad Tijani, and was commended to the Shaykh by the Prophet Muhammad himself ﷺ. In a waking vision, the Prophet ﷺ told the Shaykh, "He is for you what Abu Bakr was for me." In another vision, the Prophet ﷺ, said, "O, Ahmad, consult with your greatest servant (*khadimik al-akbar*) and your beloved, Harazim, for he is for you what Aaron was for Moses." And he was the Shaykh's faithful servant and companion until his death.

Shaykh Ahmad Sukayraj said in "Tijan al-Ghawani fi Sharh Jawahir al-Ma'ani":

> The hand of Divine care pulled him from the situations of physical commerce, and took him by the hand, causing him to travel the path of eternal bliss. Thus, he profited from his commerce. And glad tidings followed.
>
> He recited what was easy for him of the Qur'an. And he perfected his *tajwid* of that which he had memorized. So, he became majestic of speech and of helpful counsel. And he had beautiful handwriting, such that even people who were unfamiliar with his

writing could easily read his script, and beautiful speech such that even non-Arabs could almost understand his clear Arabic speech.

Then, after he had studied a portion of the Islamic sciences and attained his portion of memorization of the Book and an ample portion of beautiful script, leaving the realm of *tawhid* by imitation, through knowing the proofs and evidences, he mastered, in his youth, the art of trade. So, he was present in the markets. And he traveled between Fez and other regions, seeking to profit through buying and selling. So, he obtained a portion of worldly wealth.

However, that wealth did not distract him from his religious conviction, his innate nature and his pious intention. In fact, he was frequently distracted from his worldly affairs through his dedication to the religion. While trading, he frequently read the books of the Sufis, his soul being nourished by their lofty exploits. And he was anxious to meet one of the people of the path who could take him by the hand. He longed for that every day. And that longing was rewarded in his meeting with Shaykh Tijani ﷺ.

Sidi Ali first met Shaykh Tijani in Wajda (or Oujda, Eastern Morocco) while the latter was en route to Fez after returning from Hajj. Both had received knowledge from God that he was to be associated with the other, but Sidi Ali did not immediately recognize Shaykh Tijani until the Shaykh said, "You have been told that your Shaykh on the path will be a certain Shaykh Ahmad Tijani." Much surprised at the stranger's ability to guess the content of his previous dreams, Sidi Ali replied, "Yes, that is so." Shaykh Tijani then said, "I am he." At this time, Shaykh Tijani had not yet received his own *Tariqah Muhammadiyyah* from the Prophet ﷺ, so Shaykh Tijani instructed him in the Khalwati way.

Sidi Ali accompanied the Shaykh when he settled in Fez (1798) and was responsible for composing the "Jawahir al-Ma'ani," which remains the primary source of Shaykh Tijani's life and teachings. Regarding this book, the Prophet ﷺ told Shaykh Tijani, "This book belongs to me"; and concerning the words of Sidi Ali more generally, the Shaykh used to say, "What my *Khalifah* says, I also say." He is similarly reported to have said of Sidi Ali, "No one will receive anything from me except by way of Sidi Harazim." Although he died before Shaykh Tijani, Sidi Ali is still considered the greatest spiritual successor among the Shaykh's companions, even if the greatest successor alive at Shaykh Tijani's own passing was Sidi Ali Tamasini.

After receiving the greater illumination (*fath al-akbar*), the Shaykh sent Sidi Ali Harazim to accomplish his pilgrimage to Mecca and to visit the Prophet Muhammad in Medina. Many miracles (*karamat*) and spiritual unveilings are reported on this journey, which we are not inclined to mention here. But it is clear that his lofty spiritual zeal (*himma*) touched many who encountered him on this journey, including Shaykh al-Islam Ibrahim Riyahi of the Zaytuna University who hosted Sidi Ali for several months in Tunis. Shaykh Riyahi was no doubt inspired by meeting Sidi Ali to visit Shaykh Tijani himself on a later trip to Fez.

After accomplishing the Hajj, Sidi Ali visited the tomb of the Prophet ﷺ. When he arrived in Badr on the way to Medina, he was overcome by love for the Prophet ﷺ and fell into such a deep spiritual state (*hal*) that he came to be buried among the martyrs at Badr. At the exact moment of his burial, Shaykh Tijani told his companions in Fez, "If they did not bury him, they would hear from him sciences, gnosis and secrets such as they have never heard before and have never found in any book." His grave at Badr is no longer distinguishable, like many other tombs destroyed in the last two centuries. But Shaykh Hassan Cisse, when visiting Badr some years ago, reports having been indicated the exact spot in a visionary encounter with Sidi Ali Harazim himself.

Although "Jawahir al-Ma'ani" is his magnum opus, he had a number of different writings. Among them are "al-Kanz al-Mutalsam fi Haqiqah Sirr Ism al-A'zam"- a diary of his visionary encounters with the Prophet ﷺ, "al-Irshadat al-Rabbaniyyah bi al-Futuhat al-Ilahiyyah min Fayd al-Hadrah al-Ahmadiyyah al-Tijaniyah"- a transcribed explanation of the "Hamziyyah" by the Shaykh ﷺ and "Risalah al-Fadl wa al-Imtinan"- a short treatise on the principles of the Tijani Tariqah.

License [*ijazah*] of Sidi 'Ali Harazim Given by Shaykh al-Tijani ﷺ

In the Name of Allah, the Beneficent, the Merciful. O, Allah! Bless our Master Muhammad, the Opener of what was closed, the Seal of that which went before, the Helper of the Truth by the Truth, and the Guide to Your Straight Path and his family in accordance with his grandeur and immense worth.

All praise is due to Allah. His Majesty is illustrious, His Perfection mighty, His Names and Attributes purified, His might exalted and His generosity and nobility holy. I send blessings and peace upon the most noble of His creations, our Master Muhammad and his family.

To proceed:

The lowly slave most in neeed of his independent, majestic Lord, Ahmad b. Mahammad al-Tijani (may Allah treat him with His grace and generosity in both abodes) says:

I have licensed and given permission to our true friend, the object of our affection and friendship, who we love with our complete being, starting from the inner dimension of our heart and our secret, the writer of these words, 'Ali Harazim b. al-'Arabi Barradah al-Maghribi who grew up, lives and resides in Fez. It is a universal, unrestricted, eternal, time honored license that is valid wherever he may be, in whatever state he may be, perpetually and coloring his entire being, in all that we have of exoteric and esoteric sciences, secrets, outpourings, Divine manifestation, elevations, openings and lights; in the paths of stations, ambitions, states and phases; in all that we have taken from the Prophet ﷺ- which we took directly, of exoteric and esoteric sciences, secrets, special formulas, states and remembrances.

And we have given him license and permission in the known litany which was arranged by the Master of Existence ﷺ, which he dictated, and which has a lofty status in the Muhammadan Tariqah; in all that the secrets and Ahmadan lights that it comprises; in all the paths, remembrances, prayers, names, verses, Surahs, all the names and the Named and the Greatest Immense Name which was reserved for the Messenger of Allah ﷺ, and in all its arrangements, secrets, sciences, outpourings and lights, and all its general and special *tasarrufat*, restrictedly and unrestrictedly, with a complete, universal license and permission, which comprises all kinds of *tasarrufat* without exception; in all the supplications and their different types, secrets, sciences and *tasarrufat*, forever, unendingly, permanent until the Day of Ressurrection.

And we have erected him in our place in giving al the remembrances, litanies, prayers, sciences, secrets, states, Divine manifestations, elevations, subtleties, nuances and lights that we possess.

And we have stood him in our place as a representative of us, spirit and our holy station. Thus, he stands on our behalf in our presence and absence, in our life and after out death. Thus, whoever takes from him, it is as if he has taken from us directly. It is all the same. There is no difference. If someone venerates him, he has venerated us. Whoever respects him, has respected us. Whoever obeys him has obeyed us. And whoever obeys us has obeyed Allah and His Messenger. And whoever disobeys him has disobeyed us. And whoever disobeys us, has disobeyed Allah and His Messenger. This applies to being commanded to good and forbidden evil as much as one is able.

ABOUT THE AUTHOR

We have licensed him and give him permission in all that we have read and heard, individually and altogether, a license for learning, teaching and benefiting, from the hadiths that we narrate and other knowledge.

And we have granted him permission to grant permission to others, and to transmit whatever exoteric and esoteric sciences, paths, remembrances, special invocations, secrets, and elevation to the different stations of lights that he has taken from us, and in all that we have dictated to him from our memory and in our words, and in all of the exoteric and esoteric sciences.

He may transmit our litanies and give our Path with all that it contains. And he may transmit whatever he has heard from us, narrated from us, what we have dictated to him, with the known pre-condition which has been affirmed in its proper place.

I have granted him permission and given him license to grant others permission to transmit our known litany, with it its ordained, definitive pre-condition, throughout his life and after his death. Thus, he has permission to give our Path and our litany from this moment for eternity. And he may grant permission to anyone he deems worthy for that. And he may give that person permission to give permission to others. And that may persist forever and perpetually in the eastern and western regions of the earth, until Allah inherits the Earth and all that is upon it. And He is the best of inheritors.

He has general and special permission, generally and in a special manner, restrictedly and unrestrictedly, wherever he may be, in state and station, coloring his entire being, forever, time honored and until the Day of Resurrection.

We have forgiven him and overlooked him in what he has taken or eaten from our provisions, whether he knew it or not, in open or in secret, in all of his disobedience, inwardly and outwardly, towards us, in all of his exterior and interior states, in the past and in the future, with a complete forgiveness, universally, eternally, time honored, wherever he may be, presently and in the future, for all eternity.

And he has our greatest, complete, universal satisfaction; a satisfaction which will never be followed by anger, by way of being beloved of Allah and His Messenger. And I have treated him with the treatment of the beloved, intimate khalifahs, perpetually and forever, for all eternity.

And we have made him our Khalifah and erected him in our place in the sciences, the states, the degrees and elevations, and that he may be one of those who are safe. Peace.

Written by the sinful slave, the servant of the Tijani Presence: the Lordly *Qutb* and eternal *Fard* [Saint], Mawlana Ahmad b. Mahammad al-Tijani al-Hasani, 'Ali Harazim b. al-'Arabi Barradah. May Allah his Protector and ever Gracious towards him. 8 Dhu al-Hijjah. 1214 AH. Peace

Below this license, our Master, the Shaykh ﷺ wrote with his own handwriting the following:

The granter of this license (may Allah pardon him) says:

After praising Allah. Majestic is His Greatness, Mighty is His Grandeur, Exalted is His Might and Holy is His Majesty and Generosity. I have granted license to our beloved and close friend Sidi al-Hajj 'Ali Harazim in all that he has written in this record, exactly who he has written it, from its beginning to its end, line for line and letter for letter, with a complete, universal, unrestricted, all-encompassing and eternal license… to the end of what he wrote.

Written, given license, by Ahmad b. Mahammad al-Tijani. May Allah treat him with His grace, generosity and satisfaction. May Allah bless our Master Muhammad and his family and extend them a salutation.

Introduction

In the Name of Allah, the Beneficent, the Merciful

All praise is due to Allah, the First, the Last, the Hidden and the Apparent, who sent His Beloved Messenger ﷺ ❨*reciting to them His signs, purifying them, and teaching them the Book and the Wisdom*❩ ¹; who sent him ﷺ as a mercy to all the worlds and the Seal of the Prophets. We confess that we are unable to render Him praise and that He is as He has praised Himself. And we thank Him for the blessing of the virtuous Saints whom He has kept among His believing folk from the time of the Prophet ﷺ until now; and [we thank Him] that He will keep them among this blessed nation until the beginning of the hour.

May Allah bless and grant peace to our Master Muhammad, the Opener, the Seal, the First and Last Messenger, the Helper of the Truth by the Truth, and the Guide to the Straight Path, who has not ceased to purify his nation, with the permission of his Lord, through his appointed deputies and their respective paths; who taught us the value of the Saints before Allah, saying (while quoting Allah), *"If someone showed enmity to Me through My friend, I declare war on him."* We ask Allah to reward the Prophet on our behalf- for we are unable to repay any of the favors owed to him ﷺ, to send blessings on him unceasingly from the beginning of existence, and to bless his family, companions and all those who follow them until the Day of Resurrection.

May Allah be pleased with our Master, the Seal of the Saints, the Hidden *Qutb*, the isthmus between the Prophethood and the generality of mankind, the secret of Prophethood and the benefactor of all the Saints from

---

1   Al 'Imran, 164

the beginning of creation until its end, Mawlana Ahmad b. Mahammad al-Tijani al-Hasani.

We are delighted and thankful for the blessing of presenting, for the very first time in English, the seminal Tijani work, and main sourcebook of the Tariqah Tijaniyyah, *Jawahir al-Ma'ani wa Bulugh al-Ma'ani fi Fayd Abu al-'Abbas al-Tijani*, which we have presented as "Precious Meanings and Attainment of Hopes From the Outpouring of Sidi Abu al-'Abbas al-Tijani."

This book has been, from the time it was written, the main source of the teachings of the Saintly Seal and *Qutb*, which our Master himself had approved and for which he had given license [ijazah]. It contains a concise biography of the Shaykh, including an account of his parents, his upbringing, his brethren and his setting out on the path until he met his goal in the waking vision of the Prophet ﷺ. It also contains many of the discourses and keen insights of the Shaykh regarding various issues of importance, such as the ruling on taking a Shaykh, the description of the Shaykh who is taken as a guide, the disciple's conduct with his Shaykh, and comments on various Qur'anic Ayat and Hadith.

Jawahir al-Ma'ani has received acceptance and praise from both Scholars and laymen, consummate wayfarers on the path and novices, as mentioned by Sidi al-'Arabi b. Sa'ih in his commentary on the important poem *Munyah al-Murid*, titled *Bughyah al-Mustafid li Sharh Munyah al-Murid*:

> From that which we have confirmed from the trustworthy transmitters, and what has reached us of the excellence of this book from our Master ؓ is that the Master of Existence ﷺ ascribed it to himself, saying, "This is my book. And I wrote it."
>
> And the confirmation of this noble statement has become manifest in its gaining complete acceptance, its being spread far and wide and its lofty sciences and splendid secrets being universally beneficial for both the ordinary people and the elect, despite the fact that its author had no share in the didactic sciences.

The author of *Munyah al-Murid*, Sidi Tijani b. Baba al-Shinqiti ؓ praised the book as follows:

> Cling, o, beloveds, to,
>   This book, as long as you live,
>
> It was compiled by the permission and command of TaHa,
>   And venerate this Imam according to his grandeur,
>
> Anyone who reads it with fairness, will conclude,
>   That the characteristics of the Shaykh are unique in creation,

INTRODUCTION

> For me, there is no doubt about that,
> By my Creator, I am only speaking the truth.

And Sidi al-'Arabi b. Sa'ih said, while explaining these amazing lines:

> From the blessings of this book, which are mentioned widely among the companions and brethren, in every town and city [in which they are found], is the frequency with which people enter this Muhammadan Tariqah because of their reading and inspecting it. And this has happened so frequently that one can hardly enumerate or mention them exhaustively. And I used to frequently hear one of the companions of our Master ﷺ, who was one of the head scholars and one of the majestic, noble luminaries, say, "It has been witnessed that the place in which this book is kept has such protection, plentiful sustenance, copious felicity and beautiful conduct, as can only be negated by a stubborn divisive person."
>
> One of its manifest blessings and amazing miracles is that its author ﷺ mentioned that the Master of Existence ﷺ counseled our Master ﷺ, after he ordered him to compile it, saying to him, "And guard it so that the Saints that come after you may benefit from it."
>
> And that statement has been confirmed, and to Allah belongs all praise. For many of the Saints have benefited from it. And many of the elect have wayfared along the paths that it comprised. And they derived, from it, a number of paths, all of which cause those who travel upon them, from the people of this Ahmadan Tariqah, to arrive at the Presence of the Creator. And if the only example of that was what happened to the author of the "Kitab Mizab al-Rahmah al-Rabbaniyyah," it would be sufficient supporting evidence for that which we have mentioned.

Nevertheless, as it is said, "If someone writes a book, he has exposed himself to criticism." And this book is no exception. It has been criticized by a number of people in the past and present. The two main criticisms are:

1. Its author had no formal education and, therefore, he would have been prone to mistakes. Thus, his [Sidi 'Ali Harazim's] assessment of the Shaykh's knowledge and correctness is not accepted.
2. The author has plagiarized the book "al-Maqsad al-Ahmad."

The response to the first criticism is that the majority of the main contents of "Jawahir al-Ma'ani" are contained within the book *al-Jami li Durar al-'Ulum al-Fa'idah min Bihar al-Qutb al-Maktum*, whose author, Sidi Muhammad b. Mishri al-Sa'ihi al-Hasani al-Tijani, was indeed a Scholar. Furthermore, the Shaykh's companions included a number of Scholars, including the Shaykh of Zaytuna University, Sidi Ibrahim Riyahi. The acceptance that *Jawahir al-Ma'ani* received among these companions who were Scholars, and then Scholars who were not among the Tijanis, is a testament to its correctness.

The second criticism was answered by Sidi Ahmad Sukayraj in his *Jinayah al-Muntasib al-'Ani fi ma Nasabahu bi al-Kadhib li al-Shaykh al-Tijani*, where he said:

> Some people who seek out the book *Jawahir al-Ma'ani*, which al-Khalifah al-Mu'azzam Sidi al-Hajj 'Ali Harazim Barradah wrote, have maligned the book, saying that it is plagiarized from the book *al-Maqsad al-Ahmad*, which was written by Allama Abu al-Tayyib al-Qadiri, about the righteous Saint Abu al-'Abbas Sidi Ahmad b. Abdullah Ma'n. And do not even ask about the elation shown at this criticism by some of those who harbor hatred towards the Ahmadi Tijani presence, which they discussed openly among them and used as a weapon against the brethren.
>
> The status of *Jawahir al-Ma'ani* in this Muhammadan Tariqah and its immense importance among the brethren have been evident from the lifetime of the Shaykh until the present day. Nevertheless, the Shaykh ﷺ had ordered the author to burn the things that he had written down, for reasons that his companions had not known. Perhaps one of the reasons was the fact that he arranged it according to the order of *al-Maqsad [al-Ahmad]*, which in the last few years the critics have used to malign it [*Jawahir al-Ma'ani*].
>
> I have examined three copies of *al-Maqsad [al-Ahmad]*, comparing it with *Jawahir al-Ma'ani*. And I found that their introductions were identical. And the order of their sections, for the most part, are the same. However, regarding its content related to the path, issues related to the sciences of Hadith and Fiqh, the statements of the Shaykh ﷺ, his stations and *Karamat*, none of that resembles *al-Maqsad*, except where the two methodologies meet one another in one or more occurrences that the Shaykhs had in common. However, the same exact thing occurs with many people to whom these instances occur, and they mention them verbatim.
>
> However, this is not a blemish on every writer who sees something that corresponds to the subject that he is writing on and copies it. Nevertheless, I believe that it was not attributing it to its

source that caused the Shaykh ﷺ to burn it at first. Later, when he believed that there was no harm in it, he ordered him to compile it again, as he mentioned in the introduction. And since many of the great Scholars copied texts from their original sources, which were then attributed to them, despite its original author being known, there is no harm, and all praise is due to Allah, in the resemblance between *Jawahir al-Ma'ani* and *al-Maqsad al-Ahmad*.

I have mentioned in our explanation of *Jawahir al-M'aani*, entitled *Tijan al-Ghawani*, some of the books that were attributed to someone other than their author, such as *al-Mudwwanah*, which is the mother of the books of the [Maliki] *madhhab*. And Allah refused that it should be any other way with *Jawahir al-Ma'ani*, which is the mother of the books of the path.

He concluded:

If this is reviewed, it will confirm for the intelligent that one should not pay attention to the accusations of those who demean the parts of this book that copied the words of *al-Maqsad al-Ahmad* in its introduction, or its resemblance in the arrangement of its chapters.

So, it should be clear that, despite the author's plagiarism of the introduction, to which he admitted in the introduction itself, the accusations that the book was copied from *al-Maqsad al-Ahmad* are baseless.

About Our Translation

Our Methodology

We have tried to provide an accurate, yet accessible, translation of Jawahir al-Ma'ani. The current selection of works on Tasawwuf in the English language tends to run between two currents: works, usually academic, that use technical philosophical terminology in excess and works translated by non-native speakers. I believe examples of the latter to be sufficiently visible so as not to require an explanation. So, we will focus on the need for works that are accurate but avoid the use of technical philosophical terminology.

The prevalence of philosophical terminology in Sufi texts is problematic for a number of reasons. First, outside of academia, philosophical terminology may alienate parts of our target audience- many of whom are not native

English speakers. For this group, it is difficult enough reading texts in English, let alone texts that are meant for a certain stratum of English-speaking society. Such alienation also occurs to a lesser degree among people who have an aversion toward academia.

Another reason is that technical philosophical terminology is prevalent is because academics tend to treat Tasawwuf as a purely philosophical exercise. However, the path of our Shaykh ﷺ is one of experiential taste. In fact, Sidi al-'Arabi b. Sa'ih mentions in the Bughyah, about Shaykh Abdullah b. al-'Arabi, from the Banu Mu'n al-Andalusi, "... our Master ﷺ did not take anything from him because theirs is a path of philosophy." So, avoiding technical philosophical terms as much as possible is, in our opinion, more correct.

Connected to the previous reason is the fact that the paradigm of human thought no longer corresponds to platonic and neo-platonic models. Modern human beings are more influenced by empiricism and scientific investigation. That being the case, such language, and its connotations, cease to reach the understanding of people outside of the niche audiences, such as academics.

And all of this creates a notion that *Tasawwuf* is for the rich and elites and has nothing to offer the ordinary masses. So, we wished to avoid all of this by avoiding that language. That is not to say that academia has no place in this work. We wait with expectation a scholarly and academic edition of the book, with a full study of its sources and concepts. However, our purpose is to serve as many people as possible.

The astute reader will also notice that we have made a number of changes with regard to the sections and subsections. The original Arabic text is difficult to use for research purposes, due to the sections being written without any subheadings. And there is no detailed table of contents. We have tried to make it more useful in this regard by providing subsection headers and numbering the sections. We hope that the purists among our Shaykh's blessed companions will overlook this if they consider it an aberration. We did it after much deliberation, consultation with Shaykh Muhammad al-Mahy Cisse and seeking to serve the blessed members of this Path.

Bibliographical Information

We have gleaned the translation of Qur'anic verses from various translations, editing them as we saw fit for the text. The translations that we most utilized were of Sahih International and Muhammad Asad. We have given the Surah and verse of each of the verses mentioned in the text. We have also sourced all the Hadiths mentioned in the text. For Hadiths from the more famous Sunni Hadith texts, we have given the Hadith numbers. In certain cases, when the sources are obscure, we have only given the source book. However, there are few examples of the latter.

With regard to authenticity, Hadiths from Bukhari and Muslim are generally considered authentic. So, we did not give the verdict on them. For Hadiths from other sources, as this is a devotional work and not an academic work, we have deferred to the Shaykh's knowledge, given that the illuminated Saints have different manners of determining if a Hadith is Sahih. For some, they witness a light, as mentioned by Sidi 'Abd al-'Aziz al-Dabbagh. Others meet with the Prophet ﷺ and ask him about statements attributed to him. And the Prophet ﷺ informs them of their status.

And such *karamat* can hardly be denied, since the Prophet ﷺ is reported to have said, in a *Hasan* (acceptable) Hadith narrated in *Sahih Ibn Hibban*, *"If you hear a narration from me and your heart accepts it and you have some feeling for it, then it is from me."* Such an ability is common to both the Scholars of Hadith who have a deep intuition, and for the believers who reach high states, as attested in the Hadith reported by al-Darimi. Wabisah ibn Ma'bad reported: The Messenger of Allah ﷺ said to me, *"Have you come to ask about righteousness and sin?"* I said, "Yes." The Prophet clenched his fist and struck his chest, saying, *"Consult your soul, consult your heart, O, Wabisah. Righteousness is what reassures your soul and your heart, and sin is what wavers in your soul and puts tension in your chest, even if people approve it in their judgments again and again."* We ask Allah for understanding.

Acknowledgements

We would like to thank all those who supported or helped with this project in any way. They include, but are not limited to, our Shaykh, Muhammad al-Mahy Cisse. He commissioned and gave permission for the work. Without such permission, we would not have found the acceptance that we did. I would also like to thank Sidi Alan Abguzhinov who financed the work and graciously bore patiently with us through delays and the arduous editing process. And I would like to thank all those who participated in proofreading and editing, including Dr. Jamillah Karim. I ask Allah to reward all with the highest levels of Paradise without any reckoning. Amin.

As a final word, despite our diligent efforts, no human work is perfect and without error. Whatever we have done correctly is from Allah. And we praise Him for that and thank Him. And whatever mistakes are from our own deficiencies. We ask the reader to pardon and overlook such mistakes. And if you are so kind, please inform our publisher of any mistakes in order to correct them in subsequent editions.

License [*Ijazah*] of Shaykh Ahmad al-Tijani ◈ for the Compilation of "*Jawahir al-Ma'ani*"

Shaykh Ahmad al-Tijani ◈ wrote two *ijazahs* for the book "Jawahir al-Ma'ani." The first was written at the beginning of the text and the other at the end of the text. The text of the first *ijazah* is as follows:

> In the Name of Allah, the Beneficent, the Merciful. May Allah bless our Master Muhammad, his family and companions. The destitute slave in complete need of the mercy of his Lord, Ahmad b. Mahammad al-Tijani says: I have authorized, with a universal, unrestricted, complete, abiding and eternal authorization, our beloved, Sidi al-Hajj 'Ali Harazim b. al-Hajj al-'Arabi al-Fasi, in everything compiled in this journal, on the first page of which this [*ijazah*] is written, from its beginning to its end. [He is authorized] to narrate whatever is in it from me and to act upon all of its contents, with permission in all its special secrets, whatever they may be and from whatever category they may be. And [I have authorized him] to authorize whomever he wills, however he wills, according to the well-known foundations for permission and license, according to its people, fulfilling the rule of who is competent and deserving, keeping it away from and far from those who are unworthy.
>
> Ahmad b. Mahammad al-Tijani gave the license and wrote it. May Allah treat him with his grace. And it is from our dictation to the aforementioned person of license. And Allah is the facilitator to all good through His grace.
>
> May Allah bless our Master Muhammad, his family and companions and extend them a salutation.
>
> Thursday, 29 of Rajab, 1215 AH

The second *ijazah* is as follows:

> The slave in need of Allah, Ahmad b. Mahammad al-Tijani says: The edition and correction of this manuscript has been completed. And with the help of Allah (Mighty and Majestic is He), it was blessed with a transmission and oral authority from us. Thus, there is no doubt that the manuscript at the end of which this text is written is the master copy. And every copy besides it should be compared against it. Everything in them that contradicts this copy should be left. And I have given its narrator and compiler, Sidi al-

INTRODUCTION

Hajj, 'Ali Harazim in all that it contains, since everything in it is from our dictation to him. May Allah bless our Master Muhammad, his family and companions and extend them a salutation.

جواهر المعاني
وبلوغ الأماني في فيض
أبي العباس التجاني

Jawahir al-Ma'ani wa Bulugh al-Amani
fi Fayd Abu al-'Abbas al-Tijani

Precious Meanings &
Attainment of Hopes

From the Outpouring of Sidi Abu
al-'Abbas al-Tijani

VOLUME ONE

Al-Khalifah Ali Harazim b. al-'Arabi
Barradah al-Fasi

translated by
Talut b. Sulaiman Dawood al-Tijani

Prologue

In the name of Allah, the Beneficent, the Merciful
May Allah bless our Master and Chief Muhammad, his family,
and his companions

ALL PRAISE IS DUE TO ALLAH, who outpoured upon His friends, and His chosen loved ones, lights from the Ahmadi light. And He chose for them sciences and secrets from the hidden content of His secret and the jewel of His knowledge and abundance. And He embellished them with the adornment of His loftiness and the adornments of His beauty and brilliance. And He caused them to rise into the Heaven of Divine oneness as moons.

Thus, human beings sought light from their lights and traveled by them upon His path in the religion. And they took it as a home and a place of rest. Then they became, for the spiritual wayfarers, guidance, signposts and flags on the road. And they emerged as lighthouses on every passable road. If it were not for them, no one would be capable of passing the treacherous stretches of those roadways, of rectifying the crookedness of the souls, nor would guidance have become clear to them. Then glorified be the One who chose them for wisdom and light, opened their hearts, and made them helpers and supporters of His religion.

May blessings and peace be upon our Master and Chief Muhammad from the flood of whose ocean they came to know and from the garden of whose gifts they harvested and picked fruits and blossoms. From his lights, they sought help, and from it, they inherited and took a portion. And all of them revolve around his axis. No blessing arrives, and no prayer upon the

Prophet is dispatched, except that it was sent spouting forth through his hand. He is the greatest door to Allah, His straight path, and His abundant, beneficial rain. If it were not for his blessed appearance, and his universal benefit, which opens hearts and visions, no one would taste the sweetness or the joy of arrival. Neither the goblet of love nor its drinking companion would be known. And its sweet odor would not have been inhaled. May Allah bless him, his perfect family – whose honor is perfected through his honor and perfection, and who are consecrated to majesty and honor- and his righteous companions, both immigrants and helpers, who are chosen and elect. And may He extend them a worthy salutation.

To Proceed:

The best thing to which the human being may direct his aspiration; in which he should spend his days and nights; with which he should occupy his thoughts and actions; whose remembrance he should make his constant intimate companion; what he should take as his prayer niche that he faces and his Imam; what he should seek for his path and guide; whose immense treasure he should acquire; the beautiful unmarried bride towards which he should look; from whose niche of light he should seek (fire); from whose suns and moons he should seek light; in whose gardens and thickets he should graze; from whose wells and springs he should sip; with whose fragrant scent and perfume he should anoint himself; and of which he should remind his family and loved ones; are the excellent qualities of the elect, preferred People of Allah- His Party and the People of His Presence; who have enjoyed witnessing and seeing Him; who are pulled towards Him; who direct their love towards Him; who bow and stand before Him; whose hearts are ever prostrated to Allah; who unceasingly uphold His covenant openly and secretly; the containers of the signs of the Chosen One ﷺ, his deputies and successors who sip from his inundated watering holes; who drink from his cold, pure water; who have taken on his character and disposition; and who follow his words and actions.

That is because the hearts are refreshed by their remembrance, and by it, long for the Knower of the Unseen. And they are supported by its rope to perform acts of obedience and to serve Him. Verily, it leads many people to that until determination, strength, diligence, and vigor stir within them. And they reach the point where they consider their egos more worthless than a speck of dust, and only accept high standards and rush towards that whose end is adorned by the abode of felicity. They kept their limbs free of the blemish of disobedience and sinful behavior. And they persevered in the performance of religious duties, both obligations and prohibitions, and were diligent in obtaining the pleasure of their Beloved with their spirits and souls. Then they wholeheartedly accepted what came from Him, and their stories and characteristics began to be recorded on pages.

And it has reached us that one of them said, "By Allah! I will compete with companions of Muhammad ﷺ in actions so that they know that they left behind good men." Or he said something to that effect ﷺ.

Look then, may Allah have mercy on you, at such a grand aspiration, and how it is only satisfied with high degrees. That was after he had heard about the acts of the predecessors, such that he desired to rival them. And he diligently sought after that. Allah ﷻ said:

❴So for this let the competitors compete❵[1]

O, Allah! Provide us with a lofty ambition by which we will attain every praiseworthy thing and a sincere intention by which You will cause us to refrain from every obstruction. It is said:

> If you wish to obtain,
>   Be sincere in your love,
>
> Buckle down with your firmest determination,
>   And cast aside all close attachments,
>
> The secret of sainthood only manifests,
>   To the one who is an ardent lover.

That, o, lover, is the upshot and summary of the benefit of their existence, their manifestation, and listening to their stories.

❴And none knows the soldiers of your Lord except Him❵[2]

The blessings of Allah are completely innumerable. And the hidden ones are more numerous than those we know. But to Him is all praise until He is pleased.

If we had attempted to list all of the sayings of the People (may Allah be pleased with them), and all of the excellent qualities with which they had been blessed, we would not be able to, due to short time. Then let us refrain from seeking out all of the sayings of those who came to know from the ocean of gifts and blessings and harvested the flowers of mercies and gnosis from the abode of generosity and munificence. And how should they have

---

1   al-Mutaffifin, 26
2   al-Muddaththir, 31

not, when they are people whom the Real had chosen for His service? And He made them worthy of His intimate communication and His presence. And He caused them to witness the lights of His beauty and excellence and sat them on the carpet of His perfection and grace.

They are people imbibing his love and found pleasure in it. So, their hearts became perplexed in His greatness and withdrew. Then they attained from their Lord what they sought, and He made them and gave them in their time what they desired. Thus, though they appear to be beggars, they are commanders, princes, and kings. And they are fit to be His representatives, being obedient and adhering to His service, by His decree and His will. Then life only becomes serene through them. And hearts are only reassured through their remembrance. When the natural disposition is stirred with their love, it screams and shouts out of pride for their proximity. And it says:

> By Allah! Time has not been anointed without them,
> For if it were not for them, I would not have enjoyed life,
>
> Because life is only among them and under their shade,
> And they are my comfort, my confidence, my request and my aspiration,
>
> They had placed my heart at rest, and I have nothing other than them,
> Upon them, from the Most Merciful, be the choicest salutations.

Then give praise, o, lover of their beauty and admirer of their path and perfection! Cool your eyes by them and attach yourself to their coattails. And do not incline to anything that will prevent you from their fold. And delight in what I put forth to you in these honored pages about the characteristics and special qualities of this great Shaykh, the like of whom time has not seen, except in ancient times. How excellent was the person who said:

> The excellent qualities of the People of Allah are undoubtedly abundant,
> However, the crowning glory is only for Tijan,
>
> And his Lord caused him to live in Paradise perpetually,
> And the Garden of Eden between maidens and youth,
>
> Paradise is his abode and place of rest,
> And the seat of sincerity in gardens of aromatic plants.

PROLOGUE

And someone else said with the same meaning (may Allah have mercy on him):

I swear, and I am blessed with my portion,
  No age or time has not seen the likes of him,

Yes! Confirm it, without suspicion, and reach certainty,
  No woman in all of time had given birth to the likes of him

And among those whom Allah had blessed with this honor, and placed and erected him in its station; whom He had dispatched to its highest degree and position and blessed him with its greatest sign and virtue; and who obtained in its fertile spring rain the largest allotment and the most ample portion, is our Shaykh, our Master, our means of connection, our intermediary to our Lord, the accomplished Shaykh, the complete exemplar, towering mountain, the Knower who is firmly established in gnosis, the mountain of the Sunnah and the Religion, the flag of the God-conscious and the rightly guided, the accomplished scholar, the erudite with deep understanding, the one who joined between the Sacred Law and Reality, the one who overflows light and blessing onto all of creation, the one with clear signs and secrets, the abode of munificence and honor, the ocean which has swollen and overflowed, whose special qualities are known to the elite and ordinary folk, the *Fard*[3] of the age, the lamp of the time, the virtuous Sharif, possessor of immense worth, Abu al-'Abbas, our Chief Ahmad, son of the famous saint, the grand scholar, the Shaykh, the Imam, the magnanimous exemplar, the beneficial teacher, who followed the Prophet ﷺ, Abu Abdullah Sidi Mahammad b. Mukhtar al-Tijani, may Allah be pleased with them both.

And since Allah had blessed me to know him, to flee to his army and troops; since I saw of his character, his characteristics, his excellent qualities, and his superiorities; heard from his speech, his gnosis, his indications and subtle signs, great things that rarely occur and have no equal or resemblance, and things which should be sought after and benefitted from, which pens should write down on pages, and which scholars should compose in their poems; and since some of my beloveds requested me to, I was prompted

---

3   The *Fard* pl. *Afrad* is the unique Saint in every age. He is at the station of being the *Ghawth* and the *Qutb al-Aqtab*. It may also refer to a category of unique Saints that exist outside of the *Diwan al-Awliya'*, which is what has been described in various of Hadiths, consisting of a number of categories, including the *Abdal*, the *Awtad*, the *Nuqaba'*, the *Nujaba'*, and the *Qutb*. Others say that the *Afrad* are included in the Diwan and are four. And that there are further *Afrad* outside of the Diwan. These concepts will be explained by Sidna Shaykh ﷺ throughout the book.

to write down what is easy for me and what Allah has driven me to, of knowledge of him, his path, his gnosis, his achievements, his upbringing, his wayfaring, his conduct, his characteristics, his speech, his indications, his unveilings, his saintly miracles, and his other signs and exploits.

I have compiled in this book what I witnessed directly, but only a part of that, in response to those who sought it from me, and as a gift to those who hoped for it, assisting esteemed folk and elucidating for the seekers of insight, a benefit for the lovers and a guidance for those who are connected both by lineage and by transmission. That is because connecting oneself to the People of Allah, adhering to their fold, fleeing to them and standing at their door is (in reality) connecting oneself with the fold of Allah, the Generous, standing at His great door and placing oneself under His special and general mercy. According to the Hadith in al-Tabarani, *"Verily in the days of your life, your Lord has breezes. So, seek them out. Perhaps you will obtain a breeze therefrom and will never be unhappy thereafter."*[4] How successful are they who pounced upon that, and sought it out, and assisted themselves in those breezes!

And since, according to the famous mawquf[5] traditional report, at the time of their remembrance, mercies descend, and fragrant breezes are revealed. Then what can be said in that regard about publicizing their excellent qualities and noble traits, enumerating their exploits and accomplishments, mentioning their Prophetic lives and their Mustafawi conduct- which are guidance, light and healing for souls, medicine for hearts, removal of difficulties, illumination of insights, benefit to people's inner beings, and guidance for the wayfarer and the traveler. They stir the one who listens to their narration, and they incite one to long to be in their presence. Verses and books had not been filled, mouths had not uttered, and inkwells had not written down- after the characteristics of the Messenger of Allah ﷺ, his life, his pure attributes and his exploits- anything better than their stories, exploits and miracles. That is because they are his spiritual companions and his perpetual, eternal miracle. And how excellent was the one who said:

> O, my masters! O, best of masters!
> I will decorate my time with your mention!
>
> O, best of Muhammad's companions who came after him!
> O, best of the living and the dead!

---

4   Al-Mu'jam al-Kabir, (Hadith no. 15257).

5   A *mawquf* tradition is one that is attributed to a Companion and is not narrated from the Prophet ﷺ

And even if we are not true followers and adherents, we have at least, been in their presence and obtained a little of their blessing:

> If you cannot obtain the whole, then take what part you are able,
>   If you had not experienced a downpour, at least you would have obtained a drop.

It is appropriate for the one who repeats their stories, listens to their exploits, and loves the past and present ones among them, that he should enter their abode and obtain their good treatment, or cling to something of benefit for himself. In this same vein, it is said:

> Speak what you have heard of their excellent qualities,
>   Because speaking (about it), for us is the drinking fellow of souls,
>
> And when you have been given to drink a cup therefrom,
>   It will remove from you the anguish of every misery,

May Allah cause us to be among those who love them and follow their Path and their People, and provide us with delight through their stories, lives, and exploits.

You should know, may Allah have mercy on you, that I could never, even with all of the time of the world, encompass all of our Master, our Shaykh, our Chief, Ahmad al-Tijani's ﷺ exploits, signs, feats, and miracles. That is because every time I remembered a beneficial quality, I found other beneficial qualities. And every time I pondered a sign, I found a sign greater than it. And so it was for all of his different attributes. Not to mention, he ﷺ is still living at this time- the month of Sha'ban, 1213 Hijri. So, everything that you read in this registry is only some of what happened before this date. And others will follow.

Read with care and you will find, Allah willing, numerous wondrous and sublime miracles and new insights, which will cause you to obtain a light and will deposit secrets in your heart. That is because new occurrences sound sweet to the ears. And I will mention to you here, Allah willing, what will cool your eyes and remove from you every sadness, from what I have personally confirmed as authentic, and what is sufficient for people of understanding and contemplation. That is because the exploits of this Shaykh ﷺ are innumerable, and his feats are incomprehensible. So, reports of them have been proliferated nearly overnight. And they have no known limit or measurement. We only relate a small portion thereof, because paper and pen would be exhausted from trying to record them. They are- in the eyes of people- more apparent than a fire upon a mountaintop. He spoke the truth, who composed this:

> Ask the people of knowledge, intelligence, and understanding about him,
> And those who possess erudition and piety

However, I will mention to you some of what I heard from him and what I copied from his handwriting. I will also mention the reports I received from his companions and students, and what I witnessed myself. All of this will delight the ears of the listener, fill his eyes with tears and benefit, if Allah wills, both sinner and saint. And I have included some of what I found in others' handwriting. However, I did not write anything until I had substantiated it and verified the truthfulness of the one who related it, although I assume the best of them all, since everyone I conveyed or narrated from has been described as righteous as far as I know. And they are the people of mastery, religiousness, love and respect- all of them following his example.

May Allah make me and you among those who embark upon his Path, are numbered among his Party and know his worth- and the worth of those who love him, by the honor of our Master Muhammad ﷺ, his family, and companions. Whoever clings to their coattails attains their objective, and whatever he wishes will be easily attainable. So be respectful, o, lover, when they are mentioned. And stand humbly at their door. And say, in a state of neediness, "O, Allah! Have mercy on your weak slave, even if he is stingy and oppressive." For He ﷻ has said, upon the tongue of His Messenger ﷺ, "*I am with those whose hearts are broken for My sake.*"[6] Thus, humility and neediness are the best of what a slave acquires in this abode.

And you should know, may Allah have mercy on you, that I began this blessed book at the beginning of Sha'ban in the year 1213 Hijri in Fez. May Allah watch over it with the eye of His protection. And I hope that Allah will provide us with the best of it. Verily He is Merciful, Loving. And I have not written a single letter until I had made the Prophetic prayer for guidance, taken refuge with Him, and expressed my neediness to Him alone. So, we ask Him ﷻ that He inspire us to what is most correct. Verily He is Generous, Giving.

---

6   Narrated in "Majmu' Rasa'il Ibn Rajab," vol. 1, page 294. The author narrated, saying, "Imam Ahmad (may Allah (Exalted is He) have mercy on him) narrated in his book, "al-Zuhd," with his chain from 'Imran alQasir, who said, "Musa b. 'Imran said, 'My Lord! Where should I seek you?' he said, 'Seek me with those whose hearts are broken for my sake. Each day, I come closer to them a bow's length. And if it were not for that, they would be extinguished.'"

It is not like me to dare to collect the words of the Friends of Allah ﷻ and their characteristics, nor to delve into their affairs and talents. However, I saw that the strides of the companions of our Master ﷺ had fallen short of collecting his words, and neglect of collecting his sciences and secrets had overtaken them. And I saw that though all kinds of people attach themselves to him, effort, seriousness, and earnestness had been limited to those who are annihilated. So, I began gathering these pearls in the midst of this laxity and stagnation, so that people would exert great effort for them and make obtaining them their intention and aim. And I knew that every rare item requires a search. And the rarer the item, and the less it is sought out and hoped for, it is possible that the one who truly looks for it would not find it at times, due to its status with those who know its true price and value.

So I confined myself to working on this and put all of my energy into seeking them out and gathering them- and each person is given according to his ability and strength- hoping in Allah, through my own lowly determination, which has been tarnished by rejected acts, that He beautify it by words of the Best of Creation, when he said and declared, *"A man is with the one he loves."*[7] And also by his words ﷺ, *"Whoever loves a people, he is among them."*[8] And also by his saying, *"They are the people whose sitting companion is never disgraced."*[9]

O, Allah! Just as you have blessed us firstly to recognize them, do not veil us from loving them and seeing them, and cause us to follow their customs and their Path. And do not cause separation between them and us until you make us to rest in their place, or until you enter us where they have entered, o, Lord of the worlds! And I ask you, o, Allah! That you forgive us if we write anything in excess and for what mistakes we make. Verily You are Allah, Owner of Generosity and Openhandedness. And I ask You that You do not make what we write down a proof against us. Rather, make it a proof for us, o, Lord of the worlds! And who can attribute perfection to us, while we are the containers of deficiency, errors, and mistakes, being unable to flee from the rising tide of mistakes. However, our opinion of the spiritual masters is beautiful, since they are the containers of abundant generosity.

And far be it from them that one who attaches himself to their coattails that they should neglect him, or that one flees to them that they should abandon him. For the children of their courtyard are not turned away and are not impeded from their door. He spoke well who said:

---

7   Sahih al-Bukhari (Hadith no. 3688); Sahih Muslim (Hadith no. 2639).
8   Al-Hakim narrated it in his "al-Mustadrak 'ala al-Sahihayn," without a chain of transmission, in his commentary on Hadith no. 4294. But it is supported by the Hadith, "A man is with the one he loves."
9   Sahih al-Bukhari (Hadith no. 6408); Sahih Muslim (Hadith no. 2689).

> They are my masters. They are my repose. They are my aim,
> The people of purity who have obtained all high honors,
>
> Far be it from them that one who has loved them or visited them,
> That they, my masters, should neglect him in the Hereafter.

And someone else said:

> I have, by your companionship, superiority over humanity,
> And whoever loves you has no worry,
>
> You are my goal, and there is nothing in existence other than you,
> If it were not for you, my soul and my breaths would not be perfumed,
>
> Do not neglect me, for I am the servant of your presence,
> Your place with me, o, my master, is upon my head

I hope that whoever comes upon this book will cast aside the eye of rejection and will excuse what he finds in it of appropriation and alterations, additions and subtractions, and also will rectify whatever shortcomings he may find in it. And we hope that he will repay our ignorance with pardon, overlooking and good action. That is because we are not of the people of knowledge or those acquainted with it, nor of the people of grammar and its inner workings. Only our strong love for the People of this fold and our clinging to these beloveds compelled us to this work. And when someone excuses himself, blame has been removed from him. To this someone has said:

> When the criminal apologizes, his apology wipes out his sin,
> But whoever does not accept apologies is a sinner.

Now, the time has approached for us to mention- after what we have set forth- and to clarify for the listener the mention of the superiority of this Shaykh ﷺ that we had promised him, as well as his reports, his words, his deeds, and his traditions and those lights, secrets, supplications, litanies and remembrances of his that will cause the hearts and spirits to flow, so that the hearts and souls will be reassured by it, and so that after the night of loneliness, the day of remembrance, moons, and suns may begin. So, I say, and in Allah, I seek help. And He is enough for me! And how excellent He is as a reliance and a how excellent a Helper!

I have divided its sections, subsections, biographical reports, and elements into six sections, including a foreword and an epilog. And I ask Allah to assist us from Himself with an excellent assistance. And He is (Majestic and Exalted is He) the One, the Unique, the Eternal.

Section One: On the Shaykh, His Birth, His Parents, His Pedigree, His Close Relatives, His Upbringing, His Beginning, His Struggle, His Taking the Path of Guidance and Direction. (It has three subsections.).

Section Two: On His Ecstatic States, His Spiritual States, the Station Chosen for Him and Its Perfection, His Sunni Path, a List of Some of His Lofty Conduct and Blessed Dealings with His Brothers and People Whom He Loves. (It has two subsections.)

Section Three: On His Generosity, His Munificence, His Great Chivalry and Faithfulness, His Fear of Allah, His Lofty Ambition, His Scrupulousness and Abstinence, His Spiritual Exhortation and Consecration to the Service of Allah, His Calling to Allah and Gathering to Him and His Driving People with His State and His Words Towards Him. (It has three subsections.)

Section Four: On the Arrangement of His Litanies and Remembrances, Mention of His Path, and His Followers, the Benefit of His Litany and What Allah Has Promised Its Reciter, On the Description of the Disciple, His State and What Cuts Him Off from His Teacher, On How to Recognize the Shaykh Who Is Followed in All of His Statements and Actions, On the Method of the Spiritual Concert, On What Acts He Performs in the Day and the Night and the Various Supplications Which Allah Caused to Flow Upon His Tongue According to His Honored Habit with the Hearts of the People of His Gnosis. (It has three subsections.)

Section Five: Mention of His Responses about Qur'anic Verses and Prophetic Hadiths, His Letters, His Speech, His Direction and What I Heard from the Outpouring of His Knowledge and Statements. (It has five subsections.)

Section Six: On a Host of His Miracles, Some of His Performing of *Tasrif*, Some Unveilings of His That Occurred with Regard to Some of His Companions, and an Epilog which I have placed at the end of the book, so that it would be a perfume to its ending, so that I may include some mention of his miracles, and so that it will deliver to the lover his desire, and that it would quench the thirst of his love and ardent desire.

I have called it "Precious Meanings and the Attainment of Hopes in the Outpouring of Abu al-'Abbas al-Tijani." And upon Allah is our dependence and reliance, and from Him are success, assistance, facilitation, and help. He is the Generous and the Munificent. Through Him is all strength and facilitation, and upon Him is all reliance for its completion and perfection. For there is no power except through Him, and no confidence except through Him. And He is the Protector and the Guarantor. He is sufficient for me and how excellent a guardian. And I say, through Allah is success, and He is the Guide to the Straight Path.

Foreword

At the beginning of his "al-Tabaqat," Shaykh Sha'rani ﷺ said:

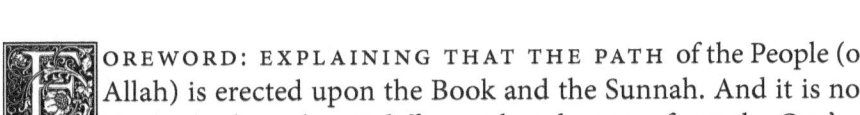

FOREWORD: EXPLAINING THAT THE PATH of the People (of Allah) is erected upon the Book and the Sunnah. And it is not blameworthy unless it differs with a clear text from the Qur'an, Sunnah or Scholarly Consensus. As for when it does not contradict them, then the most that can be said is that it is a different understanding that a Muslim person has been given. So, whoever wishes, he should act upon it. And whoever wishes, he should leave it by reason of his not understanding the action. And there remains no entry for censuring them, except having a bad opinion of them or considering them hypocrites. And that is not allowed according to the Sacred Law.

Then you should know, o, brother, may Allah have mercy on you, that the science of Sufism is a term given to the knowledge that had been kindled in the hearts of the Saints by their acting upon the Book and the Sunnah, until they were illuminated. No one acts upon them except that they kindle for him innumerable sciences, etiquettes, secrets, and realities, just as when scholars of the Sacred Law act upon what they know, rulings are kindled for them.

Thus, just as the knowledge of "*ma'ani*" and "*bayan*[10]" are the quintes-

---

10 *Ma'ani* and *Bayan* are two branches of the science of rhetoric (balaghah). *Ma'ani* is a science that deals with the structure of sentences and phrases and extracting meanings based on them. *Bayan* is a science that deals with differences

sence of the science of grammar. Sufism is the quintessence of acting upon the rulings of the Sacred Law, in a sound, non-egotistical way. And whoever deems the science of Sufism to be an independent science is correct, and whoever considers it a river from the rulings of the Sacred Law is correct, just as one who deems the sciences of "ma'ani" and "bayan" to be independent sciences is correct, and whoever deems them to be the entirety of the science of grammar is correct. However, the one who dives into the depths of the science of the Sacred Law until he reaches its limit is honored to know that the science of Sufism branched off from the river of the Sacred Law.

Then, when the slave joins the Path of the People (of Allah) and dives into its depths, Allah gives him the ability to derive rulings, in the same way that the outward rulings are derived. So, he legislates in the path obligations, recommendations, manners, prohibitions, and disliked matters that are different from the first, in the same way that the Mujtahids did. And the Mujtahid's obligating, by his legal reasoning, something that was not obligated by a clear text is not more appropriate than the friend of Allah ﷻ obligating, in his Path, something that was not obligated by a clear text. Al-Yafi'i and others have clarified this.

That all of them are trustworthy in the Sacred Law is illustrated by the fact that Allah (Honored and Majestic) has chosen them for His religion. And whoever investigates deeply will know that the sciences of the People of Allah ﷻ do not fall outside of the Sacred Law. And how could their sciences fall outside of the Sacred Law when the Sacred Law is their means of approach to Allah (Honored and Majestic) at every moment. The root of the negation of the one who has no familiarity with the People of the Path- that the science of Sufism is from the river of the Sacred Law- is his not diving into the depths of the Sacred Law. For that reason, Junayd (may Allah ﷻ have mercy on him) said in refutation of those who believed this science to fall outside of the Book and the Sunnah, in that time and later times, "This science of ours is erected upon the Book and the Sunnah."

There is consensus, among the People (of Allah), that it is not correct for anyone to embark upon the Path of Allah (Honored and Majestic), unless he has dived into the depths of the Sacred Law and knows its statements, meanings, general and specific rulings, the abrogating and abrogated, and also dives into the depths of the language of the Arabs until he knows its similitudes and metaphors, etc. So, every [accomplished] Sufi is a jurist without the opposite being the case.

The upshot is that only the person who is ignorant of the states of the Sufis denies their states. Qushayri used to say, "In every age, since the beginning of Islam, there have been Shaykhs. And the Imams of the scholars

---

metaphorical and ambiguous expressions and their meanings.

of those ages all submitted to the Shaykh of their respective age. And if the people did not have a special quality or superiority, the matter would have been the opposite."

I (al-Sha'rani) say: It suffices us as praise for the People (of Allah) that Imam al-Shafi'i ﷺ submitted to Shayban al-Ra'i when he asked Imam Ahmad b. Hanbal about someone who does not know which prayer he is praying, and the submission of Imam Ahmad b. Hanbal in like manner, when Shayban said, "The rectification of a man who is heedless of Allah is to learn the proper conduct (with Allah)." Likewise, it suffices us that Imam Ahmad b. Hanbal ﷺ submitted to Abu Hamzah al-Baghdadi al-Sufi ﷺ and believed in him. In fact, he would send him his most difficult questions, saying, "What do you say about this, o, Sufi?" And little by little Imam Ahmad would understand it, and Abu Hamzah would cause him to recognize the loftiness of the Path of the People. Likewise, it suffices us to mention the submission of Abu al-'Abbas b. Surayj to Junayd when he visited him. He said, "I do not know what he is saying. However, his words do not sound false."

Likewise, Imam Abi 'Imran submitted to al-Shibli when he imparted to him some knowledge on the issues of menstruation. He provided him with seven verdicts of which Imam Abi 'Imran was not aware. And Shaykh Qutb al-Din b. Ayman (may Allah have mercy on him) related that Imam Ahmad used to encourage his son to meet with the Sufis of his era. And he would say, "They have reached a level of sincerity that you have not reached." Imam Qushayri, in his "Risalah," and Imam Ahmad b. As'ad al-Yafi'i, in his "Rawdat al-Rayahin"- and others among the people of the Path- had written at length in praising the People of the Path. And their books are filled with that. Abu Turab al-Nakhsabi ﷺ, one of the men of the Path used to say, "When the heart becomes accustomed to distance from Allah, it is accompanied by attacking the friends of Allah ﷻ."

And Shaykh Muhammad al-Maghribi al-Shadhili ﷺ used to say, "Seek the way of your masters among the People (of the Path), even if they are few. And beware of the path of the ignorant, even if they are many." And it is sufficient honor for the science of the People what Moses (peace be upon him) said to al-Khidhr (peace be upon him):

❴ May I follow you so that you may teach me some of what you have been taught as a guidance? ❵[11]

That is the greatest proof of the obligation to seek the knowledge of Reality, just as it is obligatory to seek the knowledge of Sacred Law. And everyone speaks from his own station.

---

11   al-Kahf, 66

I say: I have seen in a letter that Shaykh Muhyi al-Din Ibn al-'Arabi ﷺ sent to Shaykh Fakhr al-Din al-Razi, (the author of the Qur'anic exegesis). In it, the Ibn al-'Arabi makes clear to al-Razi the deficiency of the latter's level of knowledge. And that was the case, even though Fakhr al-Din al-Razi was considered among the greatest of the scholars in terms of outward knowledge. Below, I quote some of that letter:

> "Know, o, brother! May Allah enable you and me (to what is good)! That a man does not become complete in the station of knowledge until his knowledge is from Allah (Honored and Majestic) without any intermediary, nor transmission from a Shaykh. Whoever's knowledge is only taken from a transmission, or a Shaykh, he does not cease to take from created beings. And that is defective according to the People of Allah (Honored and Majestic). And whoever spends his life trying to know the creation in detail, then that is his portion from His Lord (Honored and Majestic). That is because a man will perish in (pursuit of) the sciences related to created things and will never know their reality. If you, o, brother, would only travel at the hands of a Shaykh from the People of Allah, he would cause you to reach the Presence of witnessing the Truth ﷺ. And you will take from Him knowledge of different matters by way of true inspiration- without tiredness, exertion or hardship- in the same way that al-Khidhr took knowledge (peace be upon him).
>
> So, the only true knowledge is what one obtains through unveiling and witnessing. It is not what one obtains through inspection, contemplation, assumption, and estimation. The Complete Shaykh Abu Yazid al-Bistami ﷺ used to say to the scholars of his age, "You have taken your knowledge from the scholars of texts- as a dead person from dead person. But we took our knowledge from the Living One, who will not die."
>
> It behooves you, o, brother, that you should not seek any knowledge, except what will perfect your essence and travel with you wherever you may go. And that is through knowing Allah ﷺ by way of providence and direct witnessing. For example, the knowledge of medicine is only needed in the world where there are illness and disease. But if you travel to a world that has neither illness nor disease, what use would that knowledge be?
>
> You should already know, o, brother, that the intelligent person does not take any knowledge except that which will travel with him to the Interworld (Barzakh), without separating from him while he is traveling to the Hereafter. And that the traveling

companion consists of only two types of knowledge: Knowledge of Allah (Honored and Majestic) and knowledge of the stages of the Hereafter. That way, he will not deny the manifestations that occur there and will not say to the Real, if He appears to him, "I seek refuge in Allah from you."

Thus, it behooves you, o, brother, to uncover these two types of knowledge in this abode, so that their fruits will save you in that abode. And, according to the People of Allah ﷻ, you should not carry any knowledge in this abode, except that which you need in your wayfaring towards Allah (Honored and Majestic). And the path to uncovering those two sciences is only found in seclusion, spiritual exercises, struggle and Divine attraction.

I wished to teach you seclusion, its conditions and what will be revealed to you in it, stage by stage, in order. However, there was with me at that time someone who has not dived into the secrets of the Sacred Law. His riding animal is disputation, denying that of which he is ignorant. And he has been diverted by sectarianism, love of fame and leadership, and seeking the world through the religion from submission and yielding to the People of Allah. "

End of letter.

Shaykh Muhyi al-Din has also mentioned in the "Futuhat" and elsewhere: That the path to arrive at the knowledge of the People is belief and fear of Allah. He said ﷻ:

❴ *And if the towns had but believed and feared Allah, We would have opened for them blessings from the Heaven and the earth* ❵[12]

In other words, we will acquaint them with sciences connected with the higher and lower realms, secrets of Jabrut, and lights of Mulk and Malakut. He said ﷻ:

❴ *And whoever fears Allah, He will make for him a way out and will provide for him from where he had not expected* ❵[13]

Sustenance is of two types: spiritual sustenance and physical sustenance. He has also said ﷻ:

---

12 al-A'raf, 96
13 al-Talaq, 2-3

❴ *And fear Allah, and Allah will teach you* ❵¹⁴

In other words, He will teach you those Divine sciences that you had not learned through intermediaries. For that reason, He associated the teaching with the name "Allah," which indicates the Divine Essence, which gathers all of the names, actions, and attributes. Then he [Shaykh Muhyi al-Din] said ﷺ:

> "Then it is imperative, o, brother, that you confirm the truthfulness of and submit to this group, and that you do not assume that their explanation of the Book and the Sunnah involves transference of the words from their outward meaning. Rather, the outward meaning of a verse has different meanings depending on the differing understandings of people. So some of what is understood is what the verse or the Hadith indicates according to conventional language. Then there are other inward understandings for every verse or Hadith, which Allah has opened for some people, according to what has been related in the Prophetic Hadith: "*For every verse, there is an outward meaning, an inward meaning, a degree, and a point of ascent- up to seven inward levels, or even up to seventy.*"¹⁵

The outward meaning is those beneficial sciences that are intelligible and transmissible, which govern good deeds. The inward meaning is Divine gnosis. The point of ascent is a meaning that joins between the outward and inward meanings. And the degree is the path to witnessing the All-encompassing Essence. Understand, o, brother! And do not let the words of the disputant rejecter- that this amounts to changing the words of Allah ﷻ or the words of the Messenger of Allah ﷺ- deter you from accepting those meanings from this honored party, which are beyond the understanding of the general population. These meanings would not affect a change in the words as they would if they had said, "There is no meaning to this verse or Hadith, except the one that we say." But they did not say that. Rather, they transmitted the outward meanings verbatim, meaning by them their subject matters, while understanding inwardly what Allah ﷻ had caused them to understand by His grace and that with which He illuminates their hearts by His mercy and blessing.

Whenever the People say "illumination" (fath), what they mean is the lifting of the veils from the soul, from the heart, from the spirit or from the secret to what the Messenger of Allah ﷺ brought in terms of the Great Book and the Honored Hadith, since the Saint does not, at all, bring any

---

14   al-Baqarah, 282
15   Sahih Ibn Hibban (Hadith no. 75).

new law. He only brings a new understanding of the Book or the Sunnah with which no one before him had been acquainted. For that reason, the one who does not believe in the People of the Path completely disapproves of it and says, by way of reproach, "No one has ever said this."

However, it would have been more appropriate that he take from him, believing in it and trying to benefit from the one who said it. And whoever is given to censure and reproach will not benefit from any of the Saints of his age. And that suffices as an evident loss. Shaykh Abu al-Hasan al-Shadhili ﷺ has said, "Allah has indeed tried this party by people, especially the people of disputation. There is little chance that you would find one of them who Allah has opened his heart to confirming the veracity of a specific Saint. Instead, they will say to you, 'Yes. We know that the Saints and Chosen Ones of Allah exist. But where are they?'"

And you will not mention to them any Saint except that they deny him and reject the special qualities that he has from Allah ﷻ. And they will set their tongue free, providing an excuse for why he is not a Saint of Allah ﷻ. But what has been hidden from him is that only the Saints know the characteristics of the Saint. So how can one who is not a Saint deny the sainthood of another man? That is only pure sectarianism, just like the censure we have seen in our time from Ibn Taymiyyah upon us and our brethren among the Knowers of Allah. Then be cautious, o, brother, of the one who has this characteristic. And flee from their gatherings, just as you would flee from a dangerous wild beast. May Allah make us and you to be among those who confirm the veracity of the Saints and believe in their miracles, by His grace and generosity."

[Muhyi al-Din Ibn al-'Arabi] also said, "The habit (sunnah) of Allah, with regards to His Prophets and Chosen People, has always been that every time their hearts incline to other than Allah ﷻ, He sets upon them the creation at the beginning of their wayfaring and near its end. Then their turn of fortunes and victory will be the end of the matter when they have accepted Allah completely."

I [al-Sha'rani] say: That is due to the fact that it is difficult for the disciple upon the Path to be sincerely in the Presence of Allah ﷻ, due to his inclination towards the creation, and his reliance on their belief in him. So, when the people abuse him, depreciate him and cast aspersions and false accusations upon him, his soul will develop an aversion towards them, and he will not have the slightest dependence upon them. At this point, his time with his Lord will become serene. And acceptance will be appropriate for him because his dependence on all others has gone. Understand.

Then, after they return to guide people, after the end of their wayfaring, they return donning the robes of forbearance, pardoning, and covering of others faults. So they will bear the harm of the creation and will be pleased with Allah ﷻ in everything that His slaves commit against them. Thus, that will raise their esteem among the creation. And that manifests the differences in their levels because a man is tried according to his religion. He said ﷻ:

❴And We made them Imams, guiding by Our command because they were patient❵ [16]

And He also said ﷻ:

❴And certainly were messengers denied before you, but they were patient over denial, and they were harmed until Our help came to them❵ [17]

This is because each of the perfect ones is always witnessing one of two things. Either he witnesses the Truth ﷻ with his heart, being with the Truth and having no inclination towards His slaves. Or, he witnesses the creation and regards them as slaves of Allah ﷻ to be honored for the sake of their Master, even if he is devastated thereby. We are not concerned here with his responsibility before his Lord being lifted during the condition of his being devasted because it is known that whoever wishes to follow in the footsteps of the Prophets, Saints and Scholars will, just like them, inevitably suffer harm, and false accusations, and lies will be told against him just as they were told against them. So he should be patient just as they were and behave with clemency towards creation (may Allah be pleased with them all).

Sidi 'Ali al-Khawwas (may Allah have mercy on him) used to say, "If the perfect of the callers to Allah ﷻ depended on the people coming to agreement upon their veracity, it would have been thus for the Messenger of Allah ﷺ and the Prophets before him, whereas some people confirmed their veracity- those whom Allah guided by His grace- and others denied them- those whom Allah ﷻ made miserable by His justice. Because the Saints and Scholars follow the footsteps of the Messengers (blessings and peace be upon them), taking them as their exemplars, people fall into two groups with respect to them: one group believing and confirming their veracity and another disbelieving and denying it- similar to what happened to the Messengers (blessings and peace be upon them), for Allah confirms thereby their Prophetic inheritance.

None confirms their veracity, believes in the authenticity of their sciences and secrets, except a person whom Allah (Honored and Majestic)

---

16 al-Sajdah, 24
17 al-An'am, 34

wishes to place among them, be it after some time, whereas he who denies and censures them is cast out from their presence, and Allah but increases his remoteness thereby. Few are those who, as a result of Allah's selection, providence, and choosing, are able to recognize the Saints and Scholars. This is due to the prevalence of ignorance concerning their ways, the predominance of heedlessness, and the aversion most people have, because of jealousy, to anyone having any precedence over them in station or status. The Great Book has spoken of this concerning the people of Noah (blessings and peace be upon him). He said:

❰*And none believed with him except a few*❱ [18]

And He also said ﷻ:

❰*But most people do not believe*❱ [19]

And He said ﷻ:

❰*Or do you think that the majority of them listen or reason? They are but like cattle. Rather, they are farther astray*❱ [20]

And other such verses.

Muhyi al-Din ؓ used to say, "The root of people's disputation concerning Divine gnosis and Lordly indications is that these are beyond the sphere of the intellect, arriving abruptly without transmission or intellectual musing, and not by way of the intellect, which makes the method of its arrival hidden from people. They deny it and are ignorant of it; and whoever denies any of the paths, by necessity, becomes an enemy of its people, due to his belief in the falsity of that path and the falsehood of its people. He is unaware that denial is a kind of actively rejecting something. Rather, the intellect should change its wrongful denial so that it can escape from the sphere of rejection."

Then the Saints and Scholars who act upon their knowledge have sat with Allah (Honored and Majestic) with real veracity, submission, sincerity, and fulfillment of their covenants. And that is observing every breath with Allah (Honored and Majestic) until they submitted their reigns to Him and threw themselves in submission before Him. And they forsook helping their egos at any time out of shyness of the Lordship of their Lord (Honored and

---

18   Hud, 40
19   al-Ra'd, 1
20   al-Furqan, 44

Majestic) and sufficed themselves with that in which He has placed them. So He placed them in that in which they had placed themselves, rather, something greater. And He ﷻ was the one who made war on their behalf against the one who made war against them, and overcame those who had overcome them.

My Master Abu al-Hasan al-Shadhili ؓ used to say:

"Since Allah (Honored and Majestic) knew what would be said about this group- because of His previous eternal knowledge- He ﷻ began with Himself. He decreed that a group would turn away from Him in misery, so they attributed a wife, a son and poverty to Him, and they said that His hands were tired. So when a Saint or a Siddiq[21] becomes fed up due to people accusing him of disbelief, apostasy, sorcery, insanity, etc., the Real calls out to him in the interior of his soul, 'What has been said about you is what you would have been if it were not for My grace upon you. Have you not seen how your brethren among the children of Adam had impugned My honor and had attributed to Me what was not appropriate for Me?'

If he does not then understand what has been said against him, he is constricted. And the Real calls out to him again:

'Do you not have enough of a support in Me? And things have been said about Me that do not befit My majesty. And things were said about My beloved Muhammad ﷺ and about his brethren among the Prophets and Messengers that do not befit their station. It was said that they were sorcerers and insane and that they did not seek anything through their calling except leadership and prestige.'

Consider, o, brother, the medicine that the Real (Majestic and Exalted) gave to Muhammad ﷺ when his breast was constricted due to the words of the disbelievers. He said ﷻ:

❴So exalt the praise of your Lord and be of those who prostrate [to Him] And worship your Lord until there comes to you the certainty❵ [22]

---

21 A *Siddiq* pl. *Siddiqun*, as defined by Sidna Shaykh, is a person who has perfect gnosis of Allah, being drowned in His presence while outwardly showing no sign of his station.

22 al-Hijr, 99

Thus, it is imperative for you, o, Saint, to follow the Messenger of Allah ﷺ in that, since it is a Divine cure and a Lordly remedy. And it removes the constriction of the breast that comes from the criticism of others and the people of censure and delusion. That is because glorification (tasbih) is to exonerate Allah of what does not befit His perfection. That is accomplished by praising Him ﷻ for difficulties and denying any deficiency in Him, such as anthropomorphism and limitations. As for praise (tahmid), it is to praise Allah for what befits His perfection. And they are both two things that remove the constriction of the breast that comes from the criticism of the deniers and people of contempt. As for the prostration, it is an indication of the slave's being purified from seeking loftiness and high status, since the one who prostrates has perished from the attribute of loftiness while he is in prostration. For that reason, it was legislated that the slave should say in his prostration, "Glorified is my Lord, the Most High and Praised."

As for the slavehood indicated by His words,

❴And worship your Lord❵

what is meant by it is to purify one's intention and remain remote from seeking honor. And that is an indication of the annihilation of the slave's essence and attributes. And that will bring about (the donning of) the robe of nearness, being chosen, honor, and proximity, which is indicated in His words:

❴Prostrate and draw near❵ [23]

Junayd (may Allah ﷻ have mercy on him) used to say to al-Shibli (may Allah have mercy on him), "Do not reveal the secret of Allah among the veiled people." And he also used to say, "It is only appropriate for the *faqir*[24] to read the books of special Divine Unicity among the people who confirm the veracity of and

---

23   al-'Alaq, 19

24   *Faqir* is the name given to the travelers of the Sufi path. The idea is that they stand in complete need of Allah. Thus, they are spiritually poor. Different Paths demonstrated this in various ways, with some asking the disciple to give up all his wealth and possessions, becoming outwardly poor. Others took a more inward approach, where one was not forbidden to possess the things of this world. He was forbidden from letting his heart become content with them. The Tijani Path is of the latter category.

submit to the People of the Path. If he does not follow this rule, it is feared that the hatred of those who deny them will befall him." And Abu Turab al-Nakhshabi used to say about the veiled deniers, "When the heart becomes accustomed to distance from Allah, it is accompanied by attacking the Saints of Allah."

I [al-Sha'rani] say: That is why the Complete Saints among the People of the Path hid the explanations of the stations of special Divine unicity. They did so out of pity for the general population of Muslims, out of mercy for the veiled people of disputation, and out of courtesy for the great Knowers of Allah, who conveyed those explanations. Junayd would only explain the science of Divine oneness in the basement of his house after having locked the doors of his home and placed the keys on his hip. And he would say, "Would you like that people would deny the Saints of Allah and His elite folk, and should accuse them of apostasy and disbelief?"

And among the saints are those who forbade speaking on the subtle words of the People until they died. They would instead connect such speech to wayfaring, saying, "Whoever travels their path will come to know whatever they came to know. And they will experience what they experienced. And they will not need to listen to the words of people."

The companions of Abu Abdullah al-Qurashi asked him to let them hear from him a portion of the science of realities. But he said to them, "How many are my companions today?" They said, "Six hundred men." The Shaykh said, "Choose one hundred from among them." They chose, and he said, "From the one hundred, choose twenty." They chose, and he said, "From the twenty, choose four." They chose, and those four were possessors of unveiling and gnosis. So the Shaykh said, "If I had spoken to you about the science of realities and secrets, the first ones to issue a verdict to execute me would be these four."

That is the end of what was said by al-Sha'rani in his Tabaqat, by way of summary. I ['Ali Harazim] only placed it as a foreword here because of the benefit contained therein of meaning and because its benefit returns upon the one who reads it. We ask Allah that He facilitate us all, by His blessing and grace, to what pleases Him and His Prophet. Verily He is Benevolent and Generous, Kind and Merciful to His slaves. And we will close this foreword with a section on the fundamentals of the science of realities because it is very beneficial for whoever adheres to the sciences of realities.

And I say, and it is Allah who provides success, and He is the Guide, by His grace, to the right path:

You should know, o, brother, that it is imperative for every field of knowledge to have principles upon which it is established. And the problematic rulings of each science, its anomalies, its nuances and its rarities are all evaluated according to its principles. Thus, just as the science of jurisprudence (fiqh) and the science of Arabic grammar have legislative principles that are used to establish each of its rules, the People of unveiling and realization, and the science of experience have coined terms and principles upon which their authentic science is established. And thereby one knows what is authentic and what is corrupt with regards to it. And when any problem, or anomaly, or rare thing occurs, one returns to its established rulings and principles. And I have set down for you, at the beginning of this book, a foundation which gathers in it all of the principles of realization, which, if it is relied upon, will banish every issue and each corrupt assumption and insinuation. And may it be to the one to whom it arrives a basis, a principle, a resort and a means of reliance in recognizing the principles of this field in this book and elsewhere. And I say, and from Him I seek help:

The Foundational Principle

You should know that the foundation of the scholars of unveiling and realization is that rational attributes do not change and that realities are not transmuted. So when a description or an attribute is essential, it does not become non-essential. And what is necessary for His Essence does not become merely possible, nor does the possible become necessary, nor the impossible possible nor necessary. Take for example existence. Since it relates to the Essence of the Real ﷻ, Whose existence is necessary. So it is said about Him that He exists and His existence is necessary since His existence is with His Essence for His Essence. So it is essential for Him, and it is necessary.

And since the essential attribute of rationally possible things is nonexistence, this attribute does not change to something other than nonexistence. So existence for them is essential. And existence is a change that occurred to them in the sphere of possibility. And it is possible for it to return to merely possible and possible that it never return to that. Similarly, since hiddenness is an essential attribute of the Essence of the Real, it does not change to other than that. And this essential hiddenness of the Essence of the Real ﷻ is what is indicated in His words ﷺ in the Sacred Hadith, "*I was a hidden treasure.*"[25]

---

25   In his Takhrij of this Hadith, in "Kashif al-Ilbas" of Shaykh Ibrahim Niasse, Imam Shaykh Tijani Cisse said, "al-'Ajluni narrated it in "Kashf al-Khafa." [He said], "[Its attribution to the Prophet ﷺ]. However, [Mulla 'Ali] al-Qari said, 'It's

The consequence of His ﷻ being attributed and named with the name "the Hidden"- which means undisclosed, concealed and absolute hiddenness of the Essence- is that being revealed does not occur to Him ever, not in this world, nor in the Hereafter, since revelation is an indication of the manifestation of the Real ﷻ in whatever manifestation He chooses. And the limit of the knowledge of those who know by Allah is to know what knowledge has manifested and is knowable. And that knowledge, which manifested and was knowable- regardless of the manner by which it is known- is beyond the reality indicated by the attribute of hiddenness.

And the highest knowledge that is knowable is the attainment of knowledge of the existence of the Creator (Majestic and Exalted). So rather than knowledge of the Essence, there arrives at the knower the knowledge that He exists and that His existence is necessary, and that nothing whatsoever is similar to Him. How would that not be the case, when contingent knowledge is contingent? So the limit of the knowledge of the slave is to know that the Creator (Majestic and Exalted) exists and His existence is necessary, that it is an essential attribute, that there is nothing whatsoever like Him, that no one knows Him but He and that no one knows His power except Him, due to His words ﷻ:

❮And they did not appraise Allah with true appraisal❯ [26]

Also, the Scholar of Allah only obtains knowledge by way of knowledge. And his knowledge is erected upon it. So they do not obtain anything except knowledge. And knowledge does not necessitate discernment of that which is known. How should it, when everything that is perceptible is creation? And one of the well-known principles, which researchers have all agreed upon, is that attributes and descriptions are according to the one who is described by them, and that ascribing an attribute to that which it describes can only be in accordance with the one being described, and according to the possibility of ascribing that attribute to His essence. And since the Real ﷻ is high above that, His true Essence should be perceived. Ascribing what attributes and descriptions are possible to Him is not the same as ascribing them to other than Him. That is because everything apart from Him is merely possible. And the governing rule for all possible things and

---

meaning is true and intelligible from His words (Exalted is He): {And I have only created jinn and mankind that they should worship Me} [al-Dhariyat, 56]. The verse has been explained by Ibn 'Abbas (may Allah be pleased with father and son) to mean, "That they should know Me." And the narration that has become widespread among people, "I was a hidden treasure. And I wanted to be known. So, I created creation. And through Me, they know Me" appears a lot in the words of the *Sufis*."

26 al-An'am, 91

their necessary characteristics are neediness, limitation, and deficiency.

And He ﷻ is- in terms of His Reality- different from all possible things. And nothing whatsoever is similar to Him. So ascribing a description or an attribute to Him can only be according to what befits His majesty. And He is completely exalted above whatever does not befit His majesty. And ascribing descriptions and attributes to a possible thing is also according to its reality, what is appropriate for it and what befits it. Take knowledge for example. If it is attributed to an eternal being, it is eternal. But if it is attributed to an accidental thing, it is accidental. And the same goes for every other attribute and description that can be applied both to the Allah and creation.

If you have understood the ruling of this honored fundament- which is the pole around which the sciences of the People of Allah, His scholars and those researchers who are fully established in knowledge, and if you have confirmed its meaning, then know that from the perfection of this fundament is that you should know that Allah ﷻ made for everything an outward and an inward. So the soul of a man has an outward and an inward since it is among created things. So it is possible for a man to perceive what outward things he perceives with the outward of his soul, which is interpreted through vision, examples and senses, but that he should not perceive anything by its inward. And it is also possible that he perceives what he perceives through the perception of the inward of the soul so that the knowledge pertains to the inward of the soul. This knowledge- which pertains to the inward of the soul- is specific to the science of gnosis of realities, secret gnosis, and secret Divine Oneness.

If you have understood this and have known that the Real ﷻ is the Manifest and the Hidden and that hiddenness is an Essential Attribute for Him- just as has come at the beginning of this fundament-then you should know that man does not perceive with his inward self, nor with its outward, anything except what is a manifestation of the name al-Zahir (the Manifest). So when the Real ﷻ manifests His name al-Zahir to the outward of a soul, the one to whom He manifests perceives an outward science, knowledge that corresponds to that which is illuminated for him. But he does not abstain from any created thing. So he deduces what knowledge he can deduce while loving the best of this world and the Hereafter, due to what has been revealed to the outward of the soul by what has been manifested outwardly to it.

But if the Real ﷻ reveals a manifestation, by the name al-Zahir, to the inward of the soul, the one to whom it is revealed obtains perception with the eye of insight. So the perception of the possessor of that station will be by the eye of insight, not by contemplation and investigation. So he will perceive by the eye of his insight the world of realities and the world of meanings. And there will not remain- regarding what he perceives with the eye of his insight- any doubt or obscurity. And he will be relieved of the weariness of contemplation. So Divine hidden and secret sciences, as well as knowledge related to the Hereafter, knowledge of the oneness of existence and his rejection of everything apart from the Real will be illuminated for him. And the secret of Divine oneness and gnosis will be manifested to him. And he will abstain from everything apart from the Real ﷻ, and he will become annoyed with all else. And nothing but the Real will remain in him by consequence of his inner self's being filled with that revelation that has arrived to him. Thus, the realities of all things will be unveiled to his insight. And he will distinguish, by his insight, the station of the Real from the station of all others. And he will no longer deem, in his heart, anything other than the Real to have any real worth due to what he has come to know of the reality of His station.

Benefit is completely obtained from this fundament through exhortation to become fully established in the knowledge of the Stations. That is to say, that the fundament, according to the Imams of confirmed Scholars is that every existent thing has an essence and a station. And its station has different requirements that are manifest in its existence, which are specific to its established reality. Thus, the effects of those decrees on the essence of the one who possesses it are called "states." And the degree (al-martabah) is an indication of the reality of everything, not in terms of its individuality, rather in terms of the conception of the connection that joins between it and the existence of the one to whom it is revealed, and their corresponding realities, since some of the realities correspond to others. And those correspondences are states, attributes, and intrinsic qualities. That is because things do not exist because of some quality that has been added to the different realities. They manifested through one Being that was specified and multiplied according to its different degrees. And it is not that when it was considered individually of connections to those realities it multiplied in itself.

The Real also has an Essence and a Degree. His Degree is an expression of the concept of the connection of His Divinity. That connection is in terms of its being named with Divinity. And the Real has- in terms of it- vestiges among those who are His Divine subjects and necessary attributes that are called Rules of Divinity. His Essence ﷻ is not described because it is independent of all restrictive expressions, and its never being connected to anything and nothing being connected to it since that is not appropriate. But in terms of the concept of its connection to the creation and their connection to it, and according to their differing states because of their being His manifestation and appearances, different states are attributed to it, such as contentment, anger, response, happiness, and other things which are interpreted according to circumstances.

And, in terms of the mark of its level of Divinity in every sense of the term, the attributes within it- termed requisites of the degree- are contraction, expansion, causing life, causing death, overpowering, etc., and it is not possible for the universe to be connected to Allah by way of His Essence. Rather, it is connected through the outcome of Divinity being attributed to Him. Understand that Divinity being attributed to Him is a consideration additional to His Essence, and that the world's attachment to the Truth is only possible through this attribution, since all of the names, degrees and attributes return to this attribute, and because it is the foundation of every requirement, name, attribute, description, as well as whatever else can be connected to or associated with the Truth (Blessed and Exalted is He).

The human being also has an essence. His essence is his reality, which is his established origin in the presence of the knowledge of his Lord, and which is an expression of his being attributed with knowledge of the Truth. And his distinction in the knowledge of his Lord is eternal, without beginning, according to the requirement of his degree with his Lord, as well as what his Lord knew was possible for him, what He had decreed for him in it and what He had required of him in it.

The states of this human reality are the states that affect him, and in which he fluctuates, of conceptualization, growth and development, and other such states that affect his being. Such states [must inevitably] originate from the Real because the confirmed, default state of contingent beings is nonexistence and because their existence is a change that occurred to them and require one to specify that change. If He specifies that something should come into existence, it exists. But if He specifies that it should not exist, or He removes it from existence, it is nonexistent. Thus, the degree of the human being is an expression of his slavery and worship. And the requirements of this degree are those matters and attributes that are associated with him because of his being a possible slave and worshipper, as well as his being a mirror and a manifestation.

This is a precious, invaluable, foundational principle that deserves to be the chief support on which one depends when giving legal verdicts on the knowledge of the realized folk, if such a thing were possible. It should be the measure by which are known the Real's governing laws in all the degrees of Reality and of creation. Thus, let every investigator recognize its high status because of its usefulness, its benefits and all the principles and maxims that it includes, which are very beneficial, if the student puts them to use, in solving difficult matters, problems and puzzles. And success is only achieved through Allah. And from Him is assistance to reach the right path.

Section One

Information about Him, His Birth, His Parents, His Lineage, His Close Relatives, His Upbringing, His Efforts, His Taking the Path of Guidance and His Guiding Others (It has three subsections.)

1.1 General Information about Him, His Birth, His Parents, His Lineage and His Close Relatives

1.1.1 General Information about Him

I SAY, AND SUCCESS IS ONLY obtained through Allah: He is ﷺ among the Scholars who act upon what they know, the guided Imams, and those who joined between nobility in lineage and religion, in knowledge and action, between Honorable Divine States and Lofty Sublime Stations, between a lofty, celestial ambition and pure, beneficent conduct, between the Excellent Sunni Spiritual Path, spiritual knowledge and the unexhausted Divine Secret, between phenomenal feats and numerous miracles, the Encompassing Pole, the Beneficial Succor, the Beneficent Inheritor, the Divine Imam, who Allah made, in his time, mercy to the slaves and a blessing and a light in the lands, the point through which He looks at His creation, the treasure house of His secret, the vessel through which He directs affairs, the container of His assistance, the overflowing of Divine assistance and aid, the extremely beneficial to the slaves, who has a special chemistry which changes the eyes and removes the rust from those souls which are pure gold in a short time, so that their darkness becomes light and their sadness, happiness, that removes their evil desires, lightens their (the desires) thickness, that raises aspirations and gathers important matters, so that the majority of slaves can benefit from him in all of the lands, by his Divine assistance and the secret of his noble, eternal, Muhammadan litany, without any struggle or exhaustion, due to his pristine effulgence and Divine grace.

He is the magnanimous model, the lamp of the age, the essential essence, the complete Knower of Allah, who has confirmed arrival, the Scholar of Allah who supports the Sunnah of the Messenger of Allah, the one who follows the Prophetic Path and exhibits the Muhammadan character, the

Ocean of Divine Oneness, the abode of uniqueness, the comprehensive inheritor, the beneficial educator, the one who points to Allah with his state and his words, who calls to Him by His permission, in word and deed, the heart of hearts that outpours light, manifest signs and splendid karamat, the most trustworthy proof, the luminous star of the religion, our Master Abu al-'Abbas al-Tijani ☙.

1.1.2 His Birth

He ☙ was born in the year 1150 Hijri in the town of 'Ayn Madi. And he grew up there in righteousness, faithfulness, safety, protection, piety and religiousness, protected by Allah ☙, safeguarded in His care and guarded as one of His flock. He was of noble characteristics and character, was pure in soul and actions, and was very modest and polite. He was graceful in his vigilance and search, displaying both earnestness and exertion, inclining towards good instruction and solitude, seeking out the religion and its great guides. He busied himself with reading, having a habit of reciting the Qur'an. He was beautiful in manner, often silent, having much dignity and modesty. He was beautiful physically and in conduct, had a lofty aspiration and humility, esteeming both the elect and the common folk.

He memorized the Qur'an at an early age, knowing well all seven canonical recitations, according to what he ☙ informed me of himself. He memorized the recitation of Nafi' upon the hands of the righteous scholar and teacher Shaykh Abu 'Abd Allah Sidi Muhammad b. Hammu al-Tijani. And he recited it ☙ to his Shaykh Sidi 'Isa Bu 'Ukkaz al-Mudawi al-Tijani, who was a pious man who was known as a Saint. He also used to teach the children of the aforementioned town. And he related that he saw the Mighty Lord in a dream and read the Qur'an to him, according to the recitation of Warsh, from start to finish, and the Lord said to him, "That is how it was revealed." He (Sh. Tijani ☙) received the benefit of reciting the Qur'an upon his hand. Sidi Muhammad b. Hammu passed away in the year 1162 Hijri.

After memorizing the Qur'an, he focused on seeking knowledge of religious principles and rulings, as well as proper conduct, until he had mastered all of these sciences and obtained their secrets. He read, with his Shaykh, the master scholar, the accomplished Knower of Allah, Sidi Mabruk b. Bu 'Afiyah al-Mudawi al-Tijani, the Mukhtasar of Shaykh Khalil, the Risalah, the Muqaddimah of Ibn Rushd and the Akhdari. Then he dedicated his time to seeking knowledge in his town until he obtained beneficial sciences and began to teach and give legal verdicts. Then he ☙ turned to the path of the Sufis and seeking out the Divine secrets until he had dived into the depths of understanding of its sciences, states, stations, defects, as well as understanding of his time and its characteristics. And he had responses to questions in all of the fields of knowledge. Thus, he excelled in knowledge and revised it. And he clarified both transmitted and speculative knowledge.

Then he occupied himself in acts of obedience; he began to love worship and his aspiration desired asceticism. So he would often do long standing for prayer at night until, when he had reached its limit, Allah ﷻ guided him, out of His generosity, to what He wanted from him, by His preordained providence. So he began ☙ to call to Allah and advise His slaves, to help the Sunnah of the Messenger of Allah ﷺ and to revive the matters of the religion and the hearts of the believers with the gnosis, secrets, blessings and lights that Allah had blessed. Thus, Allah revived, by him, the lands, benefited, by him, the one who is present and the one who is absent, and, upon his hand, spread the Sunnah of Madinah, and manifested His clear signs.

Then he is ☙, inwardly and outwardly, a stalwart, completely illuminated and beautified, high in station, with a firm, established foothold and aspiration, who has a complete inheritance from the Messenger of Allah ﷺ, the radiant object of sight and beautiful vessel, with illuminated white hair and a great presence. He had a majestic esteem and a well-known remembrance, had a far-reaching fame, beneficial knowledge and states and words that were consumed in the habit of commanding the good and forbidding the evil. He made the Sunnah known and extinguished innovation. And an example was set by him, and by his household, for reviving the Sunnah and practicing the religion. Thus, he deserves to be given the nickname "Muhyi al-Din" (the Reviver of the Religion). He is the owner of his age, the *fard* of his time. And Allah revived by him the prestige of our Maghrib after its traces had been obliterated and its lights extinguished. And through him were revived the dedication and dependence on the remembrance of Allah and benedictions upon the Messenger of Allah ﷺ. We ask Allah to make us among those who follow his Path, of his party, by the right of His Beloved and Prophet, our Master Muhammad, his family, and companions.

1.1.3 His Parents

His father ☙ is the Shaykh, Imam, the refuge of Islam, the shelter of creation, the famous scholar, the great scrupulous one, who called to Allah and gathered people to Him, and called to Him with both his state and words, the proof of the scholars who act upon their knowledge and the destination of the wayfarers and seekers of guidance, Abu 'Abd Allah Sidi Mahammad b. al-Mukhtar. He was a scrupulous teacher who followed the Sunnah, an instructor and one who remembered Allah. Lower Angels used to visit him and offer to satisfy his needs. But he would reject that from them saying,

"Leave me. It is between Allah and me. I have no need to seek other than Allah ﷻ." He used to seek Allah and would stand upon the truth for Allah in all of his states of movement and rest, not inclining towards the censure of the critic when it came to Allah. He had a house in his estate for the remembrance of Allah, which no one else would enter. He ؒ passed away in the year 1166 Hijri due to a plague. May Allah ﷻ have mercy on him.

His mother (may Allah be pleased with her) is the honorable, pure, perfect, heavenly purified, and gracious noblewoman, who possessed honorable manners and upright conduct, who was concerned with religious matters and held on to its strong rope. She had a high position with regards to piety and a sublime degree, as well as a grand portion of righteousness, excellence, grace and gratitude. And she was always very pleased and happy with his father, along with her being extremely grateful without limit. She used to comply with the rights of her husband, Shaykh Sidi Mahammad ؒ and was obedient to his command and words and strict in attending to his needs and concerns. She would seek out his desires and concentrate on what he wished. She would exalt his esteem and honor his authority and would supervise for him his charges and what he had entrusted to them. She would speak on behalf of truth, sincerely advising people. She would persevere in the religiousness and the practices of the God-consious, instilling the same into her children and her close relatives- guiding them to what is best. She had much sincere concern for them and mercy. She would often remember Allah and send benedictions upon the Chosen Prophet ﷺ, consistently performing these throughout the day and the night. And this caused mercy from the Mighty and Forgiving to descend upon her (may Allah be pleased with her, cause her to be pleased, and make Paradise her abode and resting place).

She is the noble free woman, the Sayyidah 'A'ishah, daughter of the noble Sayyid, the great Saint, possessor of great blessing and lights (may Allah cause him to abide with the righteous and provide him with blessings and felicity), Abu 'Abd Allah Sidi Muhammad b. al-Sanusi al-Tijani al-Mudawi. She passed away (may Allah be pleased with her), due to a plague, on the same day as her spouse. And they were buried together in 'Ayn Madi on the aforementioned date. They had children besides our Master ؒ, both male and female. But all of them passed away (may Allah have mercy on them), and none remained besides a son- Sidi Muhammad- and a daughter, of whom our Master ؒ took custody.

1.1.4 His Lineage

As for his paternal grandfather ﷺ, he is the pure, confirmed, great Sayyid, who was chivalrous, vigilant, held with high regard and in great esteem, concerned for religion and trustworthy, Sidi Mukhtar b. Ahmad. He was pure, munificent and pleasant, liberally openhanded, and completely faithful. He had a lofty aspiration and a distinguished disposition. He was among the greatest noble and honorable individuals of his time. He would keep ties with family and close relatives and assist his neighbors and neighborhood. He was very generous and extremely modest (may Allah be pleased with him and cause him to be pleased and make Paradise his abode and resting place).

As for his great-grandfather, he is the confirmed, pure, great Sayyid, the diligent, erudite scholar, the reference of the scholars, the commander of commanders, who had a great status and grand importance, possessor of a strong spiritual state, thirst-quenching spiritual assistance, resplendent light, evident guidance, firm resolution, authentic insight, clear speech, awe, dignity, distinction and esteem, the scrupulous ascetic and sincere one who is followed, Abu al-'Abbas Sidi Ahmad b. Mahammad. He is the fourth of our Master's ﷺ ancestors. And he is the Shaykh, the established, exalted Saint, possessor of apparent light, clear attraction, sincere love, surpassing aspiration, dependence on and satisfaction with Allah, upright manner, and honorable conduct.

Our Master ﷺ related about him that he had a house in his estate that no one would enter but him. And when he left his estate for the mosque, he would cover his face so that no one could see it. And he would not uncover it until he had entered the mosque. Then when he returned to his estate, he would cover his face until he entered his place of seclusion.

I asked the Shaykh ﷺ about the reason for his covering his face in front of people. He answered ﷺ, "Perhaps he had reached a degree in Sainthood, which anyone who reaches it, anyone who sees him will not be able to turn his eyes away from him for the blinking of an eye. And if he were to turn away and were veiled from him, he would die immediately. For that reason, the one who comes upon its secret, which is seventy-two Muhammadan Sciences, and remains in it for twenty-three years, he covers his face from people for the aforementioned reason."

I asked him ﷺ, "Is this degree something especially for the Keys to the Treasure (Mafatih al-Kunuz), or do others also have a share in it with them?" He replied ﷺ, "The aforementioned state is for some Gnostics other than them. As for the Qutb and the Keys to the Treasure, they do not cover their faces due to their completeness. And perhaps the aforementioned Sayyid had reached this degree, and it was the reason for his covering his face from people."

This Sayyid ﷺ is the first of his ancestors to arrive in 'Ayn Madi and settle there. He built a home there and married among them. So they became our Master's ﷺ uncles. For that reason, they gave their origin to the people of Tijan. And they have no origin in the people of 'Ayn Madi. Rather, the surname and agnomen was given to them due to their relationship to them through marriage.

As for his lineage ﷺ, he is a confirmed Sharif. His lineage traces back to Mawlana Muhammad, who was nicknamed "the Pure Soul," b. Mawlana 'Abd Allah al-Kamil b. Mawlana al-Hasan, the second, b. al-Hasan (the grandson of the Messenger of Allah ﷺ) b. Mawlana 'Ali (may Allah be pleased with them all). His pedigree ﷺ is written in the records kept by their chiefs. But our Master did not depend upon that, due to his strictness and effort. So he did not suffice himself with what is mentioned by fathers and grandfathers, nor what is written in records, nor the reports of individuals, until he asked the Chief of Creation and the Signpost of witnessing (may Allah bless him and give him peace with every breath that is taken) about his lineage. "Is he from among his children, family, and descendants?" He replied ﷺ, "*You are truly my child. You are truly my child. You are truly my child.*" He ﷺ repeated it three times. And he said to him, "*Your pedigree to al-Hasan b. 'Ali is authentic.*"

This question from our Master ﷺ to the Chief of Creation occurred in a state of wakefulness and not in a state of sleep. And he ﷺ gave him glad tidings of grand, momentous things. May Allah bless him, give him peace, honor him, be generous to him, praise him and raise his esteem.

1.1.5 On His Close Relatives

As for his close relatives, they are the children of Shaykh Sidi Muhammad ﷺ. They are Sidi Muhammad (his brother)- who was nicknamed Ibn 'Umar- and his full sister, Sayyidah Ruqayyah (may Allah be pleased with her). His brother had memorized the Great Qur'an obtained a share of the knowledge of the Sacred Law, excelling in obligatory knowledge and arithmetic. He passed away (may Allah have mercy on him) in 'Ayn Madi in the year (…)[27]. His sister was older than our Master ﷺ. She used to come to his home, and he would honor her and support her and satisfy her until he sent her back to her home in 'Ayn Madi. She passed away there (may Allah have mercy on her) in the year (…)[28]. She left behind a son whose name is 'Abd Allah. He has memorized the Qur'an and participated in the field of knowledge. And he has a great capacity in the science of arithmetic. He

---

27   No date was given in the original text
28   No date was given in the original text

is also of the companions of our Master and took the path from him. And he is still living in 'Ayn Madi. These are the close relatives of our Shaykh ﷺ who are known to us.

All of the children of Sidi Muhammad ﷺ grew up in a beautiful state, in honorable treatment, with a pure nature, acting upon the requirements of his education ﷺ, such as manifesting the customs and familiar practices, as well as excess and dissimulation, while being humble within themselves and raising their aspiration above that of their counterparts. They took these things from the life of their father and conducted themselves by them and proceeded upon their practice, and realized by them (the verse of the Qur'an):

> ❴Those who believe and their offspring follow them in faith, We shall cause their offspring to reach their level❵ [29]

And Allah ﷻ rewards the slaves according to their actions and their intentions. May Allah increase them all in His grace, and may He be for them with His blessing and generosity.

---

[29] al-Tur, 21

1.2 On His Upbringing, His Setting Out on the Path and His Efforts

1.2.1 On His Upbringing

He was born ﷺ in the year 1150 Hijri, according to what he informed me about himself ﷺ in 'Ayn Madi. And that is his hometown, and the home of his forefathers (may Allah be pleased with him and with them), as had come previously in Section 1.1. He was the middle child of his mother and father. Nevertheless, he still received the entirety of their honor, purity, the seal of their majesty, and their entire focus. And this ennobled him with their good fortune and established him in their spiritual support. Allah sealed for him a pathway from their methodology and perfumed that seal.

He grew up ﷺ in piety with his two aforementioned righteous parents. They educated him, raised him and gave him an upbringing similar to their equals among the people of insight. So he grew up in preservation and chastity, devoutness, and religiosity, with a lofty soul, a lofty aspiration, good conduct, safeguarded in the Divine care, and enveloped in attention. And he grew up unaware of the habits and excesses of people. He would never intend something except that he started it, would never start something except that he completed it, and when his aspiration sought after something, whatever it was, he would not enjoy any part of life, nor would he settle for anything until he attained it and had surpassed it. I heard him say: "Part of my innate nature is that if I start something, I do not back off from it. And I do not start anything except that I complete it." He would only employ his aspiration in high matters, not being satisfied with lowly aspirations. He was like the words of the poet:

> When my soul turns away from anything, it does not,
> Incline towards it in any way for the rest of my life.

Thus, he ﷺ had an outstripping aspiration and a far-reaching resolution. His soul refused that any knowable thing should be unknown to it, or that he should fail to travel any of the paths of wayfaring. He had a natural courage and undaunted bravery. And among the characteristics that were instilled in him were grand generosity, liberal spending, upholding the rights of his close relatives and family, as well as taking care of the affairs of his friends and clients, charity to the poor, and love for religious people. So virtue and high aspirations became his character and honorable conduct his character and reality. Not a dirham ever remained with him as a matter of habit, as the poet said:

> Coined money does not remain in its purse,
> Rather, it passes by it, but it soon departs.

More on his generosity and explanation of his spiritual state will come in its place if Allah so wills.

1.2.2 On the Description of His Noble Form and His Magnificent Appearance

It is clear from his visible form, just as it is clear from the description of his knowledge, that Allah ﷻ is his custodian. And He preserved his complexion as white mixed with red, a moderate stature, and illuminated white hairs. He had an audible voice, beautiful mannerisms, exalted esteem, and beautiful, clear speech- making his point with the utmost clarity.

He is one of the guardians of the people of his time- because of the sciences that he had been granted at just the right time. He also had one of the most excellent gatherings, the highest of them in example, possessing great dignity, respect, modesty, majesty and prestige. In his early age, he had perfect intelligence, powerful brilliance, exhaustive understanding, noble astuteness and strong reasoning. Not a meaning escaped his perception, due to the Divine light, which had been kindled in his innermost being. And he was never misled by anything at any time, nor did he lack in anything, whatever it was. He would find out whatever he wanted to know at the time that he turned his attention towards it without study, due to the strength of his intelligence and the depth of his understanding. These abilities had been witnessed in him in his very nature. His abundant astuteness, his perfect intelligence- in which he is unrivaled and unequalled, and all in all his complete intelligence and understanding ﷺ, as well as the strength of his perception and reasoning, are such that they dazzle the intellect, are beyond transmitted knowledge, and it would take a long time to explain its origin. However, when Allah wills to make a slave worthy, He paves the way to that for which he was created- by way of His special will and bounty- and He perfects his natural disposition and character. Then He manifests his merits and honor, and perfects for him intelligent discernment, and paves the way, by it, to special, distinguished intelligence. And the first stages are an indication of the last, the beginning a sign of the end.

When he reached puberty ﷺ, his father, Shaykh Mahammad ﷺ married him without delay, out of concern for his affair, to preserve him, safeguard his interest, and follow the Sunnah in its procedure. His wedding ﷺ was in the year (…)³⁰. But he remained in the home of his father until the latter passed away (may Allah have mercy on him). So he attained from him blessing and a great share of piety and religiousness, as well as benefit in the Path and a great deal of good conduct (may Allah be pleased with them both). Amin.

1.2.3 On His Setting Out on the Path

As for his setting out on the Path ﷺ, and the confirmed way in which he took it, when his father had passed away (may Allah ﷻ have mercy on him), he continued on the path of studying and seeking Islamic knowledge and gathering and recording those of its pearls found in his town of 'Ayn Madi.

Then he traveled to the Maghrib, to Fez and its surrounding areas, in the year 1171 Hijri. There he listened to some transmission of Hadith. And he continued to roam about there with the intention of performing visitations and seeking out some of the people of good, piety, religion and success. Then, on Mount Zabib, he met a man from the people of unveiling. He indicated to him that he should return to his town and informed him that he would obtain what he was seeking. So he did not remain, and he returned to his town quickly. Then he left towards the white land in Sahra', where the grave of the Great Saint and Famous Qutb Sidi 'Abd al-Qadir b. Muhammad- who is nicknamed Sayyid al-Shaykh- is located. And he remained there for five years to read, worship, study and recite. During this time, he arrived at his town of 'Ayn Madi, confirming that of which the aforementioned Saint had informed him. And he returned to his place in the Zawiyah of the aforementioned Shaykh.

Then he traveled to Tilimsan and settled there for the purpose of asceticism, worship and benefiting others through teaching the science of Hadith and explanation of the Qur'an, until, when our Master was inspired with what he was inspired, there settled in his chest what settled there, and there was manifested to him what was manifested, along with that to which Allah had paved the way by His preordained care, the outpouring of His generosity, he dissociated himself from that in which he was involved. And he directed his aspiration to Allah, to fleeing towards Him, standing at His

---

30   No date given in the original text.

door and being busily engaged with Him. So he isolated his soul from all attachments and cut off from it every individual association. And he dressed anew in the garment of repentance. And he rolled up his sleeves in sheer seriousness. So Allah opened for him doors of wayfaring and removed from him all hindrances and veils. And he devoted himself completely to His affair, directed himself wholly towards Him, fled towards Him with all of himself, turned himself with his heart and his soul towards Him, and cast everything other than Him behind him at the beginning of the year 1181 Hijri.

Thus, he withdrew to Allah immediately and intensified his wayfaring and traveling. He subjugated to Him his will, placed his yoke in His hands and effaced his desire in His desire. Thus, he adhered to taking refuge and isolating himself at His door, dedicated himself to remembrance and contemplation and inclined towards seclusion, worship, and nearness. So the beginning stages of illumination and its flashes appeared upon him, and charismatic talents became evident and apparent. Then his state did not cease to become stronger and increase until he had abandoned every habit and custom, every pleasantry and desire, and there remained not with him any desire that would distract him from the goal. And he developed an aversion to the creation and isolated himself from them with the Real King, turned himself towards Him and threw all else behind him. And his aspiration continued to rise, and his Lord continued to pull him towards His Presence, surrounding him with His care, grace and generosity, until he reached high degrees and sublime stations and arrived at the goal and desire.

❰ *And that to your Lord is the finality* ❱ [31]

From his immense etiquette when witnessing the grace and blessing of his Lord is that, when certain states overtook him, he was beset by a condition that cut him off from his ego and its desires. And the effects of Divine outpouring appeared on him. Then, his speech and words began to make his inner unification of God and gnosis apparent. At that time, anyone who looked at him became enamored with him because of the augustness and radiance that they witnessed on his face. Thus, that state would seize the hearts, minds and intellects of people to such an extent that they were forced to listen to him out of etiquette with his exalted honor. When he sensed that in his brothers and companions, he forbade them that, reproached them, rebuked them, distanced them and turned away from them. He became very angry at them and turned away from them in reproach. Some traveling parties would come to him to visit him, take from him and benefit. However, he would refuse that in every way possible. He would say, "We

---

31   al-Najm, 42

are all one in benefitting [one another]. There is no superiority of anyone over the other. The claim of Shaykhhood is but the worst of innovations."

So when he had excelled all others in every way, and he had adorned himself, inwardly and outwardly, with the garments of majesty, and there did not remain with him any desire among people, except to make the pilgrimage to the Sanctified House of Allah, he raised his aspiration to seeking that and to achieve his goal, and spent all of his time and energy in bringing it about. And he gathered his efforts and stood earnestly. So his aspiration led him to embark upon that path. So he ﷺ began preparing for departure, and left behind his close relatives and tribesmen, such that nothing at all prevented him from the pilgrimage. So he visited and frequented the people of the estate and gave possession of the lands and the affairs. And he left the city of Tilimsan in the year 1186 Hijri.

1.2.4 On His Effort and Struggle on the Path

As for his efforts ﷺ, you should know that there is no disagreement among the Imams of the time who met him during his youth, that he was of the chosen of Allah's slaves and among those who had been brought up in obedience to Allah, as well as among those who were guided and who took to the path of Allah.

He is ﷺ among those who struggle in the religion and those who fear the Lord of the worlds, the foremost in observing piety (taqwa) and scrupulousness, spending his effort in that, tightening the reins of delving into what does not concern him, traveling the noblest paths. However, after he grew up and became an adolescent, and the light of his heart increased, and the clear illumination from his Lord came to him, and he was raised up, and the Divine facilitation directed him to seek out the eternal Divine secret, he busied himself with reading the books of the People of the Path, dedication to that, teaching knowledge and benefitting people with it, until he was cut off from all towards Allah. And his aspiration inclined towards Allah. So he rejected all attachments and threw all relationships behind his back. And that increased him in light upon light and raised him by his witnessing the degrees of the leaders of souls. Thus, he ﷺ has approached the houses by their doors and took the Path from its leaders. And that brought him inheritance and Imamate such that no one in his time had surpassed him.

> So he became the foundation of the era, and truth is his words,
> And not one person among humanity has reached his status.

He ﷺ took to seriousness and earnestness, to keeping away from people and fleeing from them. And he busied himself with the rights of his Lord that concerned him, that being what He sought from him of piety and scrupulousness. People would come to him sometimes to visit him and would not find him having much time due to his extreme constriction. And when someone would come to him to kiss his hand, he would become angry and refuse that. And he ﷺ hated superfluous speech, and was severe in being on guard from backbiting, slander and delving into what did not concern him.

As for his efforts in fasting, he used to fast at the beginning of his wayfaring, fasting continually during long days. As for his standing at night, he never left it for many years. And he still performs it until now. He has no relaxation except in it, since it is the rest of the worshippers, since in it, their hearts find sweetness and private communication, as well as shedding tears on the pulpit of recitation. And he knows ﷺ that his time is his life and his life is his capital, and that it is what he trades with so that he may arrive at eternal bliss. And he sees his breath as priceless jewels. So he is too stingy with them that he should pass them in that for which he was not created. So he busied himself with that undertaking.

> The race! The race! Words and deeds!
> Warn your soul of the sorrow of the one beaten!

Perpetual obedience and spending one's effort in that can only come from one who has been raised to witnessing its Creator and Originator. Thus, those who Allah has chosen for His service and has illuminated their inner being with the lights of His gnosis, their hearts are strengthened, and they embark (on the ship) before they miss it and hurry towards that which their Lord has assigned them to do. And they are those who adhere (to worship) and submit themselves. They glorify (Him) night and day. They do not disobey, and they have no choice in what they have been commanded to do. They know that their Lord is looking at them, so they tightened their belt and busied themselves with what was required.

I say that he ﷺ is of those for whom every night is the Night of Decree since he ﷺ is among those who uphold the limits of Allah and those who look at the Sacred Law with the light of Allah, whom the abuse of the abuser cannot come to in regards to Allah. And what can a man say about one whom Allah had befriended and chosen, had adorned with His attributes and preferred, and who He singled out for His gnosis and satisfaction? All praise falls short since he is higher than that which the tongue could describe him, or that which any heart or mind should conceive of him. The situation is just as the poet has said:

> Who can count (the drops of the sea) for me, while the sea is overflowing?
> And who can count the pebbles or the stars for me?

And he is among those whose attributes had been perfected, whose actions had been beautified and whose service had been exalted. He had abandoned all apart from Him and did not witness, in any of the dominions, anything apart from Him. Someone composed these verses:

> I have no methodology except the methodology of love,
> And if I incline towards anything else for a day, I have left my religion,
>
> And if there should occur to me any desire other than You,
> Because of my negligent thought, I would determine that You had rejected me.

Around this do the thoughts of the Gnostics (may Allah be pleased with them) revolve, and they have seized the opportunity in it. And they exchanged their innermost beings for it. And they did not abandon it for a second. They knew what they sought, so what they had abandoned was of little importance to them. And whoever seeks the best is not bothered by its dowry. The one who warned and cautioned us ﷺ had informed us, in what has been narrated from Ibn 'Abbas (may Allah be pleased with father and son), who said, "I heard the Messenger of Allah ﷺ say:

> O, people! Reckless hopes foreshadow the descent of the decree. And the Hereafter is where actions will be displayed. So lucky is the one who successfully earns something, and wretched is the one who lacks good action. O, people! Greediness is poverty, renunciation is wealth, satisfaction is relaxation, seclusion is worship, action is a treasure, and the world is mine. By Allah! I would not like to trade what has passed of this world for the twigs of this brush. And what remains of it resembles what has passed, just as water resembles water. And all will soon be exhausted and will come to a quick end. So work while you still have the luxury of breaths, and the advantage of leisure, before you are stricken silent, and remorse does not benefit."[32]

'Ata' b. Yazid al-Laythi related that Abi Ayyub al-Ansari said, "I heard the Messenger of Allah ﷺ say:

---

32   Narrated in "Bihar al-Anwar."

Accustom yourselves to obedience and don the weapons of fear. And make your Hereafter for yourselves, your striving for your final abode, and know that in a short time you will be traveling. And to Allah, you will arrive. And nothing at that point will benefit you, except pious works that you have sent forth, and a reward that you had earned. You will certainly only go forth to what you have sent forth. And you will be rewarded according to what you had done before. Do not let ornaments of this lowly world distract you from exalted gardens. It is as if the mask has been removed, and all doubt has been lifted."[33]

May Allah have mercy on Shaykh Imam Isma'il b. al-Muqri, the author of "al-Rawd," for what he said in his amazing, unequaled poem:

> How long will you swing between happiness and negligence,
> And how long will you do so in sleep without waking up.
>
> A life has been wasted, an hour of which has been traded,
> For the like of Heaven and Earth as an estate,
>
> Would you trade that for desire of the other,
> Which Allah has refused to equal with the wing of a fly?
>
> Would you trade a happy life in which you live,
> Among the exalted hosts, for the life of beasts?
>
> What a pearl that has been cast among dunghills,
> And what a jewel that has been sold for such a pitiful price,
>
> Would you foolishly trade what perishes for what abides,
> Or anger for satisfaction, or fire for a garden?
>
> Are you an enemy or a friend to your soul?
> Verily you cast it into every misfortune,
>
> If your enemies were to do to your soul some of what,
> You have done, mercy would reach them on its behalf,
>
> Sadly, for you, you have sold it for a low price,
> And in that manner, it was not peculiar for you,
>
> Your bond for release is that you do not eclipse it by witnessing,
> Anything in creation, if you are indeed the son of an honorable woman,

---

33 Narrated in "Bihar al-Anwar."

And in front of it is a stand and a record book,
   Which enumerates against it anything the weight of an atom,

You have caused it to become fond of a world whose deceptions are many,
   Which treats those who trust it with deception,

If it faces you, it will turn around. If it does good,
   It will then do evil. And if it is purified, it will entrust it to difficulties,

And if it obtained the wealth of Qarun, it would not feed you,
   Even a morsel of food therefrom,

And if you were able to dominate it, would it not,
   Plot to remove from your mouth whatever blessing you had?

Then leave it and distribute to it a portion. And take that,
   For yourself on its behalf because it is all of the booty one has,

And do not indulge it. One moment of enjoyment,
   Will return upon you much more regret,

Thus, your dwelling with it for over a thousand years would only seem,
   Like your living with her for a day and a night,

And take care and be prudent in what you allow it,
   For indeed you are subject to immense passion and heedlessness

That is the end of what we wanted to quote from it though it is longer. I only placed it here because it is related to it, and because it has great admonition and exhortation. We ask Allah ﷻ to benefit us by it in this world and the Hereafter. Amin.

It is said that the first thing that the People of Paradise will see in Paradise is written:

This is that happiness in place of those afflictions,
   And this is that bliss in place of that exhaustion,

There is no relaxation except that before it is exhaustion,
   Exhaust yourself, and you will find rest that will save you from exhaustion.

It is also said that the levels of Paradise are given according to actions in this world. So whoever has a lot of actions, his status in Paradise is increased. And whoever has few actions, his status in Paradise is decreased. However, He ﷻ can give to whomever He wills among His slaves, in the abode of His generosity, what has not occurred to any mind, out of His generosity and grace, since He is the doer and the chooser. And He will not be asked about what He does (Majestic and Exalted). He said ﷻ:

❴And that is Paradise, which you are made to inherit for what you used to do❵ [34]

And He said ﷻ:

❴That is Paradise, which We give as inheritance to those of Our servants who were fearing of Allah❵ [35]

The verses that convey this meaning are many. Likewise, whoever wishes to take the Path of the People will not catch even a whiff except by seriousness and earnestness, by leaving habits and pleasures, by cutting off all attachments and hindrances, and by turning away from everything apart from Allah. It is as Shaykh Zarruq ؓ said, "It is that you not see anything in existence except you and your Lord."

Junayd ؓ was asked, "What is the path to isolating oneself to Allah ﷻ?" He replied, "It is repentance which will remove faults, fear that will remove procrastination, hope that causes one to embark upon the path of action, and frightening the soul by (reminding it of) its nearness to its appointed time, and its distance from hope." It was said to him, "How does the slave accomplish that?" He replied, "With a unique heart in which is unique Divine oneness." And Sa'id al-Kharraz ؓ said, "Gnosis comes to the slave from two directions: from witnessing Divine generosity and endeavoring to struggle. So when Allah recognizes sincerity in His slave, He opens to him the treasures of His unseen and makes him among the people of His nearness and His party."

He said ﷻ:

❴And those who strive for Us, We will surely guide them to Our ways. And indeed, Allah is with the doers of good❵ [36]

---

34 al-Zukhruf, 72
35 Maryam, 63
36 al-'Ankabut, 69

SECTION ONE

You should know, may Allah have mercy on you, that if a person has a high aspiration, you will not find him satisfied except with high degrees. And he will flee from anything other than that, whatever it may be. That is because the strength of the light that Allah has cast into his heart causes him to reject anything that he sees as lower than something else. So he is always in a state of rising. And all of that is from the grace of Allah upon His slave. And if a person's desire is his Lord, he will enjoy endless bliss and the vision of His Blessed Countenance, and he will enjoy the bliss of gnosis and belief in this world, and in the next, the lifting of veils and seeing with the eyes.

Our masters the Sufis had taken hold of that since they were most ardent in following what the Prophet ﷺ had brought. They turned towards Allah, and away from everything apart from Him. Such was the likeness of our Shaykh and Imam Abu al-'Abbas ؓ. He joined between a high aspiration, safeguarding the sacred and penetrating earnestness. And anyone who has an authentic connection to him, they are all upon their upright way, and constantly displaying what they were upon of beautiful conduct. The indication that someone is beneficial is that they have followers. And the fruit of high aspirations manifests outwardly through beautiful service and safeguarding the sacred. And whoever is thankful for a blessing always uses it in obedience to the Benefactor. And according to one's diligence come honors.

Verily the Shaykh ؓ is among those who exemplified effort and obedience to the One who is worshiped, and is among those who sought knowledge in his beginning in order to uphold obedience and worship of Him, not so that he could achieve his desires by it. Rather, in his beginning, he acted upon authentic repentance, according to its conditions, in his path, by observing the Sacred Law and its limits, and by denying his desires and cutting off from his soul allotments and attachments. And he isolated himself to Allah by observing His right. So the realities were unveiled to him. He acted upon denial of dispensations and interpretations and buckled down and got to work at all times. And he restricted all ways of delving into disobedience and acts that did not concern him. And he stuck to the Book and the Sunnah, and what the predecessors of this community had erected as practice.

Thus, he turned with all of himself towards his Lord, and He sufficed him from all else. He constructed his house upon the fear of Allah and His satisfaction due to his busying himself firstly with knowledge, Hadith and Qur'an and his delving into the depths of rare knowledge and subtle understandings. And he struggled against himself with uprightness and scrupulousness. And he abandoned every created thing. And he had no greediness except for his Lord. And he had lowered his gaze from all created beings, as a whole and individually. And he isolated himself to his Lord and devoted himself entirely to Him. And he conducted himself with the good manners of the ascetics and worshippers. Nothing distracted him from Allah. He confined himself to service and cast out from his heart everything that was temporal. The affair of the *Siddiqun* is exclusivity of action for Allah, sincere turning in every state, and forgetting their actions through witnessing the Great, Exalted One.

All in all, the Shaykh ﷺ is one of the foremost Imams of his time, and is among those whom the scholars were unanimous in honoring and esteeming, as well as venerating, without rejection or slight from any of the possessors of sincerity. He was the be all of the leadership in this affair. And he encompassed the subject of training the wayfarers and rectifying the seekers, as well as removing their problems and unveiling their states. And no one in our time has achieved what he achieved. He has honorable conduct and subtle attributes, perfect manners, and a majestic status. He is extremely intelligent, always joyous, merciful, very humble and modest, always following the mandates of the Sacred Law and the manners of the Sunnah. He is a lover of the people of piety and grace and honors the possessors of knowledge. He never has a misstep and does not incline towards following any desire. And I ask Allah to seal us with what He sealed His saints, and to make the best of our days, and the happiest of them, the day that we meet Him, by the station of the elite of His saints and the elect of His chosen ones (may Allah bless him, his family, and companions and extend them a worthy salutation, until the day of His meeting).

1.3 On His Taking the Path of Guidance and Direction

1.3.1 On the Importance of the Path and of Knowing Allah, and the Importance of a Guide

You should know that the most important relationship to recognize and be cognizant of, the person whose standing and guardianship you should preserve, is the one who brought you, upon his hand, to the benefit of guidance, and who directed you, by Allah's permission, to providence. He is the true father and progenitor and has more right than any familial relationship or lineage since he was the means for you to obtain countless blessings and blissful assistance. That is because he was the means of your being brought out from the void of ignorance to that of existential gnosis, from a place of negligence and remoteness to a place of orientation and arrival, from the region of error to the home of guidance, from the darkness of disobedience and insubordination to the light of conformity and satisfaction, from the outpost of harshness and distance to the bosom of proximity and affection, from the lowest level of alienation to the highest level of communion, and from the place of polytheism and multiplicity to the station of unity and *Fardiyyah*.

Thus, he transfers you from sensual existence to pure existence, from egotistical existence to merciful existence, from existence that resembles nonexistence to firmly established existence. And he causes you to occupy these sublime ranks, and the light of reality shines forth upon you from him until you become a true monotheist and attain eternal victory. Then, spiritual parentage is more beneficial for you than your physical parents and more important in terms of consideration, more critical in terms of recognition, closer in terms of regard and a closer means. It is as Ibn Farid said ﷺ:

> The relationship between us in terms of love,
> Is closer than that of my relationship with my parents.

Then knowing him has become more appropriate than recognizing any other, and more mandatory, just as al-Sha'rani ؈ said:

> Determining the father is so that the son is not ignorant of his lineage, thereby attributing himself to- or someone else attributing him to- other than his father. He would thereby come under the Prophetic Tradition, "*Whoever attributes himself to other than his father, or allies himself to other than his guardian, then upon him is the curse of Allah, the Angels and all of mankind.*"
>
> But whoever does not recognize his father and the Path is, strictly speaking, an impostor. Due to the imperative to recognize this lineage, and its being more critical and more obligatory, you will notice that in their books, the Shaykhs undertake to recognize their fathers according to their ranks. So they mention their religious lineage before their physical lineage since their degree and closeness do not resemble each other most of the time. And recognizing the worth of the Shaykh of a man is a signpost for recognizing his worth and grade, and a proof of the immensity of his benefit and the strength of his illumination. That is because the illumination of the disciple is according to the strength of the illumination of the Shaykh. And the purification and increase will be according to the strength of his purification and spiritual state.

For that reason, the complete Shaykh, and the exemplary Qutb, our Master 'Abd al-Qadir al-Jilani ؈ said, indicating what came before, "Our eggs are worth a thousand, but our fledglings are priceless." It is not possible to recognize this without undertaking to recognize the Shaykh in detail. So for that reason, undertaking to recognize the Shaykhs of our Master ؈ is critical, and complete recognition of their worth is beneficial. And in that same vein, it is critical to recognize his Shaykhs so that we may recognize his worth. So we have embarked upon that in this section. But we have restricted ourselves to what is necessary. And Allah facilitates to what is correct.

1.3.2 On the Shaykhs That He Met and His Taking the Path of Guidance and Direction

And I say, and with Allah is facilitation:

The first one of the masters of scholars that he met, at the time of his traveling from his land to Fez and its surrounding areas, was the great Saint, the famous Qutb, the confirmed noble, the highborn leader, the possessor of distinguished miracles and great, honorable virtues, our Master al-Tayyib

b. Muhammad b. Abdullah b. Ibrahim al-Yamlahi al-'Alami, who is buried in Wazzan, in the valleys of Masmudah, where his father, his grandfather and his brother, Mawlay al-Tuhami- who was also his Shaykh (may Allah be well pleased with him and all of them)- are all also buried. He had a very great reputation, which was strengthened by his traveling and visiting distant places far from people. And his zawiyahs are many in the towns of the Maghrib and its surrounding areas, as well as the eastern lands. So his fame ؋ is such that neither he, his lineage, nor his path ؋ needs an introduction.

He passed away (may Allah have mercy on him and be pleased with him) at the end of Rabi' al-Awwal in the year 1180 AH. He was buried in his town of Wazzan (may Allah have mercy on him and be well pleased with him). Our Master ؋ took the path from him and was given permission to transmit his litany. But our Master ؋ refused to do that since he ؋ was busy with himself. And he also refused to do so due to his not knowing his place at that time. May Allah be pleased with him.

He also met the pious Saint, who was successful in all his efforts, the possessor of sound unveiling and true experience, Sidi Muhammad b. al-Hasan al-Wanjali. He was from the tribe Bani Wanjal from the mountains of Zabib. When our Master ؋ came to him, he said to him, before he spoke to him, "You will reach the station of al-Shadhili." And he revealed some things that he had hidden and informed him of what would become of him, even though it was a long time off. But at this time, that of which he gave him glad tidings has manifested. And to Allah belongs all praise for His blessings of suspension of normal laws (al-khawariq), saintly miracles and glimmers of hope. But our Master ؋ did not take from him. He passed away during the year 1185 AH.

Then, in Fez, he met the pious Saint, the descendent of the successful Knower of Allah, Sidi Abdullah b. Sidi al-'Arabi b. Ahmad b. Muhammad, who was called Bin Abdullah. He was from the descendants of Ma'an al-Andalusi (may Allah have mercy on him). He met him and spoke to him about different things. Then, when he wanted to leave, he supplicated for him to have the best of both worlds. And his parting words to him were, "May Allah take you by the hand!" He repeated them three times. He passed away in the year 1188 AH. I washed his body with my hands, wrapped him in the shroud and prepared him. He was prayed over at his grave among his forefathers and ancestors, outside of "Bab al-Futuh," near the dome of the famous Qutb Sidi Ahmad al-Yamani ؋.

Then he took the path of Shaykh Mawlana 'Abdul-Qadir al-Jilani ؋ in Fez from those authorized to transmit it. He left it soon after. Then he took the Nasiri Path from the pious Saint Abu Abdullah Sidi Muhammad b. Abdullah al-Tuzani. And he left it soon after. Then he took the path of the famous Qutb, the great scholar Abu al-'Abbas Sidi Ahmad al-Habib b. Muhammad Al-Sijilmasi, a descendant of Abu Bakr al-Siddiq, who was nicknamed "al-Ghumari." He took it from someone who had permission in that path. Then he left it after some time. Then he met him in a dream after his death, and he put his mouth over his mouth, and he was biting down on the tongue of the Shaykh ﷺ. And he transmitted to him a name in that state, according to what our Master ﷺ told us. He invoked it for a while and then left it. The above mentioned Shaykh passed away on the fourth of Muharram in the year 1165 AH.

Then he took from the pious Saint, the Malamati Abu al-'Abbas Sidi Ahmad al-Tawwash, who lived in Tazah until he passed away on the 18th of Jumada al-Ula in the year 1204 AH. He transmitted to him a name and said to him, "Adhere to seclusion, solitude, and remembrance and be patient until Allah provides you the opening. You will attain a great station." However, our Master ﷺ was not happy with that. So he said to him, "Then adhere to this remembrance and persevere in it without any seclusion or solitude. And Allah will provide you the opening in that state." And our Master ﷺ invoked that name for some time and then left it. And we saw many saintly miracles at his hands ﷺ. And we heard from him things that indicated to us his authority in those lands. And he informed me of the stations that our Master ﷺ would obtain. And we have now seen him obtain them. And to Allah belongs all praise for His blessings.

Then he traveled from the Maghrib to the Sahara, heading for the Zawiyah of Shaykh Sidi 'Abdul-Qadir b. Muhammad al-Abyad. And he stayed there for some time, as has been previously mentioned. Then he traveled to Tilimsan. Then he travelled from Tilimsan seeking to perform the Pilgrimage to the Sanctified House of Allah and to visit the grave of the Prophet ﷺ. But when he reached the town of Azwazah, near Algeria, he heard about the Shaykh, the Imam, the esteemed Knower of Allah, the exemplar of the God-conscious and the support of the confirmed Saints Abu Abdullah Sidi Mahammad b. 'Abdul-Rahman al-Azhari. He met him and entered the Khalwati Path at his hands. This Shaykh had a great reputation, many followers, and grand zawiyahs. He passed away at the beginning of Muharram in the year 1208 AH.

Then, when he entered Tunis in the year 1180 AH, he met some of its Saints. Among those he met was the famous Saint, who had great worth, Sidi 'Abdul-Samad al-Rahawi. And he was under another Saint, who was the Qutb of those lands, being one of only four men who kept the company his company.. And they would only meet him at night due to his hiding his state. They would meet him on the eve of Friday and on the eve of Monday. The Shaykh ﷺ said, "I asked Sidi 'Abdul-Samad if I could meet this Master ﷺ. He refused, explaining that he never meets anyone at all. But he sent his companion, one of his most beloved, along. And that Saint said to him, 'The beloved sends his beloved.'"

And he stayed there for one whole year, spending some of that year in Tunis and some of it in the city of Susah. In Tunis, he taught some books, among them "al-Hikam." So the governor of that land asked him to stay with him in Tunis to impart knowledge, to support the religion, and to teach it. And he appointed for him a house for him to live and the Zaytuna Mosque for his classes. And he specified for him a heavy schedule. When he read the letter from the governor, he grasped it and was silent.

The next day he started a journey by sea towards Cairo, Egypt, intending to perform the pilgrimage and intending to take from the Shaykh Mahmud al-Kurdi, to submit to him, to travel his path, and to follow his example due to a dream that he had at that time. So he asked that the servant of the Saint that we had mentioned before come to him. And he said to him, "Tell him that I intend to travel by sea to Cairo, Egypt. And seek his guaranteed protection for me from fears and anxieties." He complied with his request and said, "Tell him that he is protected in his departure and return."

Upon receiving this message, he left towards Egypt. And Allah protected him until he reached Cairo, Egypt, in safety and well-being. Then, he asked about the esteemed Shaykh, the Scholar and Imam, the noble professor, the great Sufi Muhaddith, possessor of sound thought and penetrating insight, the magnificent accomplished Saint, the known splendid ascetic, the proof of Islam, the exemplary human being, the great Knower of Allah, the famous Saint, the towering mount of gnosis, the one who is firmly rooted and established, the one who is complete in his gnosis and in his imitation, the arrived, beneficial educator, Abu al-Fada'il Mahmud al-Kurdi, who lived in Egypt, but was born and raised in Iraq. May Allah be pleased with him and outpour onto us his blessing. Amin.

When our Master ﷺ came to [Sidi Mahmud], in their first meeting [Sidi Mahmud] said to him, "You are beloved to Allah in this world and the next." Our Master ﷺ said to him, "From where have you gotten that?" He said to him, "From Allah." Then, our Master ﷺ said to him, "I had seen you when I was in Tunis and said to you, 'Indeed all of my being is copper.' You replied to me, 'That is true. But I will change your copper into gold.'" When he had told him that, he ﷺ said to him, "What you have seen is true."

After some days, he said to our Master, "What do you seek?" He said, "I seek the greatest Qutbaniyyah." He replied, "You will have more than that." He said to him, "Do you swear that?" He said, "Yes." Then [Sidi Mahmud] informed him about himself, the things that happened to him in his travels, and his meeting with his Shaykh al-Hifni and his Shaykh's Shaykh Mawlana Mustafa al-Bakri al-Siddiqi (may Allah be pleased with them all).

Then he set out by sea ﷺ to travel to the Sanctified House of Allah. And the Shaykh promised him and prayed for his protection in his journey and return. Then, when he reached the Noble City of Makkah (may Allah increase it in loftiness, highness, nobility and standing) in Shawwal of the year 1187 AH, he searched out the People of goodness, piety, guidance, and success. And this was his consummate habit so that he could be completely successful in what he sought. And he heard about the Shaykh, the Imam, the famous religious leader, the perfect full moon, the sealed musk, the sun of mankind and the moon of the circle of erudite people, Abu al-'Abbas Sidi Ahmad b. Abdullah al-Hindi, who dwelled in the Noble City of Makkah ﷺ.

Our Master ﷺ took sciences, secrets, wisdom and lights from him without ever meeting him. He would correspond with him through letters sent through the intermediary of the servant of the Shaykh. That was because he had no permission to meet anyone at all after our Master ﷺ requested to meet him. He responded that he had no permission to meet anyone at all. Nevertheless, our Master benefitted from him, and he informed him of what would become of him. He said to him, "You are the inheritor of my knowledge, secrets, gifts and lights." And when he wrote that to him, he said to his servant, "This is whom I've been waiting for. Tell him that he is my successor." His servant replied, "I have been serving you for eighteen years. And now there comes a man from the Mahgrib, and you say to him, 'He is my inheritor?'" He said to him, "I had not been waiting for anyone other than him. And this is a matter in which one has no choice. He chooses for His mercy whoever He wills. If I could choose, I would have benefitted my son with that before you. But for some time, I had been expecting him and seeing him in the hidden world. We will benefit him with something that Allah prevented me from transmitting until its owner showed up."

He wrote to our Master immediately. He said to him, "By my right upon you, please be generous to my son." And he informed him that he would die on the twentieth of the sacred month of Allah, Dhu al-Hijjah. And what he said came to pass (may Allah have mercy on him and be pleased with him). When he had been buried, our Master summoned his son. He spent the night with him, and he transmitted to him the secret, observing the trust of the Shaykh and keeping his promise.

Before the aforementioned Shaykh's death ﷺ, he had given our Master a great secret. And he ordered him to invoke it for seven days, and he would receive the illumination. However, after that, he would have to avoid people, and no one could see him at all. Due to that condition, our Master ﷺ did not use it.

When the time came near to leave for 'Arafah, our Master ﷺ wrote to him seeking to meet him, since the time of leaving had drawn near, so that he may see his splendid face. But he did not relent, and he said to him, "I have no permission to meet anyone. However, you will meet the Qutb who succeeds me. And he will suffice you from me." He was indicating that he would meet Shaykh al-Simman. And he informed him that he would undoubtedly reach the station of Shaykh Abu al-Hasan al-Shadhili ﷺ, just as Sidi Muhammad b. al-Hasan had informed him of that. And he informed him of various matters. And he is our Master's ﷺ means of support in sciences, secrets, specialties, and lights. He passed away ﷺ in the year 1187 AH.

When he had finished his rites and completed his blessed Hajj and the Sa'y, he set out towards the Illuminated City of Madinah in order to visit the blessed Prophet. When he reached the City of the Messenger ﷺ and honored its nobility, honor, majesty, and immensity, he turned his attention towards visiting the noble grave and the magnificent secret that Allah had stored within it. And he entered with reverence, a somber state, magnifying and glorifying. And he gave to that station the great etiquette, exaltation, humbleness, and humility that it requires.

When he had completed his visitation, and Allah had accomplished for him his hope and his goal, he concentrated on meeting the famous Qutb, the great scholar, the possessor of dazzling saintly miracles and noble indications, Abu Abdullah Sidi Muhammad b. 'Abdul-Karim, who is known as "al-Simman." When he met him, he informed him of his state and what would become of him at the end of his wayfaring. And that Shaykh asked our Master to stay with him so that he may put him in seclusion for three days and to bring him to completion. But our Master told him he could not stay, and he gave him a valid excuse. Then, upon our Master's request, the Shaykh gave him permission in all of the Names and what they indicate. And he informed him ﷺ that he was the Comprehensive Qutb. And he said to our Master, "Seek whatever you wish." And our Master sought a number of things, and he gave them all to him.

Then, he returned to Cairo with the Hajj caravan, safely and in good health. He arrived there lightened by the Divine assistance and generosity. And he went to visit his Shaykh (al-Kurdi) to greet him upon his return from Hajj and Visitation. He greeted the Shaykh, and he welcomed him and sat him in front of him. Then he ordered him to visit him daily. And he ﷺ would present certain problematic issues before our Master and ask him to solve them from his own knowledge. And he continued to do that until our Master's copious knowledge became manifest and the scholars of Egypt gathered around him to benefit from his great knowledge.

When he was leaving for the Maghrib, his Shaykh, Mahmud, authorized him in giving the Khalwati Tariqah to others and administering its spiritual training. He refused. So the Shaykh said to him, "Transmit it to people. And the responsibility is mine." And he agreed. So he wrote him an Ijazah with the chain of transmission of the Path. We will mention the chain of transmission here in order to fully benefit from its blessing. I say, and from Allah is all help, assistance, and facilitation:

He said ﷺ:

The Lord of Might transmitted it to Jibril (peace be upon him). He transmitted it to the Prophet ﷺ. He transmitted it to 'Ali b. Abu Talib (may Allah ennoble his countenance). He transmitted it to his son al-Hasan, al-Hasan al-Basri, and Jamil b. Ziyad. Al-Hasan al-Basri transmitted it to Habib al-'Ajami. He transmitted it to Dawud al-Ta'i. He transmitted it to Ma'ruf b. Fayruz al-Karkhi. He transmitted it to al-Sarri b. al-Mughallas al-Saqati. He transmitted it to al-Junayd b. Muhammad- the leader of the Sufis of Baghdad. He transmitted it to Muhammad al-Bakri. He transmitted it to Wajih al-Din al-Qadi. He transmitted it to 'Umar al-Bakri. He transmitted it to Abu al-Najib al-Sahrawardi. He transmitted it to the Qutb al-Din al-Abhari. He transmitted it to Rukn al-Din Muhammad al-Sinjani. He transmitted it to Shihab al-Din Muhammad al-Tabrizi. He transmitted it to Jamal al-Din al-Tabrizi. He transmitted it to Ibrahim al-Zahid al-Kaylani. He transmitted it to Muhammad al-Khalwati. He transmitted it to 'Umar al-Khalwati. He transmitted it to Muhammad Biram al-Khalwati. He transmitted it to al-Hajj 'Izz al-Din. He transmitted it to Sadr al-Din al-Khayawi. He transmitted it to Sidi Yahya al-Bakubi. He transmitted it to Muhammad b. Baha' al-din al-Arzanjani. He transmitted it to Jalabi Sultan al-Maqdis, who is famous as Jamal al-Khalwati. He transmitted it to Khayr al-Din al-Tuqadi. He transmitted it to Shaykh Sha'ban al-Qastamuni. He transmitted it to Muhyiddin al-Qastamuni. He transmitted it to 'Umar al-Fawa'idi. He transmitted it to Shaykh al-Arshad Isma'il al-Jawrumi- who is buried near the grave of the companion Bilal ﷺ in Syria. He transmitted it to Shaykh al-Arshad 'Ali Effendi Qara Basha. He was made a Khalifah at the hands of his father, Shaykh Mustafa al-Tabibi. He was the one who gave him a license to guide people. He transmitted it to Shaykh al-Arshad Mustafa Effendi al-Idrinwi. He transmitted it to Shaykh al-Arshad 'Abdul-Latif al-Khalwati al-Halabi. He transmitted it to Qutb al-Arshad Sidi Mustafa b.

Kamal al-Din al-Siddiqi. He transmitted it to Shaykh al-Arshad al-Hifni. He transmitted it to Shaykh al-Arshad Mahmud al-Kurdi. He transmitted it to the Qutb of his age, the *fard* of his time and place, our Shaykh and our example in the way of Allah, our Master Abu al-'Abbas Ahmad b. Mahammad al-Tijani.

And he transmitted it to the slave in need of his Rich and Praiseworthy Lord, the compiler of this majestic book. May Allah include us among those who follow them, cause us to die upon their love, quicken us in their company, enter us where they enter and cause us to dwell in their dwelling place: the firm position with the All-Powerful King. And may Allah bless our Master Muhammad and his family.

These are my fathers, so bring me among their likes,
When you gather us, o, You who pulls the caravans.

When he left him, he traveled in the direction of Tunis and arrived there safely and in good health. Then he traveled to Tilimsan and stayed there giving great efforts in worship and calling people to it. Then, in the year 1191 AH, he traveled to the city of Fez intending to visit Mawlay Idris. And it was on this blessed trip that I met him ﷺ in the city of Wajdah on the way to Fez. I traveled with him. He recognized me. And I had a dream two years before that indicating my keeping his company and taking from him. After two or three days, he revealed to me the dream in detail, even though I had forgotten it. And he said to me, "Do you not fear from Allah (a punishment) if you trouble me, due to my position over you? Indeed, I had no need of anything except to meet you. So praise Allah for that."

I praised Allah and thanked him. And I knew, by this explicit statement of his ﷺ, that Allah had preferred me, that He was my guarantor, and that He had taken my affairs upon Himself. And he informed me of the illumination that would occur to him and in what station he would be established. Then, when we arrived in Fez, he stayed there for some time intending to visit Mawlay Idris. And he transmitted to me the Khalwati Tariqah, as well as some secrets and sciences. Then he returned to Tilimsan and informed me that he would travel from Tilimsan to another place, because his state was inconsistent there and his soul became tight on him there. So I left him, and he said to me, "Adhere to the pact (that you have made) and to love (of the Shaykh) until the illumination comes to you, if Allah ﷻ so wills." Then, when he traveled to Tilimsan, he stayed there for some time, and then he traveled towards the Saharah in the year 1196 AH. And he alighted in the town of the great Qutb, Sidi Abu Samghun.

1.3.3 On His Meeting the Prophet ﷺ, His Receiving the Illumination and the Tariqah at His Hand and His Benefitting People

Then he traveled to the area of Twat intending visitation. And he met some of the saints there. He took some special matters from them, and they benefitted by receiving knowledge and secrets in the Path from him. Then he returned to the town of Abu Samghun and stayed to live there. It was there that he received the illumination and the Prophet ﷺ authorized him to instruct people. This was after he had been fleeing from meeting people because he was concerned with himself. And he never claimed Shaykhhood until he received complete, unrestricted permission from him ﷺ to give spiritual training to people, in a wakeful vision and not a dream.

In the year 1196 AH, he ﷺ specified for him the litany that he was to transmit. He ﷺ first specified the formula of seeking forgiveness [*istighfar*] and prayers upon him [*salat 'alayhi*] ﷺ. That was the litany until the beginning of 1200 AH when it was completed with the "Declaration of Ikhlas."

At that time, he came to the people, benefitting them and manifesting the Path and its benefit. That was after [the Prophet] ﷺ had informed [the Shaykh] of his high station and exalted status and prestige. And he ﷺ informed him of the benefit of this litany and its superiority, and of what Allah had prepared for those who love him, his followers, and his party. And that shall be mentioned in full detail in its place.

When he ﷺ had given him permission in this Ahmadi Path and the Prophetic Mustafawi way and Allah had illuminated him upon his hands ﷺ, he informed him that he was his Murabbi, his guardian, and that everything that arrived from Allah to him arrived upon his hand and through his mediation ﷺ. And he ﷺ said to him, "*You owe no favor to any of the Shaykhs of the Path. I am your confirmed intermediary and benefactor. So leave off all that you took from the other Paths.*" He ﷺ also said to him, "*Adhere to this Path without any seclusion and without avoiding people until you reach the Station that has been promised to you, in whatever state you are in, without any constriction, hardship, or copious efforts. And do not depend on any of the Saints.*"

And from the moment he ﷺ said that, he left alone all of the Paths and stopped seeking anything from any of the Saints.

Then look, may Allah have mercy on you, at the care and special love that the Master of Existence ﷺ had for our Shaykh ﷺ. And that indicates that our Master ﷺ has a high degree with Allah ﷻ, just as he ﷺ informed him on more than one occasion. That is because if one arrives and receives his illumination upon his hands ﷺ, his station is more exalted, majestic and higher, as is known among the People of the Path. And his companions will be greater in prestige, in most cases, than the companions of other Shaykhs (may Allah be pleased with them all). This was indicated by our Master 'Abdul-Qadir al-Jilani in his words that we already mentioned, "Our egg is worth a thousand…" He was indicating the prestige of his companions since his illumination and arrival had been upon his hands ﷺ. So, if one's illumination and arrival are upon his hands ﷺ, he will have a higher prestige and a greater status.

And this illumination and outpouring from him ﷺ occurred at the beginning of the year 1200 AH in Abu Samghun and Shalala. And from that time, and Allah be praised for that, secrets, radiance, manifestations, elevations, and perfect lights have flowed continuously to him. And from that time, crowds have come to him from all sides and directions to take from him, visit him and learn secrets. However, he obscured, hiding it in ambiguity. And he covered it and concealed it except from the elite among the people until his matter was perfected and completed. And if the veil between him and people was to be lifted, and his matter was known completely, every person and every predatory beast would recite the following couplets, anticipating his advent:

> You have returned and so have my nights of communion returned,
>   Because of your nearness and the sweetness of your proximity has returned,
>
> You made clear what is patience when you went away. And I,
>   Due to that, had seen error as guidance,
>
> But today my life has pardoned me by your return,
>   And performed the most pious deeds after it had turned back,
>
> May Allah not remove your beauty from my eyes,
>   O, light of my eyes, that I may complete a happy life

Among his outpourings are those things that he related to us, which we transmit, that you will come upon, if Allah so wills, in this blessed book. And you will read things that will dazzle the intellect. And he remained ﷺ in that state and in that town while we returned time after time to visit him. And we set out to visit him in that town in the month of Ramadan of the year 1203 AH. And each time we visited him, we heard sciences and secrets from him that we had not heard on the previous visit. And I am still registering what we heard from him and what he related to us.

Then, on the seventeenth of the Prophetic month Rabi' al-Awwal in the year 1213 AH, he traveled from the lands of Saharah and entered Fez on the sixth of Rabiʿ al-Thani. We accompanied him from Abu Samghun until we reached Fez. And we learned from him ﷺ, in that journey, matters such as have no number. And we saw states from him that no one else knows about. And we witnessed in that journey some suspension of normal laws, which we will relate, if Allah so wills, in the section on his saintly miracles.

And his state has matured and perfected and has included all of the Divine gnosis of which he was worthy. And all parts of the Earth have been illuminated by his noble advent. And blessing has enveloped the Maghrib north, south, east, and west.

1.3.4 On the Reason for the Compilation of This Book

When he had stayed in Fez for two months, he ﷺ ordered us to compile this book after the Master of Existence ﷺ had ordered him so firmly that one cannot avoid it. And this was after our Master ﷺ had ordered us to tear up whatever we gathered from him due to the requirements of the time and circumstance. Then, the Real (Great and Exalted is He) favored us with a command from the Master of Mankind ﷺ, which was not possible to ignore. And it is only appropriate that we compile it. After the Master of Existence ﷺ had ordered him to compile it, he said to him, *"Preserve it, that the Saints that come after you may benefit by its preservation."*

So he ﷺ ordered us to write and collect it and to preserve its different issues that may be lost. And we were extremely elated by these glad tidings. That is because they had been our most prized possessions. And from the time that we had been ordered to tear them up until Allah honored us with this perfect elation, we were in a state of depression without any happiness. So we got to work immediately in writing this book and gathering its contents and issues. We ask Allah, by the station of the Complete Full Moon (may the best blessings and peace of Allah be upon him), to complete it for us.

1.3.5 On Some Good Dreams and Visions That Our Shaykh Had at the Beginning of His Life That Indicated His High Station

We will close out this section with some good dreams and visions that our Shaykh had at the beginning of his life that indicate his exalted status and high station and place. As he informed us, he did not see any dream or vision except that it occurred, even if it was after some time. That is because the vision of the sincere person indicates where he is headed in most cases. Such was indicated by our Lady A'ishah (may Allah be pleased with her): *"The revelation to the Messenger of Allah ﷺ began as true dreams. He would not see any dream except that it would be clear as the light of day."*[37]

And among those things that our Shaykh saw ؓ, which indicate where he was headed, was that he said:

> When I was a small child, before puberty, I saw that the throne of authority had been prepared for me, and I was sitting in it. And I had a lot of ministers to whom I would administer different necessary duties as if I was a king.

He saw that dream in 'Ayn Madi. He also said ؓ:

> I saw a dream that indicated the totality of my state. I dreamt that I saw him ﷺ riding a horse. And I said that I will go towards him. And if I greet him while he is still on his horse, my goal will only be obtained through hardship. But if I greet him when he is not riding, I will obtain my goal without any exhaustion. When I caught up with him ﷺ, he alighted from his horse, and I greeted him. And the dream happened exactly how I had thought about it. When I had greeted him, he entered the garden of a man from 'Ayn Madi and made the opening invocation of the prayer [*Allahu Akbar*] and started praying. When I wanted to pray with him, I was making my intention and did not make the Tahrima until he had bowed and prostrated ﷺ. So I did Tahrima and prayed with him the second rak'ah. And I completed the prayer with him until he exited the prayer. I interpreted this dream at that time that half my life would be wasted, and I would not achieve anything, and the next half is when I would obtain my goal. And it happened exactly like that. And to Allah belongs all praise and favors.

He also said:

> I saw myself in the form of a king. And people had sworn allegiance to me. There were a lot of people with me. And they placed for me the throne of Khilafah[38] on an elevated platform. And upon me were the robes of royalty. When it came time for prayer- it was the Zuhr prayer- I wanted to command someone from among the people to lead us in prayer, as was my habit when I was awake. But

---

37   Sahih al-Bukhari (Hadith no. 3).
38   The state of being the *Khalifah*.

I thought about it and said to myself, "The Khalifah[39] should lead people in prayer." So I went ahead, and I led the people in prayer until I completed and exited the prayer.

He told that dream to one of my beloveds, and he said to him, "I think that Allah ﷻ wants Qutbaniyyah for me when I am seeking something else." That was because, at that time, he ؓ was seeking from Allah that he should be among the Keys to the Treasure, due to the high station that he saw that they had. But after that, his aspiration was averted to the Qutbaniyyah due to the elite stature that the Qutb has, which no one but the Qutb can possess- regardless of the high station that they obtain. And Allah gave him that. And all praise is due to Allah.

He also said:

> In a dream, I saw Sidi Abu Madyan al-Ghawth in a gathering. He was saying, "Who can bring us something, and we will give him in return whatever need he seeks?" I said, "I will give you four mithqals. But guarantee me the Qutbaniyyah Uzma." He said to me, "Yes. I guarantee it to you. You will not die until you reach it."

This dream is supported by the fact that the Shaykh ؓ met a man who would meet with spiritual beings in a state of wakefulness, and they would inform him of whatever he wished. Our Master said to him, "I have concealed a need from you. What is it?" And he did not mention it to him. Then, when the spiritual beings came to him, he said to them, "What is the need of this person?" They said to him, "He asks you about Qutbaniyyah." He said:

> "A man came with them, and he said to them, 'Who gave you permission to speak about this matter?' They said, 'Its owner is the one who had asked.' He said, 'I promised him this Qutbaniyyah when he was in Tilimsan before he went east. He will not die until he reaches it. So neither you nor anyone else should meddle in this.'"

The man was Shaykh Sidi Abu Madyan ؓ. And the person who was asked had never met the Shaykh until the time that he was asked. And he had no knowledge of the dream at all. This points to the authenticity of the aforementioned dream and that it is true and not made up.

He ؓ told me of various dreams that indicate his Sainthood, gnosis, and

---

39   The *Khalifah* is the knower of all the Divine degrees, names and attributes in any given age. And he gives each their proper due. He is charged with upholding the management of the entire creation. He is also known as the *Qutb al-Aqtab*, the *Ghawth* or the *Fard*.

Qutbaniyyah. All of these dreams were true as the light of dawn. Every time he saw something and related it, it came true as the light of dawn. Among them are those dreams that we have already mentioned, and we will mention some others if Allah so wills. He ﷺ said:

> I saw him ﷺ in Tunis, and he said to me, "*Supplicate for gnosis or for whatever you want. And I will guarantee whatever you supplicate for.*" So I supplicated, and he guaranteed it ﷺ. Then he recited Surah al-Duha. And when he reached ❮*And your Lord will surely give to you, and you will be pleased*❯ [40], he turned his blessed glance towards me. Then he completed the Surah ﷺ.

And among his dreams is:

> I saw him ﷺ one time. And I asked him about the Hadith that has been narrated regarding our Master 'Isa (peace be upon him). I said to him, "There were two authentic Hadiths narrated from you about him. In one of them, you said, '*He will stay after his descent for forty years.*' In the other, you said, '*He will stay for seven years.*' Which one of the Hadiths has been authentically narrated from you?" He said ﷺ, "*The narration of seven.*"

Another is:

> I saw Mustafa ﷺ, and I asked him about the Zakah that the leaders and oppressors of the Muslims take by force. "Does that suffice them for Zakah?" He said ﷺ, "*Did I not command them to obey them (the rulers)?*"

The Shaykh ﷺ said, "I asked him ﷺ about a situation in which one is able to give it to someone else and does not fear that their evil will reach him. He said, "*If he gives it to them, then upon them both is the curse of Allah.*""

And another is:

> I used to be extreme and hard on myself about water that had been changed due to the leftovers of Wudu. I would not perform Wudu with it until I saw him ﷺ performing Wudu from a container and the water had changed due to the leftovers of Wudu. And he said to me, "*I am Muhammad, the Messenger of Allah ﷺ.*" From that time on, I left off being extreme and rested from it.

And among his dreams is:

---

40   al-Duha, 5

I saw our Master Musa (upon him and our Prophet blessings and peace). I said to him, "It has reached us that Qarun saw the place where you wrote the Greatest Name and threw it into the sea to uncover the grave of our Master Yusuf (peace be upon him). So Qarun took that Earth in which the Greatest Name was written and started to throw it on the places of treasures. And it would come out to him. And that is how he attained what he attained of wealth." He said to me, "That is true." I asked him, "Does the Knower of Allah have any choice in acting or refraining from acting?" He said, "Yes, until he reaches such-and-such station."

The Shaykh did not name the exact station.

Then consider, may Allah have mercy on you, the states of this Shaykh with Allah's elect among His creation. His sleep was just like his being awake. He would ask about whatever he wished. Such are the states of the men of Allah due to the spirit's dominating their being. That is because the origin of the spirit is purity and virtue. We ask Allah that He write all of us among all of His elect, chosen and beloved people. And he had many dreams and visions. But these are those that we were present to hear. He would see them at the beginning of his journey. As for now, it is very rare that he mentions any of them at all.

And the aforementioned dreams of our Shaykh were before the Master of Existence started informing him of things in wakeful visions and not in dreams. As for today, and Allah be praised for this, he has informed him of his arrival at his station and what Allah had promised him in it- a station that no one else can bear or reach. And he guaranteed him everything that he sought, even worldly matters, just as will be explained in detail in its proper place, if Allah so wills. We ask Allah, by the status of His Beloved Prophet and Chosen One, that He write us in the circle of the elect people who are recipients of His love and adoration. And we ask Him that He raise us upon the love of this Noble Master and the practice of His Great Prophet. Amin.

Section Two

On His Noble Qualities, His Spiritual States, the Station That was Chosen for Him, His Completeness, His Emulation of the Prophetic Way, and a Description of Some of His High Conduct and His Beautiful Interaction with His Brothers and Loved Ones (It has two subsections[41].)

---

41   The author's original words were that there were three subsections. Perhaps he had planned to make three subsections but did not. At any rate, we have changed it to two subsections so as not to confuse the reader.

2.1 On His Noble Qualities, His Spiritual States, His Station and His Completeness

2.1.1 Introduction

I say, and from Allah is all success:

OUR MASTER ABU AL-'ABBAS ⌘ IS the possessor of high states, lofty stations, blessed gifts, Divine ecstatic states. He is one who has effaced and annihilated himself. He possesses serenity, perpetuity. He is absent from all besides his Lord and witness to all that He has given him. He is among those who have been immersed in the sea of Reality, those who have been given true Divine attraction. He is among those who have been given strength, establishment, and a firm foothold in gnosis and certainty. Just as His verses are recited to you and His clear signs are manifested to you, he drank from that beginningless wine with delight. And he frequented its thirst-quenching watering hole and drank therefrom thirst-quenching, nourishing, and strengthening cups.

He followed the most correct and straightest path of the Sunnah. He boarded its ark, which embarks and makes berth with Allah, and rode in it. Thus, his lights were strengthened, and his secrets flowed. And his degrees and realizations came in succession. And he was ceaselessly assisted with an immense support.

❴*That is the bounty of Allah, which He gives to whom He wills, and Allah is the possessor of great bounty*❵ [42]

It is not possible for someone like me to reveal this station, nor to uncover the reality of the matter, really or imaginatively. I will only mention a sufficient portion of his gifts, manifestations, flashes of brilliance, events,

---
42   al-Jum'ah, 4

as well as reports about him to indicate it. That is because spiritual states are Divine effulgence. And the ecstasy of the heart can only be described by the one in that ecstatic state. May Allah have mercy on the person who said:

> Longing is only known by the one who endures it,
> And ardent love is only known by its sufferer.

Ustadh Abu al-Qasim al-Qushayri ؓ has defined the spiritual state as a constriction or expansion, or any other change that overtakes the heart without reflection, procurement or appraisal. He also mentioned that they proceed from pure Divine generosity while stations are obtained through strenuous effort. And he said that the possessor of a station is stationary while the possessor of a state is ascending. And it has been narrated from some Shaykhs that spiritual states are like flashes of lighting. If they remain, they are an invention of the ego. Others have said that they should perpetuate and remain. If they do not remain, they are impulses and showing off.

In this hagiography, what is meant by "spiritual states" are those things that fit into the category mentioned by al-Qushayri (may Allah have mercy on him). They are his numerous states of ecstasy and continuous outpourings that occur time after time- exactly how we have seen it with our own eyes. It does not refer to a continuous state, which is the same thing as a station. What is meant by the "station" that was chosen for him is the Gnosis that his station comprised of, just as we knew it from his speech and indications and his affirmations and informing us about himself through his outpourings.

2.1.2 On His Ecstatic and Spiritual States

As for his ecstatic and spiritual states ؓ, in his beginnings, whenever something would be revealed to him, or something would descend upon him, he would be completely detached and absent, the gravity of his state not leaving him. And even in that, he was in the utmost completion. Then, after the state subsided, he would speak about things whose meanings those present did not understand, the linguists did not comprehend; things whose meaning were only known to the one who experienced them. But at times, he would speak at the onset of a spiritual state about unveilings of hidden characteristics and occurrences in of the era. But only the most elect of the brethren would understand them. And there are many more stories, occurrences, and signs like this.

Then, after that, he became fully composed and settled. And his state became hidden and established. And the states began not manifesting in him outwardly like before. And he became perpetually in simultaneous states of movement and stillness, agitation and settlement, inebriation and sobriety, presence and absence. His sobriety did not distract him from his inebriation, nor did his inebriation prevent him from being sober. Rather, his inebriation provided him with sobriety and increased him in perfection and strength. Thus, he obtained through his dedication a firmly established place. It is as has been said:

> He gives to drink, and he drinks. And his inebriation diverts him not,
> From his drinking companion. Nor is he distracted from the cup,
>
> His inebriation obeys him until he is established in,
> The state of sobriety, to the astonishment of people.

His spiritual states' overcoming him ﷺ was only due to the strength of what was being revealed to him. This, by proof that what he would speak about were matters of gnosis, sciences, and secrets, which cannot be numbered, and which the intellect and reflection are incapable of producing. And he would relate things to us orally, from his memory and in his words. And those things will be related in their proper place if Allah so wills. Another proof is in those things that would occur to his companions due to him, such as spiritual assistance and *tasrif* in their states. And they would realize that it was from him, just as we had witnessed from them, and just as they had informed us of that about themselves.

People are not equal in regards to overwhelming states. The difference in those who are overwhelmed due to their weakness and those who are overwhelmed due to the strength of the revelation is that the sign of those who are overwhelmed due to their weakness is that their states do not spread to others. It is limited to themselves. However, the sign of those who are overwhelmed due to the strength of what is revealed is that their states spread to others. And even stronger than that is the one who can take away what he has given.

Such is the Complete Saint. He gives and takes away, all according to the Divine decree and determination. And we have seen that more than once with some of the brethren due to their bad manners, or due to some other reason. And we have seen him, on more than one occasion, do this with some of the brethren, due to their evil conduct or for another reason. We ask Allah for safety and freedom from that and that He provide us with beautiful conduct with Him perpetually by the status of our Prophet ﷺ. And being overwhelmed by a spiritual state due to its intensity used to occur to many of the great Aqtab, in ancient times and more recently. May Allah be pleased with them all.

And our Master ﷺ continues to experience strong spiritual states and outpourings of light. Most of the time he is receiving great outpourings and weighty blessings. And we have witnessed, on many occasions, the moment of his outpouring and what descends at that time. But only the most elect of those who are attached to him, and those for whom Allah wishes good, understand it. But in the majority of cases, the people who are present do not understand what is going on. Rather, he enters into a spiritual state and does not speak to them about it.

And the Divine attraction of our Master ﷺ is a very clear matter and a perpetual state. Absence continues to manifest from him in his states of sobriety, and even more so in his states of inebriation. We had sat with him on more than one occasion, and he asked about someone who was present and seated with us at the time. This occurs a lot.

And other matters make manifest the traces of the Divine attraction and the strong spiritual state of our Master ﷺ, such as his body becoming big, his body becoming full, his face glowing, and things becoming so heavy upon him that he cannot move. Recall what used to happen to the Prophet ﷺ when the revelation would come to him and he would receive the Divine command. He would become very serious and distressed. Then, when the Angel separated from him, beads of sweat could be seen on his forehead. Or his body would become visibly heavy due to the heavy weight of the words being revealed to him. It has also been related that revelation descended to him one day while he was sitting and his thigh was pressed against the thigh of Zayd b. Thabit ﷺ. And it became very heavy to the point of almost breaking Zayd's thigh.

And these (great Saints) (may Allah be pleased with them) are the repositories of his signs and the recipients of his spiritual assistance and revelations. They sought assistance from him and drank from his sea.

It is common for him, when his spiritual state strengthens, that his resplendence and beauty increase, his face glows, his teeth gleam, and the traces of his inner reality and secret show. Thus, a brilliant beauty, a brilliant light, would show upon him. Thus, onlookers would be dazzled by his beauty, majesty, resplendence and completion, and he would seize their essence and their entire heart so that his presence would control them, and they would not incline towards anyone else; this was a spiritual beauty and a Divine secret. How excellent was the person who said:

> Look and you will see that the Sun of gnosis has risen,
> With his most noble, resplendent and exalted brow,

> Every Shaykh had been clothed in resplendent states,
> However, he surpassed them with the beauty of Yusuf.

And someone else said:

> Look at the beauty garden. Its roses were brought,
> Forth by his beauty and his resplendence,
>
> Whoever is able will see the Reality. By him,
> Was seized the gaze of every person,
>
> And by his heart, the Divine light was manifest,
> And upon his face appeared His secrets.

Someone else said:

> Look at the face of his beauty and elegance,
> His lights had shined forth from his brow,
>
> His heart has encompassed the secret of gnosis,
> And the halo of his face manifests its traces,
>
> He is their overflowing sea. Can you not see that his,
> Secrets flow incessantly through his flood.

And this frequently appeared on him whenever he would hear the hidden and manifest attributes of the Prophet ﷺ, or reports and Hadiths about him. What was hidden in him would appear, and the traces of his inner reality would manifest. And he would enter a state of ecstasy, ardent love, inebriation, and outpouring. And there would appear upon him lights. And secrets would pour off of his tongue, and sciences and understanding would gush forth from his heart. May Allah afford us His pleasure. Amin.

2.1.3 On the Station That Was Chosen for Him

As for the station that was chosen for him ﷺ, it is confirmed gnosis, being established in certainty, perfect tawhid, *Fardiyyah*, isolation, and witnessing love from Allah. And it is that he is a beloved slave, who has been pulled into the Presence of his Lord, and sought out. His consummate habits are relying upon his Lord, being uniquely for Him apart from all else, the love of His command and hate for that which He has forbidden, perpetually standing at His door and being preoccupied with Him. He is restless with everything other than Him. He does not concentrate on anything other than Him. And he has no refuge, in any of his movements, moments of rest, moments of wakefulness, sleep, or any other state, except Allah.

Whenever he comes or goes, stands, sits, or awakes from sleep, he remembers Allah with such a remembrance that indicates that he has a living heart, filled with the wisdom of belief, and a light that captivates for him the listener and reassures the hearts and the listeners. He is not completely absorbed by his sleep. Rather, he turns constantly while asleep. When he moves or turns in his sleep, he remembers Allah. His reality has been mixed with being occupied with his Lord, taking refuge with Him, love of Him. And he is completely at peace with Him, in certainty, gnosis and belief.

He does not depend on anything other than Him, does not lean on anything other than Him, and he is not concerned with the acceptance or rejection of the creation, nor with their love or hate. He has been given complete happiness with whatever Allah does to or wills for him. You will only find him satisfied with the decree and will of Allah, happy with His judgment and actions, speaking of the blessings and favors of Allah.

He does not like to self-direct or elect anything alongside Allah. He says, "No chosen act is better than the act of a slave who never has any intention other than what Allah has willed and decreed for him."

Therefore, you will see that he likes all of what happens with the passage of time, due to his intense patience, fear, and trust, which forces others to be content with it, and to submit to its afflictions. And when things change, his intention does not change with it, nor does he lament anything he may have missed. And he has stated this and indicated this on numerous occasions. And he guides with his state and words towards it, and recites the following couplet as a similitude to his state:

> With me is the complete full moon,
> Which turns my heart towards wherever it inclines.

That is because he ﷺ has erased all else. And he does not witness anything alongside Allah. He does not see any benefit or harm in anything other than Him. Rather, he witnesses that all acts are truly from Allah, and that He is the decider of affairs, that He directs and informs by His actions, and that all of His actions are accompanied by a Divine wisdom and lightened by the Divine mercy. He sees the creation as containers that are grasped in the hand of someone else. And he counts a person's witnessing himself as duality. He says, by way of example, with the tongue of his state:

> If I say, "I have not sinned," a respondent says,
> Your existence is a sin that no sin can equal.

His state revolves around this concept ﷺ. Thus, it can be seen that his actions, words, explanations, and allusions revolve around annihilation in Allah, absence from all else apart from Him, witnessing His attributes, names, honor, greatness, beauty, perfection, and His beautiful actions and generosity. That is his practice, his slogan, his home, and his place of residence.

And, by that, he has traversed all of the stations of certainty, such as repentance, abstinence, patience, thankfulness, fear, hope, dependence on Allah, love, and contentment. And he encompassed entirely all of the attributes of the Knowers of Allah, such as love of Allah, being wholly for Him, leaning on Him in everything, submitting to the Divine decrees, abandoning self-direction and election, and other attributes and signs of theirs, some of which we have mentioned before.

Thus, he cannot be reduced to a spiritual state that visits him, nor limited to one station, because you will not find him perpetuating in any state, nor stopping with any matter. Rather, he is always changing according to the requirements of the times and what state Allah brings upon him. And that is the state of some of the Knowers of Allah ﷺ. Junayd was asked about the Knower of Allah and he replied, "The color of water is the same as that of its container." After mentioning this in his "Risalah," al-Qushayri said, "He means that his description fits the requirements of his time." He also said that Abu Yazid said, "The creation has states. But the Knower of Allah has no state, since his traces have been effaced, and his essence extinguished in the Essence of his Master. And his traits have been obliterated in his Master's traits." And Shaykh Zarruq said, in his "Qawa'id," after having mentioned the description of the worshipper, the ascetic and others, "And if he subjugates himself to the Will of the Real, he is a Knower of Allah."

And the People of the Path have likened the difference between the Knower of Allah and the person of a particular spiritual state to that of one who has memorized the Qur'an when compared to someone who has memorized a Surah or some Surahs. So if you say that someone is a Knower of Allah, you have attributed all of the stations to him, and you have exonerated him of being described with any one of the stations alone, such as asceticism, reliance on Allah, entrustment, or any other, since they are all included in him.

And if someone gathers all his efforts towards his Lord, and subjugates to Him his love and desires, until he becomes extinct to all else besides Him, he will inevitably be grateful for His favors, patient with His tests, pleased with His decree, entrusted to Him, relying on Him, cut off from other than Him, gathering all of the stations, but rising above all of that. He will not witness or look at anything after he has encompassed and consumed it. Thus, the people of Gnosis are those who are absent from everything, present with Allah, witnessing the majesty and beauty of Allah, and knowledgeable of His attributes and names, since real gnosis is what was described by Shaykh Zarruq ؓ in one of his explanations of the "Hikam," "The emanation of the knowledge of the majesty of the Real ﷻ, His beauty, or both in the whole being of the slave, until no trace of himself remains. Thus, he witnesses everything as coming from Him, with Him, and for Him. And according to him, there remains no connection for the existence of anything except Him."

And our Shaykh, Abu al-'Abbas al-Tijani, has so much of all of this what we have mentioned, that it is not hidden from anyone who adheres to him, or pursues any of his states, indications, or words. And what we have described of this matter should suffice you. Indeed, he ؓ is of those who possess Khilafah, those who are attributed with guiding the creation and gathering the creation to Allah, and causing them to reach Him. And he is from the kings of the hearts and rulers of the spirits. His command is obeyed, and his worth exalted. His words benefit and his arrows hit their targets. He gives life to the hearts and cures them of defects. He grants freedom with a glance and causes one to reach the Presence. When he turns his attention to something, he profits, acquires, and reaches his goal. He controls all of the states of the hearts, by the permission of the Knower of the Unseen. In such a way was he found by anyone who attached himself to him, gathered his spiritual energy towards him, so that his fruits, influence, and manners were manifest upon him. May Allah be well pleased with him, he with Him, and may He grant us His satisfaction.

2.1.4 His Perfection

As for his perfection ؓ, it is his perfect gnosis of Allah ﷻ, the proof of which we have already mentioned, his inner and outer fortitude, both in rapture and wayfaring, and his joining between them both in the most complete way and the most perfect manner. The proof of his inner fortitude is those states of his that we already mentioned. And the proof of his outer fortitude will come later, if Allah so wills, in the section on his spiritual travel and his acts. And no one, among the Knowers of Allah, is equal in that. And to Allah belongs all praise. And you will read about them all in their proper place, if Allah ﷻ so wills.

But from his perfection ؓ is the penetration of his lordly insight and his illuminated discernment- which makes manifest whatever it seeks to uncover- in recognizing the states of his companions, as well as uncovering hidden matters and unseen realities. Also, it is in his knowledge of the end results of things that they seek, whether they would bring about corruption or rectification, and other matters that would occur. Thus, he would know the states of the hearts of his companions, what would change their states and main objectives, as well as their state of acceptance or rejection, and all of their faults and illnesses. So he would know their inner and outer states, and what would cause them to increase or decrease. And he would make that clear at times. And at times, he would hide that out of mercy towards them, not wanting to test them by informing them. This has happened to more than one person and on more than one occasion.

Many times, a person may sit with him, and he (our Master) will speak about that which he has hidden within himself and those desires and worldly concerns that occupy his heart. And he will mention those things directly and specifically. Or he may speak about some ugly act that someone had done just before sitting with him. But, he will do all of this by way of general speech or parables. For example, he may say ﷺ to one of his companions, referring to an ugly act that he had committed in the past, "You are as they say, 'He swallows a big piece of iron, but leaves the needle.'"

But he makes this reference obscure to his companions by not mentioning the person by name or referring to him directly. Likewise, he may say something like, "What is wrong with a person who does such-and-such a thing?"

And the person who does it will confirm within himself that he is such a person. He would do this to cover the person's fault, just as the wisdom of Divine mercy requires and as the Sacred Law and the Sunnah have specified. That is because one's insight is like his glance. It is imperative to restrain it.

❴ *Tell the believing men that they should restrain their vision* ❵ [43]

However, he is ﷺ a mirror for those who sit before him, displaying his good and base qualities. And none of that is hidden to his insight. And there is no exception to that. In fact, when we sit with him, each one of us fears exposure and seeks safety and well-being, due to his repeatedly knowing our evil, ugly actions.

And when anyone comes to him, consulting him on a matter, be it religious or worldly, such as the matter of seeking a livelihood, for example, he clarifies for him what is profitable for him. And he guides him to that which will rectify him. And he assigns him those things in which lie his spiritual success and the attainment of his goals. Thus, he achieves his goal and obtains what he had hoped for. And he clarifies for him the best result from his hopes or expectations. Thus, his insight ﷺ reveals things for what they are, since it springs forth from the Divine light that was perfected within him.

---

43   al-Nur, 30

And it is very well known that when someone consults him, what is most correct, according to him, and the most relied upon option, is that which he mentions first. And this has also been demonstrated on more than one occasion. That is because the knowledge of these men ﷺ (may Allah be pleased with them) does not come from transmission or contemplation. It is a spiritual knowledge and a Divine opening. Thus, what first comes to them is what is correct. And all that comes to them is what is truly wise and correct. Thus, if the one who is consulting takes it, he discovers the wisdom of the matter on which he consulted. And he enjoys increase and profit.

But, if he does not take it, and he disputes with him about what he has said, he adjusts his speech for him until he goes away. Then, if he acts upon the last thing that he said, he will be detached from the correct decision, destroying the benefit that he sought. His work and hopes will not yield success. And it is also possible that his work will prove impossible. Then he will return to the first instruction that he was given, knowing that the wisdom of Allah was in it. And the matter will become completely clear to him after he had seen for himself. And that is the most common and well-known situation with the majority of his companions as it relates to deriving, and being prevented from, benefit.

Also among those things that indicate his perfect insight, the fortitude of his light, and the completion of his gnosis is his informing others about the Saints of the past, whether they are great or otherwise. It was as if he ﷺ was a contemporary of each of those about whom he informed people. He had ﷺ spoken about more than one of them and described them in a way that indicated their station, and what special gifts Allah had exclusively granted each one of them. And if someone asked him about one of the Saints, he would inform him about his state, his station, and what he obtained, and if he was among the people of *tasarruf* or not, as if he was seeing his state with his eyes. And at times, if someone asked him, he would remain silent and reject the question.

An example of this is his speaking on the special qualities of Malway Idris al-Asghar, who is buried in Fez ﷺ, about his great prestige, his majesty, his station, and his perfection. And he also informed about the special gifts of *tasarruf* that Allah had chosen for him in his life and after his death. Thus, he exalted his mention and venerated him. And he adhered to visiting him, paying his respects to him, and showing him reverence. And the proof of that is in what we have mentioned. And since our Shaykh entered Fez, he never stopped visiting him and going to him for even a day, except when he was sick.

Another example is his speaking about the perfect *Qutb*[44], the exempla-

---

44   *Qutb* pl. *Aqtab* literally means pole. It is the point around which something resolves. And a *Qutb* is the focal point of the sevants of Allah. There are many *Aqtab*

ry *Ghawth*⁴⁵, Mawlay 'Abd al-Salam b. Mashish ﷺ. He would mention his blessings and his signs. And he would describe him as granting spiritual assistance to the droves that went to him. And he would venerate his station. And another example is his speaking about the famous Saint, the great Qutb, Sidi Abu Ya'za ﷺ, about his perfect gnosis of Allah, his satisfying the needs of the droves that went to him, the *tasrif* that Allah had granted him, and his strong spiritual assistance to the old, the young and the weak. He would say, "Anyone who sought him out for a need was satisfied, whatever that need may have been." And he adheres to visiting him, venerating him frequently.

Another example is his explaining the states of other great Saints such as Sultan al-Awliya, Malway 'Abd al-Qadir al-Jilani ﷺ, Ibn 'Arabi al-Hatimi, Abu al-Hasan al-Shadhili, Abu al-'Abbas al-Mursi, Sidi Abu Madyan al-Ghawth, Sidi Ahmad b. Yusuf, and others (may Allah be pleased with them all). And we will not be long-winded by mentioning them all.

And I have heard him ﷺ mentioning the majority of those who had attained the Qutbaniyyah after the Prophet ﷺ until our time. He mentioned each one, describing his spiritual state, the high maqams and lofty spiritual states that he attained. And mentioned each one according to how his Lord had befriended him, chosen him, and was satisfied with him. This all occurred from him ﷺ before the current time. As for now, he is mostly silent about these things. May Allah be pleased with him, he with Him, and grant us His pleasure.

Also from his perfection ﷺ and his complete gnosis is his deep knowledge of the Greatest, Immense Name of Allah just as he informed us of that. And we will explain that, if Allah so wills, at its proper place.

And from his perfection (may Allah (Exalted is He) be pleased with him) and the loftiness of his noble rank is the station of Khilafah and the position of *tasrif* that he was granted. He entrusted him with authoritative representation and an unrestrictedly carried-out command in pulling and pushing away, harming and benefitting. He pushes away and pulls by His might. And lowers and raises by his spiritual influence. And he causes to ascend or descend by the permission of Allah. And he befriends and ignores by His command ﷺ, according to that of which his Lord gave him control, strengthened him, and entrusted him. Thus, his ruling is discharged on behalf of Allah, and his command is by the command of Allah, without

---

in any given age. Some are *Aqtab* of different lands or cities. Others are *Aqtab* of different circles of *Awliya'*.

45   The *Ghawth* is also called *Qutb al-Aqtab*. He is the focal point and the *Khalifah* of Allah in every age. Sidna Shaykh ﷺ explains his role later in the text as being the one that upholds all the rights of Lordship and creation perfectly, without exception.

any power or choice from him. Rather, it is by the power of the Mighty Compeller.

An example of his *tasrif* that has remained, become famous, manifested and appeared to the eyes is his taking charge of affairs with regards to the rulers and governors of the time and place. This is a matter that has become widespread and much discussed. And it has become common for the people of unveiling and others, even the ordinary people, to speak about. And one of the respectful lovers among the nobles of Fez (may Allah prolong his life) has described him as having Khilafah of *tasrif* and being the container of the Divine command, and even more signs that indicate his spiritual state and station, in a poem that I would like to present due to its brevity and beauty. It is:

> Praise has stretched forth its neck in,
> Praise of an Imam whose light and secret overflow,

> And the tongue of the state said, "How can I praise him?" when,
> His heart has become a stronghold for Him, the container of the Command,

> And all that remains in it is the remembrance of its God,
> And it has become a house that has been purified of all else,

> And it has been extinguished in Divine unity in its essence and became hidden,
> In the seas of realization. In their waves it swims,

> It was fertilized with an eternal secret. And there was thrown,
> Upon it the garment of approach, arrival and piety,

> And it was said to it, "You are the Khalifah. So take care,
> Your command is My command. And whatever you decide will be,"

> The prophetic lights encompassed it. Thus, it went forth,
> With them, inheriting every perfection without exception,

> And they purified its character. Thus, there flowed forth springs,
> Of secrets, gnosis, grace, and blessing,

> And there appeared upon him the anointment of their beauty,
> For that reason, the hearts of the lovers go towards him,

And lovingly long for him, and are given life through his mention,
  And before him is the perfume of remembrance and diffusion,

And he earned a place of reverence in the hearts,
  That pushes whomever it affects to seriousness and remembrance

Listing all of his attributes would be impossible,
  So how can one truly praise him? Then accept my excuse,

These are the contrived words of an intruder,
  Trying generously to hold my own with the container of wine,

May the satisfaction of the Most Merciful be upon him wherever the lover yearns,
  To see his magnificence and his outstanding beautiful qualities,

And his gathering and companions, all of them without exception,
  The young and the old, the living and the dead.

But the true description of his station, his perfection, his spiritual states, and his raptures ﷺ is only known by the All-Knowing, All-Informed, and whomever Allah informs of the people of vision and insight. But even then, it is not possible for him to express his reality. He can only mention its upshot, which will infer and indicate it. And we have only mentioned parts and portions of it that are outward indications of its totality. That being the case, he is the immense, wide, vast ocean which has no shore, and which can never be crossed. And that is the station that cannot be explained, nor described in full. And blessed is Allah, the Best of creators and the Greatest of benefactors and providers. So fill your ears with his beautiful qualities and words, and let the heart enjoy his secrets and lights, even if it cannot be encompassed by continued speech. And you have not even heard a tenth of it.

May Allah ﷻ provide us with his blessing, cause us to obtain his love, and place us, in the two abodes, among his party and traveling companions, and among those who drink from the watering place of his gnosis and reality. And if we are not worthy of that, if we should be the furthest of people from its path, then the Loving Merciful One is certainly capable of blessing and being generous with us. Indeed, it is He who opens for the one who hopes the door of attaining those hopes. And He is generous to the destitute person through incessant kindness. And He gives, without measure, any means that issue forth from the slave, even without the slave's seeking it. And He answers the one who calls upon Him, even if his ego and desires divert him from His obedience. There is no God but He. And there is no one who shows mercy apart from Him. And may Allah bless our Master Muhammad, his family, and companions, and extend them a worthy salutation.

2.1.5 The Reward of the Greatest Name

As for the reward of the Greatest Name that we alluded to before, our Master ﷺ said, "I was given a number of formulas for the Greatest Immense Name of Allah. And I was taught the method of extracting whatever formula from it I wished." And he ﷺ informed him of its immense benefit which has no limit and cannot be approximated. Then he ﷺ informed him of its immense special qualities, the method of supplicating by it, and the modality of its wayfaring. And this is a matter that we have not heard of anyone else attaining, except our Master ﷺ. Indeed, he has said ﷺ:

> The Master of Existence ﷺ gave me the Greatest Name that was reserved for our Master 'Ali (may Allah ennoble his countenance) after he had given me the Greatest Name that was reserved for his own station ﷺ.

And the Shaykh ﷺ also said, "The Master of Existence ﷺ said to me, 'This is the name that was reserved for our Master 'Ali (may Allah ennoble his countenance). And it is only given to one who has been decreed in sempiternity that he will be a Qutb.'"

Then he said ﷺ, "I said to the Master of Existence ﷺ, 'Give me permission in all of its secrets and all that it contains.' And he did so ﷺ."

As for what he ﷺ informed him of the reward of the Greatest Immense Name, which is the station of the Qutb al-Aqtab[46], the Shaykh ﷺ said, narrating what the Master of Existence ﷺ said:

> Its reciter receives with every recitation seventy thousand stations in Paradise. In each station exists seventy thousand of each thing that exists in Paradise, except for maidens and rivers of honey. He will have seventy of each of them. And every time it comes out of his mouth, four of the Angels drawn near will descend upon him and write it from his mouth. Then they will ascend with it to Allah and show it to Him. And the Majestic (Exalted be His Majesty) will say, "Write him among the people of felicity and record his station

---

46   Pole of poles. This is the *Qutb* that both holds the station and controls it. He is the one that is in charge of the madad of the universe, as the Scholars have said. He is also called the Ghawth. There are many *Aqtab*, or Poles, but only one Ghawth.

in the 'Illiyyun as a neighbor of Muhammad ﷺ. He will receive all of that with one recitation.

And for every recitation, he will also receive the reward of all the remembrance of Allah upon the tongues of all of His creation in all of His universes. And for every recitation, he will receive the reward of all of the glorification of our Lord performed upon the tongues of every created being from the beginning of the universe until its end. And for every recitation, he will receive the complete reward of six thousand recitations of Salat al-Fatihi. And he will also receive the reward for the recitation of Surah al-Fatihah and the entire recitation of the Qur'an. In other words, for each recitation of the Name, he will receive the reward for a complete recitation of the Qur'an. And that complete recitation will include Surah al-Fatihah and Surah al-Qadr with their respective rewards. And for each recitation, he will also receive the reward of all of the supplications that have occurred in the universe, deserving of a great or small reward.

And each time that he recites it, all of the Angels in all of the universes will recite it all together with him. And all of those Angels will recite it with all of their tongues. Indeed, among the Angels are those who have seventy tongues. And some of them have sixty tongues, and so on. And the smallest of them is the Angel that has one tongue. And they are the Angels of the Earth that we live upon.

Then he ؓ narrated from the Prophet ﷺ: *"The upshot is that as long as he recites it, the Angels of the entire universe recite it with him with all of their tongues. And the reward of their remembrance, with all of their tongues, is awarded to its reciter for every recitation, whether he recites it a little or a lot."*

Then the Shaykh said ؓ:

I asked the Master of Existence ﷺ if the reward for the remembrance of the Angel was equal to the reward for the recitation of the son of Adam, such as seventy thousand stations in Paradise and all of the glorification, remembrance, and *Salat al-Fatihi* and all. Or is the reward for the remembrance of the Angel less than that of the son of Adam?

He responded ﷺ, *"The reward for the remembrance of the Angel is multiplied by the reward for the remembrance of the son of Adam by ten. In other words, whatever reward the son of Adam receives for one recitation, the Angel's remembrance brings ten times that. And all of that reward- meaning for the remembrance of the Angels*

> *with all of their tongues- is obtained by the reciter of the Name according to how much he recites, whether a little or a lot."*

The Shaykh continued ﷺ, "One of the first things that the Master of Existence ﷺ said to me about the Name is":

> As for its reward, if anyone among the ordinary folk of my nation recites it, with every recitation, he receives the reward of one complete recitation of the Qur'an only, without anything being added to that. And that is for whoever knows that it is the Greatest Name when he recites it. As for the one who knows that that Name is the Name of the Essence, which has been reserved for it, and that it alone is the Name of the Essence apart from all other names of Allah; if one knows that and recites it, then he will have all of the rewards in addition to the reward of a complete recitation of the Qur'an. If he does not know that, then he will only have the reward of a complete recitation of the Qur'an alone. And whoever recites Surah al-Fatihah without being cognizant of the fact that he is reciting the Name with it, he will have the reward of Surah al-Fatihah alone. And if anyone recites it believing that he is reciting the Greatest Name with it, due to the fact that its letters are within it, he will receive the reward for reciting it (al-Fatihah) and the reward of reciting the Greatest Name with it.

What he meant ﷺ by its being the Name of the Essence apart from all other names is that all of the other names of Allah are names of His attributes and perfections. But the Essence only has this Name. Our Master ﷺ also said, "Contemplate this, and you will know that no worship can equal the recitation of this Name."

And our Master also said ﷺ:

> I asked Allah to give me, that for every recitation that I perform of the Name, every Angel in existence should recite it one billion times, and that every recitation upon the tongue of each Angel should equal sixty thousand *Salat al-Fatihi*. And I was given that and guaranteed it. And the Master of Existence ﷺ said to me, "*All of that is one eleventh of the owner of a special gift because he is granted all of that benefit with the recitation of but one letter of the Name.*"

And it was said to our Master ﷺ, "Is that benefit reserved for you, or is it for anyone who possesses a special gift?" He replied ﷺ, "That is for anyone who has a special gift." Then it was said to him, "And what about the benefit that whenever you recite a word of any remembrance, whatever it may be, that seventy thousand Angels recite it with you, with their remembrance multiplied by your remembrance seven thousand times, each word being worth ten good deeds?" He replied, "That is reserved for me. And it was not given to anyone else."

And I heard him ﷺ say that if all of the Knowers of Allah, from the time of Adam until the beginning of the Hour, recite the Name that was reserved for him, for one hundred twenty-seven years, reciting it every day one thousand times, and all of that remembrance were to be united, it would not equal one recitation of the remembrance that was reserved for him. May Allah benefit us by him, his sciences, and secrets. Amin.

And our Master ﷺ has conferred upon his companions the gift of this immense benefit: that seventy thousand Angels perform each remembrance with them. He said that in the month of Jumadi al-Thani in the year 1213 AH.

And our Master ﷺ was asked to confirm the benefit of the *Da'irah al-Ihatah*. He responded ﷺ:

> Consider if a person were to perform remembrance by mentioning all of the Names of Allah in every language. It would amount to half a recitation of the Greatest Formula of the Name (al-Kabir), and one full recitation of all else. What we mean is that it would be half a recitation of the Greatest Name that is the station of the Messenger of Allah ﷺ and one full recitation of all of the other formulas of the Name. That is because there is no limit to the number of formulas of the Name. And its benefit is multiplied by the remembrance of every Angel ten times. Then that benefit is multiplied seven hundred million times. Thus, if a person recites the Greatest Formula ten thousand times, it is a portion of the two hundred million twice over. And that is the benefit of the Greatest Formula. As for other formulas, they all contain half of this immense benefit.

Then he said ﷺ, "This is not known by women. Rather, it is specifically for men because it is an immense degree. And it is only given to one who has been written as beloved to Allah. May Allah make us from among them by His pure grace and generosity. Amin."

And among that which he dictated to us ﷺ is:

> If all of the recitations of the (Prophetic) nation, from the time that he was dispatched ﷺ until the blowing of the trumpet, it would not equal one pronunciation of the Greatest Name. All of that is

like a drop in a deep ocean compared to the Name. And this is a matter of which no one has knowledge. Allah kept that knowledge from His creation. But He unveils it to whomever He wills from among His creation.

Then he said ﷺ:

The Greatest Name is reserved for the Essence alone. Nothing else. And it is the Encompassing Name. And no one obtains all that is in it except for one person per age. That person is the Fard Jami'. But that is only the hidden Name. As for the Greatest Name that is manifest, it is the name of the Degree (of Divinity), which unifies all of the Divine attributes and qualities into the degree of Divinity. And below it is the degree of the different names. The outpourings of the Saints come from these names. Thus, if someone actualizes a Divine attribute, his outpouring is from that name. And for that reason, all of their spiritual states and stations differed. And all of the outpourings of the different degrees are portions of the outpouring of the Greatest Name of the Essence.

Then he said ﷺ:

Whenever someone recites the Great Name, Allah creates from that remembrance many Angels, whose number only Allah knows. Each one has the same amount of tongues as the number of Angels created from the remembrance of the Name. They are engrossed in remembrances at every blinking of an eye. In other words, at each instant, each one of them is engrossed in remembrance with all of his tongues. And they continue like that until the Day of Judgment.

Then he said ﷺ:

I asked the Master of Existence ﷺ to confirm for me the benefit of the *Musabba'at al-Ashr*; that if someone recites it once, no sin is written against him for one year. And he ﷺ said to me, "*The benefit and secret of every single remembrance are in the Great Name.*" And I knew that what he meant ﷺ was that all of the special qualities, benefits, and rewards of all remembrances are contained within the Great Name.

Then he said ﷺ:

The reward that is recorded for the reciter of the Great Name is that for every Angel that Allah has created in the universe, he receives the reward of twenty Nights of Power. And for every recitation of this Blessed Name, he receives the reward of every supplication, small or large, multiplied thirty million times.

Then he said ﷺ, "Consider if someone were to recite all of the names of Allah in all of the languages that exist. It would only equal one-half of the Knower of Allah's recitation of the Name."

As for the recitation that was reserved for the *Fard Saint* meaning our Shaykh Abu al-'Abbas ﷺ, one of his recitations is equal to the reward of any other Saint's recitation of the name one billion times over. And each of the Angels that we have mentioned, his reward is multiplied one billion times over. And each one of those multiplications is equal to all of the remembrance that has occurred in the universe from its beginning until the time that he recites it.

Then he said ﷺ, "That is as of right now. But when I reach the station that I have been promised, all of that will be granted to me with every letter of the Name. And that is reserved for me alone. And no one else can attain it."

Then he said:

> The reward of the Greatest Immense Name that was reserved for the Messenger of Allah ﷺ is that for each recitation, the rewards that have been mentioned, which had been multiplied by ten thousand, would be only one-seventieth of its reward. And that reward is obtained by anyone- even if they have not received the illumination- if he knows its degree. This means that one word of remembrance from all of that is multiplied seven hundred million times.
>
> As for the reward of the Fard Jami', when he recites it once, it is multiplied one billion times over. And the reward of one word of remembrance from the *Fard Jami'* and the remembrance of all of those Angels with all of their tongues is worth sixty thousand recitations of *Salat al-Fatihi*. And all the remembrances of the *Fard* and the Angels are first multiplied one billion times over and then multiplied by eleven. And the result is the reward that is given to the Fard Jami' is for each of the essences of the Fard Jami'. And he has three hundred sixty-six essences. And all of that reward is multiplied for his essence that is in Makkah one hundred times. That is the reward of the Fard Jami'. As for the ordinary person, if he knows its degree, when he recites the Greatest Name once, all of those Angels recite it with him with all of their tongues. And the reward for what is recited with each tongue is equal to six thousand recitations of *Salat al-Fatihi*.

Then he said ﷺ, "The Master of Existence ﷺ said to me":

> The Greatest Name has a veil cast over it. And Allah does not inform anyone of it, except the one who He has chosen for His love. And if people were to know it, they would become preoccupied with it to the exclusion of everything else. And if anyone knows it and leaves reciting the Qur'an and sending prayers upon me, due to the numerous benefits that he sees within it, he should fear for himself.

He also said ﷺ:

> Consider if each of one hundred thousand men were to recite the Great Name one hundred thousand times per day, and each one of them was to live one thousand years, it would not equal one-half of a recitation of the Owner of the Station. And for comparison, consider that if all of the names of Allah, the simple and compound of them, in all languages that exist, were to be recited all at one time, it would only equal one-half of the benefit of the Great Name.

And he said ﷺ:

> Indeed, the aforementioned benefit of the Great Name is reserved for the formula that is reserved for him ﷺ. And it is not transmitted, nor is permission given in it, except to the *Qutb Jami'*. As for the other formulas of the Name, each one of them contain one-half of the reward of the Great Name, as was mentioned. And that reward is obtained by anyone who receives a formula of the Greatest Name with a contiguous chain of transmission. As for the person who discovers it in a book, or anywhere else, and he recites it, then he will only have the reward of ten good deeds for each letter, and nothing else. And of the special qualities of the *Da'irah al-Ihatah* is that if Allah teaches anyone its formulas of utterances, without imparting its secrets, he will be safe from being robbed. And no one will be able to defeat him, even if he is not of the Saints of illumination. And only the Qutb will be able to take anything away from him.

Then he said ﷺ:

> The Messenger of Allah ﷺ gave me the Key to Qutbaniyyah [*Miftah al-Qutbaniyyah*]. And it is not given or mentioned to anyone, except those whom Allah has ordained to be Qutb. And this *Miftah*

al-Qutbaniyyah has an especially great benefit. And part of it is that if someone keeps to its recitation for eleven days, he will obtain any need that he asks for, even once, during those eleven days. And it has a response like that of the Greatest Name. And even if an ordinary person should do this, he will obtain a response, not to mention the person with illumination. But our Master ﷺ did not mention it to anyone because it was reserved for him.

And he said ﷺ, "The Knower of Allah becomes a letter from the letters of the Essence." It was said to him, "The letter has an Essence and the Knower of Allah has an essence. So how can they become one and the same essence?" He replied, "The meaning is that the Knower of Allah begins to perform *tasrif* with his essence, like the letter. It does not mean that he becomes the letter itself." Then he was asked, "Why does he not perform *tasrif* through the Exalted Names or the Subordinate Names?" He replied ﷺ:

> As for the Exalted Names, only the Fard Jami' knows them. As for the Subordinate Names, and other names of Allah, the Knower of Allah knows them. However, the Knower of Allah is too bashful before Allah to seek a need by the names of Allah. Rather, when he seeks a need, he turns his spiritual concentration towards it. And it is satisfied for him.

Then the Shaykh ﷺ said:

> My heart used to inform me that if anyone knows for certain the Owner of the Age [*Sahib al-Waqt*], meaning the Fard Jami', and knows the Name that is reserved for him, and he supplicates by them both, his supplication will be granted immediately. And I continued in that state for a time, until the Master of Existence ﷺ informed me of that, the same way that it had occurred to my heart.

Then he was asked ﷺ, "Is the Greatest Name what is meant by the name reserved for him ﷺ. Or is it another name?" He replied ﷺ:

> No. Rather, it is another name. That is because every individual creation has a name from the Exalted Names, by which its essence was brought into being. And it has a Subordinate Name by which it is distinguished from other creations. Shaykh al-Akbar ﷺ said, about His words ﷻ ﴿*And He taught Adam all of the names*﴾ [al-Baqarah, 31]:
>
> "The meaning is not what the exegetes have concluded. And if it had been that way, the special quality of Adam (peace be upon

him) would not have manifested. Rather, it means the Exalted Names. That is because every creation in existence has a name that corresponds to its greatness and worth. And by that name, it came to be."

About this same verse, the author of the "Ibriz" said, transmitting from his Shaykh:

> The names that are meant are the Exalted Names, not the Subordinate Names. Every creation has an Exalted Name and a Subordinate Name. The Subordinate Name is that name by which the one that is named is known in its entirety, while the Exalted Name is the name by which the origin of the one that is named is known, from what it was made, and what its benefit is. For example, all the proper uses of an ax are known. And the method of making it is also known. Thus, by simply hearing it pronounced, all of the sciences and gnosis connected to the ax are known. And it is the same for every creation. And the meaning of His words ﷻ ﴿*All of the Names*﴾ is those names that Adam was capable of bearing, that all human beings need, and that are connected to them. And it is every creation from below the Throne to below the earth.

And al-Busayri ؓ said:

> Yours is every science from the Knower of the Un-,
> Seen. And from them, Adam was taught the names.

I asked our Master ؓ, "Is the meaning of the couplet what was mentioned by the author of the "Ibriz" and Shaykh al-Akbar (may Allah be pleased with them both)?" He replied ؓ:

> Yes. As for the origin of the couplet, it is the special place of witnessing reserved for him ﷺ, in which no one, neither Prophet nor Saint, has a portion. The author of the "Hamziyyah" spoke truthfully when he said:
>
> > Degrees which hopes, in weariness, fall short of,
> > Well below them. And what is beyond them is beyond.
>
> He said this after saying:
>
> > He ascended by Him to the point of "Two bows-length,"

And that is mastery that befits him."

And I asked him ﷺ about the words of al-Busayri ؓ:

Your attributes were only portrayed to people,
As the stars are displayed in water.

He ﷺ replied:

Its meaning is that the Prophet ﷺ was only manifested to the Prophets and Messengers like the stars manifest in water. That is why Uways al-Qarni ؓ said to the companions, "You only saw his shadow." They said, "Not even Ibn Abi (Abu Bakr)?" He said, "Not even Ibn Abi Quhafa."

All of the great Saints were kept from perceiving the reality of his secret. Abu Yazid ؓ said, "I dove into the deep sea of gnosis seeking to discover the Muhammadan Reality. But there was between me and it one thousand veils of light. If I had lifted even one of them, I would have burned, as hair burns in a fire."

And this suffices for the benefit of some of the *Da'irah al-Ihatah*. And the intellect cannot bear what is beyond that, and texts cannot encompass it. And all that you have read here of reports, it is only from the Messenger. May Allah bless him, his family, his wives, his offspring, and his companions.

2.2 On His Emulation of the Prophetic Way, and a Description of Some of His High Conduct and His Beautiful Interaction with His Brothers and Loved Ones

2.2.1 His Adherence to the Sacred Law and the Sunnah

Allah ﷻ perfected our Shaykh and Master Abu al-'Abbas al-Tijani ؓ in the Sacred Law just as He had perfected him in Reality. And he traveled the most beautiful straight path that joins between them both. And he drank from them both a pure, delightful milk. And he inherited from them both a perfect, outstanding station. He became established in both spiritual states, ascended to the level of perfection in them both by complying with the requirements of both, adhering to the upright methodology of both. He took hold of both ends. He took the middle road between the two. He was a mountain between the two valleys and a barrier between the two seas. His sea did not dispel his piety, nor did his piety stray far from his sea. That was a strength and reinforcement from Allah to him, as well as a support and protection.

Allah reinforced him greatly in his emulation. And Allah caused him to inhabit fortified habitation. Thus, he is ؓ a signpost that directs towards adhering to the Sacred Law and following the Sunnah. And he has reached the highest state of preserving them both. He stops at and preserves the limits of Allah. And he obeys Him in His commands and prohibitions. There is no one that can either come near to him or equal him in that. He has made the Sunnah a ruler over himself and his family. And he made it his distinguishing mark in all of his actions and states.

He masterfully adhered, in the leading of the people of his house, to the concern that those who came before him had for preserving the religion and its distinguishing characteristics. Thus, he added perfection to perfection, beauty to beauty, until examples of this became very widespread, and men became needy of following them. And he modeled himself with conduct that conformed to the Sacred Law, and all of its observed etiquettes. In fact, his character is the Qur'an, and and all to which the Most Merciful commanded He is pleased with everything that pleases Allah. And he is angered by all that angers Him. He commands all that which Allah commands. And he warns of everything of which He has been warned. Thus, his wayfaring and characteristics were beautified for him. And his disposition and conduct are pleasant. And his exterior wayfaring and actions correspond to his interior character and attributes. And he was confirmed as an inheritor of the Messengerof Allah ﷺ. Thus, he caught up with the foremost of the people of the Party of Allah.

As for his conduct, he is extremely firm in the religion, having a lofty aspiration in it. And he is very concerned with the most important aspects of it after he has complied with its obligations. He is foremost in stopping at the limits and the commands and encourages others to stop at them. He very often says, "The best of remembrances is to remember Allah at the time of complying with his commands and prohibitions."

He is always fulfilling and respecting the rights of Allah. And he is ever on guard and scrupulous in matters of the religion. He is ever persevering in the religion and observing its ordinances. I have not seen anyone who is more firm or scrupulous in the religion. His whole being is firmness and resolution. He does not like explanations, nor does he incline towards looking for dispensations. He is knowing, scholarly, and studious in all of the sciences, as well as the life of the Prophet ﷺ in its entirety. And he has insight in what has been added to it and what has been removed. He tries to reach perfection, strives to be of the foremost, and hurries towards good action. He listens when people speak, adopts what is most excellent therein, and strives to put it into action. He is anxious to enact Allah's commandments and wary of falling into prohibited things. He venerates the mighty command of the Sacred Law and exalts the command of the Prophet ﷺ far too much to disobey them. And he is often heard quoting the words of Allah ﷻ:

❴*So let those beware who dissent from the Prophet's order, lest fitnah strike them or a painful punishment*❵ [47]

He loves to imitate the actions of the Prophet ﷺ, even if that action was not something he prescribed for us. And he often says, "It is imperative for a person if they hear of some of the modes of conduct or purely permissible acts of the Prophet ﷺ, that he perform that action, even if only once in a lifetime, seeking to conform to his state."

---

47 al-Nur, 63

And he adheres to the Sunnah in all of his states and circumstances. He loves to conform himself to it in all things. And he does not like to leave it in anything at all. And if some necessity prevents him, even though there is no blame on him, he says, "All good is in following the Sunnah. And all evil is in contradicting it."

He often incites people to act upon their knowledge. This goes especially for those who busy themselves with knowledge. That is because the speed and distance traveled by any ship depend on the strength and goodness of its wind. And the longer iron is heated, the easier it is to shape with exactitude.

And He ﷻ has been provided strength in following him ﷺ that is commensurate with his copious light and immense spiritual state. And how great is his concern for the religion! And how extreme is his love for it and seeking perfection in it, following the Master of the Messengers ﷺ! He loves to worship his Lord, and he venerates His commands. He worships Him in the perfect way that the Knowers of Allah, who humble themselves before His Majesty, worship Him. And he obeys Him with the same obedience as those who are happily and madly in love with Him. He puts into action leaving pleasures and desires and is ever directing others to that by his spiritual state and his words.

He observes obligatory and Sunnah acts, performing them in the best manner, being neither negligent nor slack in them. And he perseveres in performing the prayers at their proper time, always performing them in a congregation. And he performs their bowing and prostration with perfection, in a complete manner, and in a perfect way, with devotion and tranquility. Its likeness is the prayer of the submissive Knowers of Allah. And do not ask about his abundant submissiveness, humility, and excellent conduct and manner in the prayer! Anyone who knows his state finds it impossible to stand next to him in the rows, for fear that he may disturb him.

And he often incites people to perform the five prayers at their proper times and in a congregation. And he also incites to performing the night prayer, especially at the end of the night. He calls to it and encourages people to do it with emphasis. And he is zealous to perform it, saying, "In it descend mercies and benevolent Divine breezes." And he also says, "If Allah wakes someone up (in the last part of the night), He has summoned him to His mercy."

And he always performs the ritual bath [ghusl] on Fridays. And he emphasizes it due to its emphasis in the Sunnah. And he performs it according to the Sunnah, performing it just before he departs. And he puts on clean clothes if they are available. Otherwise, he goes to the Jami' Masjid with whatever he has. He does not put on the fragrance of musk or any other on the day of Jum'ah- even though it is preferred to put on a fragrance that day. And he does not put it on any other day either, even though he loves it greatly and is attracted to it. But, perhaps the reason he does not use it is the proliferation of its use among the people of luxury and those foolish people who seek luxury. He walks with ease to all of the prayers. He loves to do that to act upon the Hadith, "*When you come to the prayer, come to it with tranquility and dignity.*"⁴⁸

His consummate practice ﷺ is to seek verification and painstaking accuracy in all things, great or small so that he may arrive at the truth. Thereby, he has removed from himself the bridle of imitation and blind faith in every individual matter, to the point that he has encompassed, with his investigations, probes, contemplation, and deliberation, all of the formal sciences, removing difficulties and puzzling problems. Thus, he became a relied upon Imam in all of the sciences, whose clarification is sought out, a knower of its explanations and verdicts, principles and rulings, its derived, understood, and stated principles, as well as its abrogated and abrogating rulings. And he studied deeply ﷺ all of the transmitted and conventional sciences until he became unparalleled, the breadth of his ocean being neither equaled nor surpassed. And his manner with the science of Reality is the same, following all of the same principles. Thus, with that he gathered the conditions of Shaykhhood and leadership completely. And he displays its reality and essence. And he remembers Allah (Mighty and Exalted is He) at all times. His prayer beads are never separate from him. And he loves to do many remembrances of Allah. And he incites others to that.

And he says, "Allah prescribed for us, in everything, an amount and a form, except His remembrance ﷻ. For He said (Mighty and Exalted is He):

❴*O you who have believed, remember Allah with much remembrance*❵ ⁴⁹

And He said ﷻ:

❴*Who remember Allah while standing or sitting or [lying] on their sides*❵ ⁵⁰"

And he ﷺ adheres to his litanies after the Fajr prayer until mid-morning in seclusion. Likewise, he adheres to his litanies from the Maghrib

---

48   Sahih al-Bukhari (Hadith no. 600); Sahih Muslim (Hadith no. 945) with slightly different wording.
49   al-Ahzab, 41
50   Al Imran, 191

prayer until the time of the Isha prayer. And he also does this in seclusion. He also has a set of litanies after the Asr prayer until sunset. And he has said ﷺ, "I only perform the remembrances that the Messenger of Allah ﷺ has arranged for me."

He also sticks to sending a lot of prayers on the Messenger of Allah ﷺ in all of his states. And to this, he incites his companions, especially *Salat al-Fatihi*, due to its immense benefit- the explanation of which will come in its proper place if Allah ﷻ so wills. If anyone asks him for something other than the well-known litany, he says to him, "Perform a lot of prayers upon the Messenger of Allah ﷺ with *Salat al-Fatihi*. For in it is the good of this world and the Hereafter. By it, all wishes are attained. And the student attains by it all kinds of desires." This is his state right now ﷺ.

He guards his limbs against that which Allah has prohibited. Thus, he turns away from vain and improper speech. And he guards his tongue against it. And he does not listen to anything false. No one can mention falsehood in his gathering. And if anyone mentions anything prohibited (in his presence), he unfailingly corrects him, whoever it may be or whatever he may have mentioned. He has no tolerance for that. And he warns very severely against backbiting. And he flees from it without fail. And he mentions the verses of the Qur'an and the Hadiths that have been revealed regarding it. And he is very excessive in prohibiting it.

He strives to tell the truth when he speaks ﷺ. And he invites others to strive for it. Those who speak the truth make him happy. And he is displeased with those who lie. He is impressed with those who do what they say, even if it is an ugly action. And he deems him good. And those who speak the truth are in his utmost good graces. And he does not like a lot of swearing by Allah, out of fear of breaking the oath. And he says, "One should accustom himself to say, 'If Allah so wills,' whenever he wishes to swear an oath." He fears that his swearing may be effectual, and he may not be exonerated, or that he may break his oath and not expiate for it.

He ﷺ lowers his gaze. So you will not find him traveling any path, except that he is looking where he is walking. He does not look around. That is his natural disposition as well as his habit. Thus, when he sits with the people, most of the time he is unaware of their states. And he teaches all those who are present with him to do the same.

And he does not like to meet people a lot. Nor does he like to be engrossed with them in what they are doing. And when he meets one of his companions, he does not say more to him than "Peace be upon you." And none of them is able to kiss his hand, teaching them not to overburden themselves, and preferring them to incline towards having good character inwardly. And that is the true good character, different from the emphasis on kissing the hand of any respectable person that people have become accustomed to. That is his way with those who he knows or who frequent his presence. He only makes an exception for the person who cannot resist or a negligent person who does not know what he is doing. As for those who do not know him, he pardons and excuses them for fear that he may break their hearts. Thus, when he walks down any street, people bow their heads towards him and greet him by kissing his limbs. And at times, they crowd around him due to the awe and reverence for him that overtakes them and the love that Allah has for him that flows to their hearts, as was related in the Hadith. "*When Allah ﷻ loves a slave, He calls Jibril and says to him, 'Indeed, I love so and so. So you too love him.' Then Jibril loves him and makes a call throughout the Heavens saying, 'Indeed, Allah loves so and so. So you too love him, o, people of the Heavens.' Then he is granted acceptance in the earth.*"[51]

Before this time, he ﷺ would prohibit many people kissing his hand. And he would reprimand anyone who did it, whether that person was close to him or not, as we mentioned in the section on his beginning. As for now, he has stopped that because Allah has transferred him to the state of religious Khilafah. And his state became that which we have just described. May Allah be pleased with him and he with Him. And may He grant us His satisfaction. Amin.

2.2.2 His Keeping and Strengthening of Family Ties

As for his keeping and strengthening of family ties, he keeps ties with both religious and blood relations. As for blood relations, he keeps ties with anyone who has a close family relationship with him. He satisfies their needs and is concerned with their conditions. He supports them and advocates for them. And he shares with them what Allah has provided him. He relieves them of their burdens and fulfills their needs. He helps them with the loss of wealth, burdens, and calamities. So there is not any issue that concerns them, except that they bring it up with him and find relief and a way out through his blessing.

He does not neglect them in any worldly or religious matter. And he is gentle with the elders among them and merciful towards the young. And he educates them the way he educates his children. If he sees any one of them perform an ugly act, he rebukes him. And he goes to extra lengths to sincerely advise them. And he fulfills their rights in the most beautiful way, being adamant and steadfast in that.

---

51   Sahih al-Bukhari (Hadith no. 3209); Sahih Muslim (no. 2639).

He incites people to fulfill the rights of their close relations. And he counsels them to begin with their family before wanting to give charity to others. And in this, he is acting upon what has been narrated in the Hadiths. And how much does he give exhortations regarding parents, emphasize their rights, and warn against disobedience to them both! He often says, "If someone is not kind to his parents, then traveling this Path will not be easy for him. And whoever persists in disobeying his parents, after having entered into this Path, it will cut him off from it." And then he will not obtain anything from him. And how often a person who violates their rights acts arrogantly, and then this fact is proved true upon him.

As for his religious relations, he is among the people most insistent on keeping their ties. And he is the most charitable and giving person to the people of his fold. He gives charity to his brethren and companions, and whoever has a relationship with him in Allah, with all kinds of charity. And he is benevolent with them. So he feeds their hungry, takes those of them that are lost under his wing, clothes those of them who are naked, aids the destitute among them, and assists the weak among them.

Then he is very concerned with the people of religious brotherhood. He is hurt by what they suffer more than he is hurt by the suffering of his close relations. The closest of people to him are those who love Allah the most. So a person becomes close to him through that, even if he is the furthest from blood relations. And the person who is distant from Allah is distanced from him, even if he is of the closest blood relations. And he views leaving them as impossible. I have heard him on more than one occasion saying, "If someone is afflicted with violating the rights of his brethren, he will inevitably be afflicted with violating the Divine rights."

We ask Allah for safety and freedom from such an enormous affliction, which has become the general attribute of those who claim brotherhood in this contemptible age.

2.2.3 His Moderation

As for his appearance, he dresses in moderate clothes as long as they protect him from heat and cold, just as the ordinary people dress. He does not like to be distinguished either by excessively beautiful dress or ugly clothes. And he does not allow anything in his house except what has been narrated in the Sunnah. Indeed, he has cut them off from all excess and luxury. This way of his is clear. And explaining it in detail would take some time.

And he exonerates himself completely from all claims. And he renounces them completely. And he does not allow anyone to make claims. If for some reason he narrates any good action that he has done, or he indicates some high state that he has had, he attributes it to an unknown person. So he says, "Such and such a thing happened to one person, or to a man." But he does not say that it happened to him. Later perhaps we may meet with a person who was with him at the time that that thing occurred, so he narrates to us that it was him. And in such a way do we find out about that state of his.

He does not like for anyone to attribute anything to him, or to claim assuredly that he has any secret. Nor does he permit anyone to praise him in his gathering. And if anyone directs any praise towards him, he only pardons him if it is concealed or if the person is ignorant and unaware. And he rebukes severely the claim of complete dependence on Allah, or anything that indicates this claim. He often says, "Until now, we have not even attained perfect repentance and faith." Or he says something to the same effect, as a warning to the listeners and a lesson for the followers. And teaching by action is the most effective and most successful form of counsel. May Allah reward him greatly on our behalf and increase him in blessing and grace.

And that method has shown success. And to Allah belongs all praise for that. And it has taken effect among his companions who are here. They do not like claims or people who busy themselves with claims, due to his known spiritual state, what they hear in his words, and what they witness of his fleeing from claims. That is because claims are a greater test than calamities. And we frequently hear him seeking refuge in Allah from that. He often says, "Indeed, the punishment for claims is to die in a bad state. May Allah ﷻ be our refuge."

He reprimands with these words those who listen. And these words are proven true upon those who claim what they do not have. They are requited with a bad ending. We ask Allah for safety and freedom from such a great catastrophe. He seeks obscurity and does not like notoriety. Nor does he like people to give him gifts, just as will come in the section on his asceticism if Allah ﷻ so wills.

2.2.4 His Love of the People of the House of the Prophet ﷺ

As for his love of the People of the Prophetic House, he loves them greatly and has a deep affection for them. And he is concerned with all of their affairs. He is ever eager to do good to them. And he humbly beseeches Allah for that which will cause them good. He is extremely generous and kind to them. And he humbles himself greatly before them. And he has the most beautiful manners with them. He sincerely advises and reminds them. And he instructs them to conduct themselves with the character of the Prophet ﷺ and to act upon his Sunnah. And he often says, "The noble descendants are the most appropriate of people to inherit from the Messenger of Allah ﷺ."

He incites people towards loving them, raising their status, and being humble and courteous with them. And he makes clear their immense majesty and high status. He sees being slack with their affairs and their love as a deficiency in faith. And he does not love anyone who antagonizes them, competes with them, or has poor manners with them. And he rebukes severely anyone who does any of that. May Allah be well pleased with him, he with Him, and may He cause us to enjoy His satisfaction.

From his great love and courtesy towards them and his humility before their high status is that he does not relent to any one of his companions who wishes to marry (the Prophet's ﷺ) female relations into their families out of fear that he will neglect or violate some of their mandatory rights. And I have seen him one day being very harsh with one of his companions who wanted to marry a noble female descendant. And he denied him that and said, "If you do that, I exonerate myself from you in this world and the Hereafter."

We seek refuge in Allah from disobeying him in his absence or his presence. And that (denying companions marriage to a noble female descendant) was because he feared that he would do something that they would hate or be hurt by. And thereby Fatimah, the daughter of the Prophet ﷺ, would be angered. Thus, he ﷺ would be angered. And this he derived from the Hadith that was related by Imam Ahmad in his "Musnad," al-Hakim in his "Mustadrak," al-Tabarani, and al-Bayhaqi, from al-Miswar b. Makhramah ؓ, when al-Hasan al-Muthanna proposed to the former's daughter as a second wife after his paternal cousin Fatimah b. al-Husayn (may Allah be pleased with them both). And he offered him a pretext in the way of the Hadith, *"Fatimah is a part of me. What hurts her hurts me. And what makes her happy makes me happy."*[52]

And he stated that he was already married to his paternal cousin. And that would anger her and anger her grandmother (may Allah be pleased with her), the daughter of the Messenger of Allah ﷺ.

So our Master's ﷺ actions with those who sought his counsel correspond to the action of that noble companion. And he followed his methodology in exaltation and veneration of them. That is because the one who marries into their families may see himself as somewhat the same as them. And thereby he will belittle their dignity. And many a time he counsels people to dignify them, venerate them, and be careful to venerate their station by not intermarrying with them, out of fear that a person may think himself worthy of that. And as a consequence, he will marry from them just as they

---

52 Al-Mustadrak 'ala al-Sahihayn (Hadith no. 4848).

married from him. And he will not see them as having any special status, and he will belittle their high station. That is a sickness of the heart and a hidden weakness, of which only the masters of their hearts are cautious and watchful.

And from his great veneration for their status and jealousy for them is that he does not like anyone who associates with them for some gain, those who deceive them in any way, or those who hide any sincere advice from them. He considers that very ugly and hates anyone who does that. The upshot is that his love and veneration for the People of the Prophetic House is so great that we have not seen anything like it among the people of our time. Nor have we heard of anything equal to it. Rather, it is something that he alone has and in which he alone has been firmly established. And even though love is an attribute of the heart, its increase is known by states and situations that indicate it. And we do not know anyone, in our time, who loves and venerates the noble descendants the way that he does. But that is not something odd in a person like him.

Love of the People of the Prophet, may Allah grant us the greatest portion of it, is from the results and fruits of true faith. And such are all of the Muhammadan ways of our Shaykh ﷺ, in whose explanation, traces, and dissemination are lessons for those who take lesson, reminders for those who are reminded, a reinforcement for the God-conscious, a strengthening to those with God-given success, a support for those who turn, an awakening for those who take heed, a proof for the followers, and an evidence against the rejecters. May Allah provide us with his blessing and increase our love for him.

2.2.5 His Excellent Character

As for his excellent character ﷺ, it comprises all of the possible majestic attributes and praiseworthy character that fall under the category of noble character. They are intelligence, cleverness, bravery, courage, compassion, loving care, kindness, mercy, perseverance, sufferance, humility, good manners, and high aspiration. It also comprises of those attributes of nobility and generosity, such as virtue, chastity, and faithfulness. And finally, it comprises chivalry, which comprises generosity, munificence, forbearance, deliberateness, pardon, altruism, and eagerness to fulfill the needs of the righteous. They are twenty-one qualities. But we have already discussed four of them, namely his intelligence, cleverness, bravery, and courage. The others will be discussed from here on if Allah so wills.

Allah ﷻ had honored him with noble traits that were inborn in him and part of his natural disposition. So when he received what illumination he was to receive, they became a means of approach to Allah and a connection to His Presence. And each one of them took its rightful place in it (the Presence) and inclined to that for which it was created. Thus, all his traits became for Allah and in Allah. So his goal is to understand what Allah has willed. His deliberateness is his perfection of worship. His patient perseverance is his tranquility with the enactment of the Divine decrees. His sufferance is his fulfillment of needs and desires of others. His bravery is his strength in the religion. His assisting is his helping in the path of the rightly guided. His liberality is his selling himself for Allah and in Allah. His high aspiration is his cutting himself off from everything apart from Him. His chivalry and faithfulness are his way of dealing with his Lord. Each of these qualities was a preparation for the other. And he ascended by them to a great station. Everyone is facilitated towards that for which they were created.

Just as his noble, universally beneficial characteristics, which include compassion, loving care, kindness, and mercy, you will only find him compassionate and sympathetic, caring and gentle. He is compassionate with the Muslims and at the service of the indigent. He is pained by their afflictions and cares for their state. And he is gentle with those in need and generous with those in need. He is more affectionate with those who are strangers than he is with those who are close to him. And he inclines towards them. He is compassionate with them, sits with them, befriends them, and associates with them. This goes especially for those of them who possess a sound disposition, who do not conceal any of their states, no matter how small or great they may be.

We often see him being generous and gentle with them, having mercy on them, and honoring them. Their state amazes him. And he praises them beautifully in their absence. Not one of them complains of any sickness or ailment, except that he becomes concerned for him and turns his concern to his situation. And he does not cease remembering him and supplicating for him. And he asks about his state until Allah removes that from him and relieves him. He never sees anyone who is enduring an affliction except that he feels great sympathy for him and supplicates for him. And he will say, "May Allah, out of His generosity, give us refuge from His calamities. Amin." That is his habit. May Allah be pleased with him and he with Him. And may the Noble Countenance be his orientation and place of return.

And from his excellent character, in which he has excelled those who came before him and which those who come after him are unable to duplicate, is his humility, good manners, and beautiful character and social interaction. He is gentle of heart, merciful with every Muslim. He smiles in the face of anyone who meets him. Everyone who meets him assumes that he is closer to him than anyone else because of the cheerfulness in his face, his beautiful manner of speaking to him, and his constantly facing him. In fact, if a sad person should meet him, his sadness is removed just by his meeting him. He is easygoing and flexible in all matters, even in walking. He would remind you of His words ﷻ:

> ❴And the servants of the Most Merciful are those who walk upon the Earth easily, and when the ignorant address them, they say, "Peace"❵ [53]

I have not seen anyone more beautiful in character than him, nor anyone greater in compassion, more generous with himself, more gentle of heart, more loyal to friends and allies, or more knowledgeable and understanding. And despite his great status, he supports the young, reveres the old, sits with the weak, and humbles himself to the poor, following in that, like the Messenger of Allah ﷺ.

No one seeks to argue with him about any science except that he silences him. And he remains dumbfounded and astonished at his amazing knowledge and understanding. And he is of those in whom Allah has joined knowledge, action, and greater sainthood- in which he ascended unto the highest levels, concern and earnestness for the creation and that which will draw them near to Allah ﷻ, the highest level of patiently bearing their abuse, and the great reverence and respect that he enjoys in the hearts of people- the like of which has not been given to any of the contemporary Gnostics, Saints, Ascetics, or anyone else. For that reason, people travel to him from far-off lands, seeking blessing through him, taking from him, and relying on him in religious, worldly, and otherworldly matters. Thus, you will not find anyone who comes near to him, much less equals him, in mercy and guidance.

Despite all of this, he ﷺ humbles himself to Allah. And he is humble, for the sake of the Essence of Allah, towards those slaves of Allah that are close to Him, the People of the Prophetic House, and anyone with whom he has a religious relationship, or whom he loves for the sake of faith. As for his humbling himself, he does not see himself as having any status, associate himself with any authority, nor does he believe that he has any right upon anyone- even his family and children. Rather, he places himself in the service of his family. And he does not consider himself above doing anything, no matter what it is. Nor does he like to distinguish himself or consider himself worthy of anything. Rather, he sees everyone else as more distinguished than him. He often says, "Perhaps Allah will show us mercy through the gatherings of Muslims." He attributes to himself lowly things

---

53   al-Furqan, 63

and does not exonerate himself of any blameworthy trait or ugly action. And he witnesses the rights that people have over him. He will say, "We have not yet fulfilled the rights that we know others have upon us. And we will never be able to fulfill them." He also says, "The believer is the one that sees everyone else's rights over him while he does not believe he has any right over anyone."

As for his humility, for the sake of Allah, before the servants of Allah, he places himself at the service of all those around him, whether he is one of his companions or anyone else, in all circumstances. And under no circumstances is he bothered by hardships that befall him. And he does not let anyone occupy himself with venerating him or distinguishing him in any way, such as kissing his hand. Nor does he allow anyone to do that forcefully. He does not deem himself deserving of any of that.

As for his decorum, inwardly and outwardly, in the Muhammadan Law and in his dealings with Allah (Exalted is His Majesty), it is something in which he has reached the highest limit. And in it, he surpassed both the beginners and the experts, just as has been known from his state and speech. And the proof of this is in those attributes and actions of his that have been mentioned.

When the jurists mention decorum, it refers to performing those extra and desirable acts that are beyond the obligatory and Sunnah acts, which are related to the different situations of a person's life, such as life and wakefulness, eating, drinking, remembrance, supplication, etc. And when the Sufis mention it, it refers to gathering all of the good characteristics and noble attributes. Thus, it is an attribute that comprehends majestic attributes and praiseworthy character, by the attribute of slavehood and the majesty of Lordship. And whoever joins between them has been characterized by decorum.

And he was refined, displaying decorum with Allah ﷻ and His Messenger ﷺ. And decorum in the former meaning is included in the latter. And our Master ﷺ has gathered all decorum, outwardly and inwardly, secretly and openly. May Allah have mercy on the person who said:

> When he spoke, he was completely pleasant,
> And when he was silent, he was altogether lovely.

From his outward decorum is his perseverance in adhering to the decorum of the Sacred Law, related to different life situations, as narrated in the Sunnah and his steadily applying it as much as he is able in his standing, sitting, lying down, walking, and posture. He has never been seen stretching his legs towards the direction of prayer [*qiblah*]. And he has never spit while he was sitting in the mosque. Nor has he raised his voice in it. And if he hears anyone raising his voice in the mosque, he stops him. And if he sees anyone lacking in the decorum of the Sacred Law, he cautions him. If it is someone who should know better, he will say, by way of reprimand and censure, "Has that been narrated in the Sunnah?" And he does not like to adhere to any of the customary mannerisms of people, which have neither been narrated nor forbidden in the Sunnah, sufficing himself with that which has been narrated in the Sacred Law, and inculcating the high character of the Sunnah.

And from his inward decorum ﷺ, which his words and deeds indicate, is that he does not choose anything alongside the choice of Allah. Nor does he seek to direct anything alongside the direction of Allah, just as we have mentioned. In fact, anytime he supplicates for himself or anyone else, for anything whose ending is unknown, or in which there is any enjoyment, his supplication is to seek that which Allah chose for him. And he says to us time after time:

> I only supplicate with my tongue and heart completely submissive before Allah ﷻ, saying, "'I do not want anything. Nor do I seek anything. Do as You wish. And decree what You wish." And I only comfort the creation with (what I say on) my tongue so that their hearts will not be broken.

And sometimes, when someone seeks his supplication, he will say, "I do not supplicate," out of good conduct with Allah (Exalted is His Majesty) and because he knows ﷺ that what Allah chooses for the slave is better for him than what the slave chooses for himself or anyone else.

Yet, he is ever dedicated to the supplications that have been narrated from the Lawgiver, which include things that are hoped for or feared, drawing near or connecting with Allah (Exalted is His Majesty), or the attribute of slavehood by manifesting neediness, flattery, begging, and humility towards Allah ﷻ, as well as seeking repentance, forgiveness, mercy and acceptance from Him (Majestic and Exalted is He). And his heart and tongue remain wet with them. He says, "There is no choosing alongside what Allah chooses in any of that because it has been commanded in the Sacred Law." And many times, we have heard him supplicate, "May Allah accept you through His sheer grace and satisfaction."

And from his decorum ﷺ is that he does not like to involve himself in taking charge of the decrees of Allah (Blessed and Exalted is He) or speaking in opposition to what has already occurred. Nor does he hope for or wish to change any of the situations that befall him. He considers becoming involved in any of that as turning away from Allah ﷻ and bad manners with Him.

And he attributes all shortcomings to the ego and he only considers any shortcoming from it that afflicts the slave to be from the Divine decree. The practical application of his considering the shortcoming to be from the Divine decree is as follows: After recognizing that it is from Allah, conducting himself with the character of the Sacred Law, and confirming that completion is only attributed to Allah, he does not attribute to anyone else. But he only attributes the effects of His decree to himself, observing the station of moral conduct with Him ﷻ. And he tells a famous story regarding that, about one of the past kings:

> He had a servant boy who he honored greatly. His ministers asked him about that. So he decided to manifest (the boy's) superiority over them. He brought out to them a beautiful jewel and commanded them to crush it. So each one of them began to indicate to him that he should keep it. Then he commanded the servant boy to crush it, and he crushed it immediately without arguing. Then the king censured him and rebuked him for breaking it. So he began to humbly implore him, "O, my Master! O, my Lord!" The king then said, "I commanded you to do it first. But you tried to talk me out of it. And if you had done it, and I had blamed you, you would have said, 'You commanded us.' However, he obeyed first and then humbled himself afterward. That is why I love him."

This should give you an idea of his inner decorum. As for what is beyond that, such as observing his thoughts, breaths, and orientations, as well as his decorum with Allah in all of that, it is something that we cannot perceive. And there may be some modes of inner conduct whose indication was manifest, but that we were unaware of its indication. And decorum is commensurate with gnosis. And his complete gnosis ﷺ, which requires perfect decorum and these perfect character traits in which he achieved the highest limit, and which are all included in decorum, should not be hidden from you after all that we have mentioned.

In summary, his decorum with Allah and His Messenger ﷺ, and his humility within himself and to the elect and the ordinary people, is ingrained in his being. And his patience, forbearance, gentleness, kindness, great chivalry, and high aspiration- all of these characteristics especially, and all of his character traits in general- are something that hardly exists and rarely manifests. It only occurs to the elect of the elect among the people of *siddiqiyyah*[54], exclusivity of worship, gnosis, and special Divine

---

54 The state of being a *Siddiq*.

unity- those who have been engrossed in the mercy of the Most Merciful and who are included in His grace and generosity. Whenever he decides to manifest His grace upon a slave, He makes him worthy of His love and affection. And He annihilates him in Himself and effaces his attributes with His attributes. Then his limbs bear beautiful fruit of many different kinds. And He inculcates every beautiful attribute and noble character trait. Blessed is the Merciful Lover, full of grace and generosity, who has honored His creation and increased the provision of whomever He wills. There is no God but He. And the only good is His good. There is no giver other than Him. And no one shows mercy other than Him. And may Allah bless our Master Muhammad and his family.

Section Three

On His Knowledge, His Generosity, His Munificence, His Nobility, His Faithfulness, His Fear of Allah, His Patience, His High Aspirations, His Scrupulousness, His Asceticism, His Spiritual Counsel, His Independence, His Guiding to Allah, His Gathering People in His Way, and His Leading People to Him by His Words and Spiritual State (It has three subsections.)

3.1 On His Knowledge, His Generosity, His Munificence, His Nobility, and His Faithfulness

3.1.1 His Knowledge

AS FOR THE OUTWARD SCIENCES, he obtained an abundant share. And he gained an ample supply and portion of its principles and rulings. Then he cast towards every excellence and nobility an arrow that struck its target. There is no knowledge that is expounded upon except that he has expounded upon it to the point that it has been said, "No one is better than him."

It is the same whether it is the science of Theology, Qur'anic Exegesis, Hadith, Biographical Research, Sufism, and States, or any others of the literary sciences, such as grammar, jurisprudence, and poetry. He is a partner of the jurists in their outward knowledge. But he has no equal in the spiritual sciences. Rather, he has excelled the jurists, regarding removing doubts and difficult, ambiguous matters, in an indescribable way, just as will be seen, if Allah so wills, in the section on his responses to certain questions.

Whenever he ﷺ speaks about any subject from the outward sciences, whether it is Qur'anic Exegesis, Hadith, or anything else, he extracts from it knowledge of the Hereafter, due to what his inner reality encompasses of fear of Allah ﷻ, vigilance of Him, and never inclining towards the adornments of this world. It is as if he is witnessing the Hereafter directly in front of him. So his reading of the exoteric sciences, in reality, have become his reading of the esoteric sciences. He often says (what means), "The (real) scholar is that person who brings out the complexities of what seems clear and clarifies what is complex. That is due to his immense knowledge, varied understanding, and excellent insight and investigation."

Then this is the person whose gathering it is imperative to attend so that one may hear his rare and unique knowledge. About this, Shaykh Ibn 'Arafah said in the couplet that is attributed to him:

If in a gathering of knowledge there is little,
   Clarification of that which appears difficult,

Investigating rare text or removing doubt,
   Or ambiguity revealed by pure contemplation,

Then abandon eagerness for that gathering inspect your soul and struggle (against it),
   And beware of leaving it because it has the evilest disposition.

As for his hidden knowledge of reality, which is supported by the Divine light, he is the Qutb around which it revolves and the sun of its morning light. Whenever anyone hears his speech about it, they say, "This is the speech of someone who has no residence except Allah's unseen world." The place of these sciences is the heart and they are the treasure of secrets and the beginning of lights. For that reason, it is impossible to express them. Only those who are attributed with it and experiment with it know the sweetness of it. For that reason, he ﷺ prefers the love of his great Lord to anyone else. He maintains awareness of Him and does not enjoy the company of anyone else. Rather, you will find him most often fleeing to seclusion. His contemplation has excelled in gnosis of Him ﷻ. Thus, the rarest secrets were unveiled to him and lights manifested to him, just as was said by someone:

And solitary with Allah, enchanted by His love,
   So for him, there is no intimacy with anything besides the Lord,

He is unmatched in the world in obedience to his Lord,
   So He caused him to inherit the knowledge of the Book without doubt,

And he prefers the love of Allah. Thus, there were unveiled for him,
   The rarest of secrets as a reward for his love,

Because whoever is sincere in his claim to love,
   Lights are manifest to him without any veil,

Thus, he graces in the garden of gnosis forever,
   Whose sweetness is more desirable than eating or drinking,

Spiritual states address him from every direction,
   So he understands it with his mind and with his heart,

> He uncovers the secrets in their hidden kingdom,
> So there comes to him a flood from the hidden world.

And other things have been said.

And there is no doubt that the Masters who have been characterized by the spiritual states of the attributes are those who have inherited the Prophets in a real manner. And they have followed them inwardly and outwardly. Thus, they join between the Sacred Law and Reality in the best of ways. And our Master ﷺ has surpassed them. And he obtained what he obtained. So he is ﷺ an example for the followers and guidance for the seekers of guidance, due to his joining between subtle states, truthful statements, and genuine acts. His inner reality comprises the Reality of Divine unity, and his observable reality is asceticism and divestment. And his speech is guidance to every disciple.

3.1.2 His Generosity

As for his generosity ﷺ, from his blessed character and natural disposition is his frequent spending and giving in the way of Allah. He fulfilled that perfectly from his youth, and he continues in that however he wills. Allah made generosity an inborn attribute. Then He made him discharge it in a way that corresponds to the Sacred Law until Allah ﷻ caused him to ascend to the height of completeness. And He made him of those who witness for themselves neither authority nor wealth. Thus, Allah joined in him the two states with a joining that was done by Allah. And who can be better at acting than Allah? His efforts in spending are great, examples of it are numerous, his acts of generosity are amazing, and his exploits are extraordinary. He is one of the rarities of the age and a sign of Allah that has appeared to the eyes.

He gives as a person who is not afraid of poverty. And he does not mind being excessive or immoderate. And how should he care, when his heart has been emptied of transitory things, ascended to the station of excellence and gnosis, risen to the height of perfection and the degrees of men of excellence- who have abandoned luxuries and profits and given spirit and soul. They are the most generous of creation and truly the most munificent. So there is no grace except theirs. Nor is there any benefit theirs

That is because their spending is from the source of generosity. And their munificence is from His overflowing benefit. They do not see themselves as owning anything that they should give it or refuse to give it. So how can their situation be described? And their status in that is unknowable. However, we will mention something of what we have seen from our Shaykh and teacher ﷺ- some stories and occurrences, and some of his great generosity and giving. That is because the goal is to mention and spread some stories and anecdotes that illustrate these instances of generosity.

His habit ﷺ is to spend in the way of Allah and to feed for the sake of Allah. And he separates portions of his wealth here and there at all times, between charity, family maintenance, keeping of family ties, or other charity, in ease and hardship, when he is traveling or at home, from all of the types of wealth that he obtains, such as cash, assets, fruits, and vegetables. He often says, "All wealth belongs to Allah. And I am only the treasurer of Allah, His employee, and representative in that."

That is due to His words ﷻ:

❴And spend out of that in which He has made you vicegerent❵ [55]

And his words ﷺ, as narrated in Bukhari, Muslim, Tirmidhi, Ibn Majah, and Ahmad- all from Abu Hurayrah ؓ: *"The hand of Allah is full. It is not exhausted by His spending throughout the night and the day. Have you not seen what He has spent since He created the Heavens and the earth? And still what is in His hand has not been exhausted. And His Throne was over the water. And in His hand is the scale. He lowers, and He raises."*[56]

And his habit in all of that ﷺ, especially with charity, is to go to extremes to hide it. In fact, at most times and in most situations, people are not aware that he is the one giving because when he gives anything to a person, he does not give it to him in his hand. Rather, he orders for it to be done and sends it. Then he orders the one with whom he sends it to conceal it, seeking the most perfect manner in which Allah had preferred in His Book ﷻ by His words:

❴It is better for them❵ [57]

It is also for the preservation of the one to whom he is giving, hoping to raise his aspiration so that he may be grateful for the blessing of his Lord and not look expectantly at the one upon whose hands the blessing came. He says:

> Whenever someone looks to me expectantly, my heart withdraws from him, and I do not want to give him a thing. But if he stops looking to receive something from the creation, I am the most eager of people to help him and give to him. And I find the offer-

---

55   al-Hadid, 7
56   Sahih al-Bukhari (Hadith no. 7411); Sahih Muslim (Hadith no. 993).
57   al-Baqarah, 271

ing more pleasant when I give the wealth of my Lord to the slave of my Lord while he does not turn towards me or notice what I have in my hands.

And sometimes he may give something with his hands if the person to whom he is giving does not know who is giving. He also gives with his hand if the person to whom he is giving is from among his companions that frequent his company or others that he is sure will not speak about it, nor reveal his secret. And all of his companions, without exception, have received some of his favors, beneficence, and bounties. And none of them meet each other except that, more than anything else, they speak about his instances of giving. However, no one can praise him for that in his presence. Nor can one even mention it to him or spread news of it. And if anyone eats with him and says, "May Allah increase your good deeds," he diverts him towards giving thanks to Allah for His bounty and witnessing how He ﷻ had granted His grace and blessing. And He says:

❴*Eat from the provisions of your Lord and be grateful to Him*❵ [58]

And [our Shaykh] also says, "All blessings are from Allah alone."

And from his charismatic feats that often go along with these instances of giving is that it sometimes arrives at a person at a time when he is in dire straits and need, finding neither strength nor help against his situation. It is as if our Master ﷺ spent the night looking at him or spent his day with him, getting to know his situation. So all of what he gives falls into the proper place and circumstances, due to a light from his Lord and an insight into His command. And he fulfills completely, in all of his instances of giving, the rights of every person, near or far, joining between justice and charity and taking care of the states of all people. So he first provides for his children, his family, and his dependents and turns his charity and beneficence towards them. Then he extends his generosity towards his close relations and companions, fulfilling the obligations of ties of kinship. Then he turns towards those who are further away from him in generosity and charity. His situation in all of that is admirable and his state in its entirety is exalted.

3.1.2.1 His Home and Family Life

As for his generosity in his home and with his family, it is an abundance of food and feeding, generosity, favors, grace, and munificence. He does not leave anything except that he causes them to enjoy it in a lawful way seeking to meet their needs, causing them to enjoy the blessings of his Lord

---

58   al-Saba', 15

and not purely for luxury and enjoyment. They are covered by the good that suffices and surrounded by the best care. The blessings of their Lord are manifest upon them, and the traces of them- such as what you see of virtue, contentment, the nobility of self, and high aspiration- upon them are clear. He has shown them generosity until their souls became accustomed to it and their seeds brought forth fruit from it. He gathers for them more than what they need so that they are made self-sufficient.

He sometimes makes clear that if it had not been for his concern for them, his doing what they had expected of him, and his protecting them from inclining towards what other people possess, he would not have accumulated anything. Thus, he stores provisions throughout the year for them- food, condiments, honey, and fruits- sufficient enough to suffice them, his guests, and the weak and feeble, so that his guests, the weak, the destitute, and those who attach themselves to Allah among the people who frequent him and stick to his side or those who come to him unexpectedly, all depend upon him and are among the people he supports.

And he supports a great number of people. So a load of wheat is consumed with him in two or three days on a normal basis. As for when caravans of people come to visit him, one cannot estimate how much is consumed. And no amount of sustaining is too much. And he gathers all of that and seeks it from far off lands due to the absence of agriculture in his place of residence. That is because the land is very weak. And he is never free of a multitude of guests. The men of his family are outside of the homes as much as possible. As for women, they stay in his home. Those related to him seek out visitors and feed them. And he ﷺ counsels them to do that.

From his habitual practice is that nothing leaves his home to be given to guests or anyone else except after the people of his house have been satisfied. And if anything of food leaves his home, being the last of its kind, he invariably replaces it with something similar. And he instructs and educates others to do the same out of fear that he will fulfill one right through neglecting another.

Also among his habits ﷺ is preserving and respecting food. Whenever anything is left over, he immediately searches out someone to eat it. And anytime food is left over from what is given to guests, he gives it to charity. And no food ever comes back to his home. That is because it left for the sake of Allah ﷻ. And among his habits ﷺ is to give charity throughout the night and day. And every Friday, he distributes wheat to the weak inhabitants of the city. He gives each one among the weak, the orphans, widows, and any other needy person what befits his state.

Likewise, every day, at midmorning, he distributes bread to the children gathered at the gate of his home. And that is also how he ﷺ treats those companions of his who are unable to help themselves or earn a living. And all blessing is from Allah ﷻ. He only habituates His Saints to grace. And He only confers good upon them. And that is his state ؓ in all of his states.

If you were to contemplate how much he spends and gives, you would find that it is something only possible for those like him who are Divinely aided; who give themselves, their spirits, their wealth, and their earnings to Allah and in the Path of Allah. They are those who want nothing other than Him. Nor do they depend on anyone else. And that is his situation ؓ.

As for what occurs from him in his dealings with his distant relatives, his great charity and maintaining of ties, it is greater than all of that. That is because, with what he gathers, he withholds some of it; then he gives it all at one time. However, no one knows about that except the very perceptive. And I had found out about it on various occasions. On those occasions, he spends such wealth that his companion would fear poverty thereafter. And that is due to his habit of concealing his charity ؓ, as we have already mentioned. However, we were only able to know about some of it. And that was the smallest portion of it. But, for example, when someone seeks him out for some dealings or exchanges letters with him, we are unaware of any charity he may give him in secret.

And from his great, habitual generosity is his freeing of servants. At one point, he freed, in one day, all of the female servants in his home. And they numbered twenty-five at that time. And he freed them all at the same time. And after that, he freed thirteen male servants who had reached maturity. And he wrote a letter for each one and placed it on his neck. And he said to each one, "You are free in the Path of Allah." And there are many other examples of his generosity that we may not know at all, or that we may not know its cause. May Allah be well pleased with him and he with Him. And may He cause us to enjoy His satisfaction.

In all, his generosity ؓ is immense and his charity tremendous. It is not something that is normally observed. Rather, it is a break with the norm and beyond ordinary affairs. No one can compare with him in that, neither from the elect folk nor anyone other than them. That is because it is from the habit of the Shaykhs who do such to withhold and to give. And they spend what they have been given of Allah's wealth upon the slaves of Allah. They do not store anything. And he ؓ does not store anything. And before now, he would not take anything from anyone at all.

That was until he received the permission from the Messenger of Allah ﷺ. At this time, he does not reject anything from anyone at all. Now, vast wealth and grand gifts, the like of which is not easy even for wealthy traders, leave his hands. And that is only one of the signs of Allah, a Muhammadan blessing from the vestiges of the blessing of our Master and Chief, the Messenger of Allah ﷺ, an inheritance from him, a station in which Allah has erected him, and a guarantee from him ﷺ of complete, abiding wealth which will not be followed by any poverty.

One of the elect among his companions had been giving away whatever wealth entered his possession. Then he intended to give away all that he had at one time. But when our Master ﷺ found out about it, he said to him:

> "Do not do that. And keep your wealth with you, because if you were to do that, you would find that your heart misses it. And that would influence you greatly. And thereby you will suffer a great affliction, and your love will be cut off at its root. So do not follow me in my method of giving because if you see me doing anything, it is a station that Allah (Honored and Majestic) has placed me in."

3.1.3 His Nobility

As for his nobility ﷺ, some of it had been indicated in the previous section when we began the section on some of his good character ﷺ. And chivalry is a portion of it. Nobility is among those character traits that gathers all types of praiseworthy attributes and righteous character traits, such as forbearance, pardon, patience, generosity, faithfulness, covering the faults of friends, helping them, and dealing with them in an excellent, beautiful way. It returns to altruism and a grand generosity, which is the generosity of the souls. Its origin is as was said by al-Qushayri ﷺ, "That the slave should be ever concerned with the situations of other people."

And the People of the Path have explained it with different interpretations, which he [al-Qushayri] transmits in his "Risalah." So if one wishes to know them, he should read that book. But they explained it many different ways, each one according to the predominant trait or some of the traits that comprise it. So they explained it as "warding off harm and responding to the call." This is the way that al-Junayd ﷺ explained it. Others have said that it is "to pardon the faults of your brethren." It has also been said that it is "to be just and not to seek vengeance." And "when you are given to, you share, and when you are denied, you are grateful." And "that you not see yourself as superior to anyone." It has also been said that it is faithfulness and protection, or that it is " grace that you are given, but you do not see yourself in it." And it has also been said that it is good character and following the Sunnah. It is most used in regards to charity and pardoning the wrongdoing of others. Shaykh Abu Madyan ﷺ said in his poem the "Ra'iyyah":

"In giving to your brethren, be ever openhanded, in body,
  And spirit. And lower your gaze if ever they should slip."

And our Shaykh and Teacher ﷺ has the greatest portion of these traits, in which he has no partner in this era. He inherited it along with the crowning inheritance that was apportioned for him. And he attained in that the highest degree, the most sublime post, the highest station, and the most complete aspiration.

3.1.3.1 His Forbearance and Pardon

As for his forbearance and pardon, it is his nature ﷺ to pardon those who busy themselves with attacking him, never taking them to task. Rather, he looks towards them with the eye of Reality and makes excuses for them. He often says, "If you look both at people and at the decree of Allah enacted upon them, you will pardon them. Blame comes only from failing to witness the command of Allah that is being enacted."

In that way, he is gentle and has pity on their circumstances, out of fear that they may be ruined due to their transgressive act. And he associates with them hoping to remove their grudge and erase what they have in their heart.

Any time one of his companions complains of the attacks of anyone, he diverts him from that, encourages him to forbearance and pardon, and incites him to occupy himself with that which concerns him. He does not like those who are concerned with giving victory to themselves, nor those who busy themselves with the affairs of other people. And he does not like harshness, crudeness, or their people. He usually says, "Allah will be gentle with the gentle." And he uses as proof the Hadith that Imam Ahmad, Abu Dawud, Tirmidhi, and al-Hakim in his "Mustadrak" all narrated from Ibn Umar ﷺ that the Messenger of Allah ﷺ said, *"The merciful will be shown mercy by the Most Merciful ﷻ. Show mercy to those who are in the Earth and the One, who is in the Heavens, will show mercy to you."*[59]

He shows mercy to the old, the young, and every truly weak person. And he counsels the rulers who come to visit him to be kind to those who are destitute. He tells them, "You are shown mercy due to the weak among you. And none of you does an act that is more excellent than that. And whoever is kind is shown kindness."

He overlooks the ignorant person's ignorance. He is patient with the coarseness of the brutish person. And he pardons the attacks of those who attack. Indeed, rather, he treats well those who treat him badly. And after he overlooks his acts, he is compassionate and gentle with him. He is ever

---

59   Sunan al-Tirmidhi (Hadith no. 2037); Sunan Abu Dawud (Hadith no. 4941).

pleasant with him in word and deed. And he treats him beautifully and with that which is more excellent than the treatment he received. And he is generous with him and eager to cause good to reach him out of mercy and kindness to him.

In fact, the person who wrongs him comes to feel the utmost shyness due to that and feels very ashamed. And he is amazed at his pardoning him and then treating him generously, and at the fact that the evil that he had previously done became as good deeds before him. This is what we had witnessed when this happened between him and one of the brethren. He continued to show him forbearance and generosity until he became one of the most beloved of people to him. But the speech about his forbearance and pardon is more plentiful than this. And some of it has already been mentioned in his wayfaring ﷺ.

3.1.3.2 His Faithfulness

As for his faithfulness, and faithfulness is a category of nobility whose inclusion in this biography is a matter of explaining a specific type of nobility, part of it is that if he borrows anything, he pays it back quickly. He does not delay and is never neglectful at all. No one at all can remember him ever delaying paying off debt, as a protection and sufficiency from Allah to him.

Also, from that is his faithfulness in dealing with the brethren, maintaining their trusts and the trusts of the companions at all times, just as we have mentioned before regarding his strengthening their ties in a most complete way, being gentle with them in the most beautiful way, and being completely generous with them. And he ﷺ continues to reserve affection for them. And he does not forget their trust throughout the passing of time. And he gives every effort to be generous with those whom he is able. All of this is from his excellent pact, complete faithfulness, and beautiful love of Allah and his brethren.

And from his faithfulness is his relationship with his Lord, his worship of Him, and his standing for Allah in all of his movements and moments of stillness, never ceasing to perform an action that he has taken up. And he never reneges on anything that he intends to do for Allah. Then consider how great is this faithfulness and how great a blessing and gift from Allah it is.

There is no one who can come close to matching his good attributes such as great nobility, altruism, his benefitting others greatly, and his high aspirations. All of that, his generosity and altruism are a fortification from Allah. And the speech about our Master and Teacher ﷺ is so extensive that we could not encompass the smallest part, much less cover the greater part of it. Thus, we limited ourselves to that which was needed and imperative.

SECTION THREE

And may Allah bless our Master Muhammad, his family, and companions and extend them a worthy salutation.

3.2 On His Fear of Allah, His Patience, His High Aspirations, His Scrupulousness, His Asceticism, His Spiritual Counsel, and His Independence

3.2.1 Introduction

Along with the praiseworthy attributes, proper character traits, exalted stations, and lofty stations to which the highest aspirations of preceding generations had fallen short and which the limits of the aspirations of succeeding generations were unable to attain, as well as scrupulousness, asceticism, spiritual counsel, and independence such as have no equal at all in our time and in which he has not left any portion, or even hope for a portion, for anyone else, our Master and Shaykh ﷺ has attained such fear of Allah, patient perseverance, high aspirations in the Path, as has made him preeminent in all of that over the people of this group. If you examine his wayfaring in all of that, you will find that he is unique in his time and the Master of the scrupulous people and ascetics in his time. In all of this, nothing comes close to his finishing point nor obtains his favored position. Likewise, the ocean of his gnosis never subsides, and his racehorse is never overtaken. His high aspiration was fixed to the highest of affairs. Thus, he traversed those of average loftiness and reached their essences. He was not satisfied with anything else. Nor was he veiled from any guarded secret.

> He has aspirations, the greatest of which has no limit,
> And his lower aspirations are greater than life itself

His objective is only his Lord and Master, having left behind him every limit. And indeed, unto your Lord is every ending. And there is no aspiration greater than that. So his aspiration is not detained. Nor can any exposition explain it. It has gathered every aspiration altogether, as well as the highest affairs to the exclusion of others, such as keeping oneself free from frivolous affairs, and avoiding disliked matters or claiming nobility and dignity for himself. He is also self-reliant, leaving preoccupation with people, and sufficing oneself with the One, the Real, disregarding what is from people. Also, he has many other noble traits and adheres to what is upright.

Such is the abode, foundation, and building blocks of high aspiration. And what has already been mentioned should have informed you that our Master ﷺ surpassed their foundations and rose to their highest point. And he possesses all of them, the foundations and branches. And what we have chosen to mention in this section, and what is most appropriate that we disseminate and explain at this point, is his fear of Allah, his patience, and his high aspirations in the path of wayfaring, which he raised above every subjugated being.

3.2.2 His Fear and Patience

As for his fear ﷺ, it is having much fear of Allah and extended periods of melancholy for the sake of Allah. And many times, people hear the sounds of moans and groans coming from his chest due to his extreme fear of Allah. This especially happens when he is alone in his seclusion and consumed with the remembrance of Allah. But it also happens when he is among people and does not notice who is present with him in his gathering due to his being consumed and absent in the One whom he is remembering. And on various occasions, I have entered upon him in his seclusion and not been able to address him due to his extreme fear.

As for his patience ﷺ, his firmness in the station of patience is well known. He ﷺ continuously repays those who treat him badly with good, to the point that everyone who denies him begins to declare his grace, knowledge, forbearance, great sainthood, immense station, and sheer excellence. When they had witnessed this from him, and that this was his constant practice, and that he paid no attention to their abuse and ill treatment, they returned from the abuse and harm that they had been doing, repented to Allah, and asked Him [Allah] to overlook, pardon, and forgive their wrongdoings. And they return to the best state and the most perfect words. And they seek from our Master ﷺ to overlook, pardon, and forgive their wrongs. Thus, he forgives them, supplicates for them, has mercy on them, and pities them. And he shows them affection, engages them, seeks to know their states, and asks about them. That is his state ﷺ, of which only the greatest *Siddiqun* and most elect Knowers of Allah are capable.

Despite his being busy with all of these matters, he does not neglect any category of acts of obedience. Nor does he miss any opportunity to draw near to Allah. Rather, he has only been increased in earnestness and effort in acts of obedience. So whenever he has free time to engage in worship, he casts all else behind his back and turns to Allah as much as Allah has facilitated and willed for him.

And from his great patience is his patience throughout illnesses that affect him or his home and dependents. And there is no one more patient than him in that. For there is always some illness that affects him or his home throughout the days and nights. And his patience ﷺ with difficulties and his bearing of afflictions is something of which not even the mountain peaks are capable. And anyone who complains to him, he diverts to be patient. And he informs him that this abode was only created for trials and calamities.

3.2.3 His Lofty Aspiration

As for his lofty aspiration ﷺ in the path of wayfaring, we have already mentioned, in the section on his beginning stages, that which indicates that he has reached the lofty summit and the limit of perfection. So by reading this, his firm foothold in that should be clear to you. But it is also indicated by his allusions, his speech, his realization, and his station. For the elect (may Allah be pleased with them all) only speak through their spiritual state. And they inform people about the Path according to their wayfaring and traveling upon it. And you will only find that our Master's speech ﷺ raises your aspiration to Allah and turns you away from all apart from Him. He does not let you stop short of Him. And he does not like that anyone should rely on anything other than Him. Nor does he like that anyone should look to him (the Shaykh) for anything at all. And he speaks on that with lofty, priceless words, which the intellects are incapable of grasping and the pens incapable of encompassing and writing down.

His declarations, speech, expressions, subtle indications, and removal of doubt- when he responds to different questions in all the disciplines of the Islamic Sciences- all make this known. A barrier has been placed between the people of the exterior sciences and the sciences of the Knowers of Allah. And there has been cast between them a curtain and a veil. And Allah opens whomever He wills among His slaves. And He chooses whom He wills to know His gnosis and Spiritual effluence. It has been said:

> The sciences were only made clear to you so that,
>> You may see them with the eye of the one who does not see them,
>
> So rise above them with the ascension of he who is not pleased,
>> With any state except that he should see his Lord.

The Knowers of Allah all drink from one ocean. Their sciences are the fruits of certainty and faith, not the fruits of evidence and proofs. May Allah place us in their sanctuary and provide us with their love and satisfaction.

As for his raising his aspiration above the creation, he ﷺ is in the utmost disconnection from them and connection to Allah ﷻ. They hope only for His grace and generosity. He has rejected (everything) in creation and turned towards his Lord. He placed them firmly behind his back so that he is paying attention neither in acceptance from them nor their rejection, neither to their anger nor satisfaction. The one who accepts him is the same as the one who rejects him, the one who draws near to him the same as the one who distances himself, the one who abuses him the same as the one who praises him, and the one who confirms what he says the same as the one who denies what he says. He is completely independent of them and turns not towards them, being free of need of them, by his Lord's leave, and sufficing himself with that which He has entrusted to him. He does not befriend them outwardly. Nor does he share their hidden states. He cut himself off from their favors all at one time. And he disregarded all benefit or harm from the creation.

So he does not accept anything from anyone, regardless of who he is, near or far, noble or lowly, or whether he is giving a little or a lot. In fact, no one can impose any gift or offering upon him. He ﷺ came upon that lofty wayfaring and these noble states corresponding to the Sunnah. And he continued like that until he was given permission from the Messenger of Allah ﷺ to accept everything and reject nothing. When that happened, he stopped rejecting. However, he takes possession of some things and spends it however he wills in his home and on other expenses. And other things he takes possession of and spends it on any charity to the destitute and needy that occurs to him. And he is never negligent of rewarding those who give him anything. He accepts what they give outwardly. Then he rewards them by supplicating for them or in other ways so that no one will have any favor upon him. That is because his aspiration ﷺ refuses to let anyone have an advantage over him due to the corruption of the time, its people, and their aims.

One day I even witnessed, while I was present with him, that a man came to him and said, "My Master! I have given you this wealth of mine out of love for you and as a gift for you." So he accepted it from him, and he presented it to him. Then he whispered to him in his ear, "My Master! I seek from you that you do such and such thing for me." And our Master ﷺ replied to him, "Take back your offering." And he did not accept it from him.

I was also present and sitting before him when a man came to him and greeted him with the greeting of peace and kissed his hand. And he paid me some coins so that he could visit our Master ﷺ. And he said to him, "My Master! Accept this charity which I have brought to you." So he said to me, "Return his offering to him." And he said to him, "It is not lawful for me to accept charity. I am free of need of charity." And he tries his best to avoid the aims of the ordinary people. But he wards off their schemes in the best of ways.

One day, he was asked ﷺ about his not accepting gifts even though the Prophet ﷺ would accept them. He said:

> "In that time, gifts were gifts. In our time, they are bribes. Indeed, when a person gives something to someone else or fulfills his need, he waits a little while and then he returns to him seeking that he should accomplish for him some aim. And people only give, in most cases, to a person who has some worldly or religious authority. But if someone has no authority, they will never give to him. In our time, this is the state that we have observed in people. They do not give anything for the sake of love, affection, or brotherhood in the religion. They only give to accomplish their corrupt aims as we have mentioned. Even their wedding banquets are observed with these corrupt intentions."

For that reason, he ﷺ avoids the ordinary people and their nefarious aims. And he does not associate with them due to their frequent mixing of intentions. And perhaps if he is requested, he tries to rectify their relationships with one another. But he never tries to force anyone to give up his right. And he informs them of that beforehand because it is not befitting of his preserving ﷺ the limits of the Sacred Law.

3.2.4 His Scrupulousness and Asceticism

3.2.4.1 His Scrupulousness

One of his attributes ﷺ is that he does not lead anyone in prayer, except if it is his family or in his home. Rather, he prays behind the Imams unless there is some legal impediment, such as their being corrupt or taking bribes. He never prays behind them. This was in his beginning stages.

And he had an Imam: the erudite, astute, successful scholar who has united between the Sacred Law, Reality, beneficial knowledge, and the sciences of the Path, the guardian of his secret, the keeper of his covenant, the object of his love, and his bosom friend, the completely virtuous, noble Sharif, Abu Abdullah Sidi Muhammad b. Muhammad b. al-Mishri, Saihi

Suba'i in origin, whose residence is in Takartah on the outskirts of Jaridah. It is a well-known town in the district of Iqsamtinah, a district known as an abode is one of knowledge, rectitude, piety, integrity, and success. And to this day, its people are among the scholars who act upon their knowledge and they are among the guided Imams. The majority of them have taken the Tariqah of our Shaykh ﷺ. And they travel to visit him from their land, which is a journey of twenty days or more. They bring great wealth to our Master ﷺ in the form of dirhams, clothes, and dates. I have come to them many times while they were with our Master ﷺ, and I have not seen anyone more excellent than them in manners, religion, and knowledge. And the majority of them are scholars. As long as we have known our Master ﷺ, caravans and gifts come to him from all directions. But I have not seen anyone better than them in decorum, veneration, and good intentions. Our Master ﷺ treats them differently than he treats others, in that he does not turn away from them or ignore them like he does with others. So I asked him ﷺ about that. And he said, "They are not like others. They only seek lofty stations and exalted spiritual states."

May Allah be pleased with them. And may He not deprive them or us of the good of this Noble Master. This noble [Sidi Muhammad b. al-Mishri] ﷺ has remained with our Master ﷺ from the year 1188 AH until now- the year 1213 AH. But when our Master ﷺ arrived in the year 1208, he assumed the position of Imam for himself ﷺ due to a personal necessity he had. And he has never left that position because his prayer is not valid behind anyone else unless he has a legal excuse. Thus, until now- Ramadan in the year 1213 AH- he ﷺ leads people in prayer as an Imam, not praying behind anyone except for the Jum'ah prayer.[60]

As for his extreme cautiousness, which he enforces on himself and his family, in dealings and transactions, he does not buy anything from anyone who he knows earns profits from what is unlawful or anyone that associates with anyone from the people of the treasury or mixes other people's wealth with his wealth. This is his habit and consummate practice. And he often prohibits his companions from associating with those people. And he exhorts them to adopt the strong mount of scrupulousness in all of their affairs. And he never gives them any dispensation in anything that is unlawful. He often says, "If I am not pleased with something for myself, then

---

60 The Shaykh ﷺ stated that this was an order from the Prophet ﷺ. In Kashf al-Hijab, in the section on the Biography of Sidi Muhammad b. al-Mishri, Sidi Ahmad Sukayrij said, "It has reached me, on the authority of some of his ﷺ trustworthy Companions, that he began leading prayers with the permission of the Prophet ﷺ. And he ﷺ would say, "One who I cannot disobey commanded me not to pray any prayer behind anyone, except the Jumu'ah (Friday) Prayer."

I am not pleased with it for anyone else. And if I do not do something, I do not command anyone else to do it."

And from his scrupulousness ﷺ is that he does not accept anything he has a need for, no matter how trivial, from anyone who does not avoid the unlawful or examine closely his earnings. He does not accept any of that. Nor does he let anyone else accept it. And from his scrupulousness ﷺ is that he does not use anything in his acts of worship or religious matters except that which is completely, utterly, and perfectly pure, placing great emphasis on being careful with his religion and perfection in his worship which is the means of connection between him and his Lord. This is the nature of the elect who have made their religion exclusively for Allah. So he seeks water and wells in the cleanest and purest places.

And from his scrupulousness ﷺ is that when he gives something up, he does not want it ever to return to him, neither through buying it nor as a gift. As a whole, his scrupulousness in all things has reached the limit and arrived at the summit. His dealings only revolve around this. And it is only fashioned around it and with insight to its method and intimate knowledge of its indications. He says, "If a man takes dispensations for himself in consuming the doubtful, he is on his way to consuming the unlawful." He also says, "The essence of scrupulousness is avoiding doubtful things and perpetually consuming the lawful, being completely sincere with Allah in that."

3.2.4.2 His Asceticism

As for his asceticism ﷺ, we have not heard or seen anyone greater or more frequent in fleeing from the world and its people. And he has attained the most outstanding portion of all three of its degrees. The stories about our Master Abu al-'Abbas that evidence this are many, their proofs and examples manifest, and his actions that emanate from that are copious. Not the smallest portion of it or any of its signs can be enumerated. But some stories that indicate this reality have been mentioned before in the section on his generosity and openhandedness.

As for his abstinence from position and fame, he ﷺ continuously seeks out obscurity and hiddenness in neglected and disregarded sectors. He is not concerned with whether the people turn towards him or away from him. And he flees from meeting with those who possess political influence and authority. And he cautions others from meeting them, saying, "It is a trial in the religion." He hates for any of them to acknowledge him unless he is revealed to be sincere or he knows that his coming is for the sake of Allah. In that case, he wishes him well, exhorts him, reminds him, and counsels him sincerely. But his habit is that which we have mentioned before. And from his abstinence ؓ from position is that which happened between him and one of the rulers. When he requested to meet him, he rejected their request completely.

So look, may Allah have mercy on you, at this majestic noble and the perfect benefit that he gives for the sake of Islam. And that is sufficient. And our Master Abu al-'Abbas ؓ has ascended to an unshakable platform. And an evident light has emerged in his Heaven. All of this is evident to anyone who keeps his company, associates with him, and examines his states and actions.

This indicates his absolute independence, which al-Qushayri has defined with the following words:

> "It is that the slave should not be subservient to any created thing. And he is absolutely independent, being subject neither to this temporal world nor the Hereafter. Nothing dominates his heart. And he does not see any king other than Allah. Nor does he entrust his heart to anyone else."

And our Shaykh and Master ؓ was asked about absolute independence And his reply will come at its proper place if Allah so wills. But you will not see anyone who embodies this description more completely than our Master Abu al-'Abbas ؓ. And he is some one who is absolutely independent in a real sense and has attained the attribute of absolute independence over all creation. It has been said:

> I hope upon ages that I cannot conceive,
>   That my two eyes may see the appearance of freedom.

And let not the thought occur to your mind, nor assume with your thoughts, that anyone among the people of your era, your city, your land, or your region can match our Shaykh ؓ in absolute independence or resemble his completion and perfection in it. That is an attribute in which his lights have become apparent and his traces evident. And his standing in that ؓ and in other attributes is well known. It is not hidden to any intelligent person, young or old. May Allah grant us His satisfaction in this world and the Hereafter. And may Allah bless our Master Muhammad, his family, and companions and extend them a worthy salutation.

3.3 His Guiding to Allah, His Gathering People in His Way, and His Leading People to Him by His Words and Spiritual State

3.3.1 His Methods of Guiding

Our Master ﷺ has imbibed this noble love until it quenched his thirst. And he drank from its immense ocean and exalted effulgence that which seized his entire being, overpowered him, annihilated him from all known and decreed things, and made him perpetually absent in the Eternal One. Thus, his reality was immersed in Divine unity and his essence and existence mixed with it. And his spirit, soul, physical and nonphysical self, his form and heart, his intellect, and his mind were all conformed to it. And his spiritual states, statements, thoughts, actions, movements, moments of stillness, orientations, and behaviors all became indicators of Allah and His Messenger ﷺ, summoning people to Him, and a door to His communion. He only calls to Him. He only revolves around Him. And He will not place you except at His door. Nor will He cause you to rely except on His Exalted Essence.

When you see him, you remember Allah and forget all apart from Him. And you are awakened from the first instant. And the clouds of negligence disperse. Then you find in your heart awe, reverence, and veneration. If you sit with him, his luminance will captivate you, his breaths will penetrate you, and his fragrant scent will cling to you. And you will witness his evident beauty, and you will know that he is a devoted sitting companion and that [the inherited] light of Prophethood is visible upon him. His sitting companion is never disappointed. And those who associate with him never miss any good. It was said in one of the eulogies dedicated to him, "He is of those men whose sitting companion is not disappointed."

Light pierces the heart of anyone who sees him. And love for Allah is disseminated in those who visit him. And whoever comes to him is forced into remembrance. And whoever meets him is cast into earnestness. The sight of him is an antidote for the hearts, and his words are a cure for all defects. His gathering is a gathering of mildness, sobriety, veneration, and respect. For the most part, no one can initiate a conversation with him. Rather, if speaking is appropriate, he initiates if he wills. And he obtains his objective and aim thereby.

Those who are present with him do not speak a lot. Nor do they compete with each other in front of him. Rather, their habit is silence and decorum, unless he addressed him or seeks something from him. He is very awe-inspiring and has a majestic state. He possesses a manifest reverence and an overpowering authority. If anyone confronts him, he is struck with fear. And no one enters upon him, except that his love overpowers him, as a Muhammadan inheritance and a Prophetic favor. The more one increases in nearness to him, the more he is increased in awe of him.

When we have problems that we wish to mention to him, but we are unable to do that, he informs us about that problem. And many times he informs us of that which we wish to mention before we can start speaking. That way, he opens the way to speak to him. So we follow his lead and pursue what we want. And he speaks to people about what is within them. And he clarifies what he experiences and what overtakes him. And he clarifies for him, in a complete manner, that which is hidden from him of those things that harm his religion. And he presents him with a cure and a remedy that relieves his affliction and banishes his difficulties. His lights efface the darkness of the souls and remove from them all troubles and misery.

He reminds people through Qur'anic verses and Prophetic Hadiths. And he draws from them subtle indications, hidden meanings, aphorisms, and gnosis. And he causes them to experience that directly. And he increases those who are present in love and longing. And he fills the heart with joy, happiness, and felicity until one would swear an oath that when he hears his words, it is as if he is hearing the words of the Prophet ﷺ and is witnessing directly his perfect light and his greatest secret. Upon his words is an authority that subjects the souls to them and causes heads to bow to them. In some states, he responds with his spiritual state more than he responds with quotes.

Whenever anyone- especially one who is inclined to acceptance- hears his words, his heart is turned in that instant. And his innermost reality soars towards Allah. A man may come to him in difficulty, sadness, denial, disbelief, misguidance, rebellion, impurity, and filth. And his sadness is transmuted to happiness, his denial to gratitude, his remoteness to presence, his impurity to purity, and his darkness to light. Thus, by him, the real essences within the hearts are changed and all time periods beautified. You may find him speaking aggressively with a man while he is doing work on his heart in secret. And by that he causes him to journey a long distance towards Allah.

He may respond to someone with only a word or two and, by that, the person will obtain his wish, and get what he aims for and desires. It is as if that need is the cause of his speech. Another person may complain of a spiritual defect or a sickness of the soul, mentioning it to himself while he is before him. And he will respond to him about it in specific terms as if he had heard his words. Thus, his defect is remedied, and his vision turned. And he witnesses the grace, blessing, generosity, and benediction of Allah, while before that he had not noticed or perceived it at all.

And his spiritual state is effective on all kinds of people- attentive or negligent, worldly or otherwise. And his words have an effect on all of them, grants them all happiness, and removes all weariness, until one of them would believe that he will never have concern for the world, nor will he ever incline towards it due to the certainty about Allah and the happiness about Allah's blessings that emerge within him at that moment. Even those who come to him having been tested with great difficulty and affliction in their wealth, health, and family, when they listen to his words, all weariness departs from them, and happiness and relief seize him- as if he has been given goblets of wine to drink.

Once, one of the brothers came to him, having been tried with his wealth being seized by the ruler. And his manners, his state, his hidden and apparent reality, and his actions were all wrong. So he sat before our Master ﷺ among a group of his companions. And he started to listen quietly to his words. And the habit of the Shaykh ﷺ is to guide towards Allah, to remind people of the manifest and hidden blessings of Allah, to show them that whatever trial occurs to the slave, which outwardly appears to be disgrace, it is, in reality, all mercy, grace, and blessing from Allah and that He ﷻ only does anything due to His wisdom.

He began clarifying this and the man's state immediately changed. And the traces of happiness and felicity shone upon him. And he said, "All praise is due to Allah." And he repeated that out of happiness for the blessing of Islam, whose worth he had not previously realized, and out of disdain for the worldly means of which he had been deprived. And he said, "I have not seen or heard anything like this at all. And I have visited several of the leaders of the righteous of this era. But I have never heard the likes of these words from anyone."

Such things have happened time after time. People come to him in states of worry and distress, and their state changes to the relief of the heart and mind. And on seeing him, their distress changes to joy. And those who are present look at his signs with wonder. This is because of the light of Reality to which he has conformed and the attribute of mercy to the creation that he has adopted.

I have been present on innumerable such occasions because he is generous with people with his spiritual state just as he is generous with them with his wealth. He blesses them with the gnosis that he has been blessed with and the realizations that he has been granted. He outpours spiritual assistance and benefit on the slaves, which shines on the one present and the one absent. It is as if all people are his children, brothers, and loved ones. He is always eager to benefit them and push them and urge them towards Allah. And he uses as evidence the Hadith, "*All of the creation are the dependents of Allah. And the most beloved of people to Him are those that are most beneficial to His dependents.*" [61]

And he devotes his speech to that due to his spiritual state inclining towards that at all times. And he drives people towards Allah as much as possible. And he suffices himself with whatever inclination towards good that he finds in people, even if he only finds one good quality within him. And he says, "When the Knower of Allah finds one good characteristic in a person, such as modesty, generosity, a portion of love, a good heart, true devotion, or anything else, he treats the person in accordance with that characteristic." And he says, "Indeed, Allah has mercy on a slave due to one good quality. And the mercy of Allah conquers all else. And it obliterates causation. Thus, if the smallest portion of mercy is present, it descends [upon the person for whom it is meant]."

And when anyone complains about himself, mentioning his evil state or actions, he turns him away from witnessing that, toward witnessing the mercy of Allah. And he informs him that Allah shows mercy without cause. And he mentions the words of al-Shadhili ☪, "If we are not worthy of obtaining Your mercy, Your mercy is capable of reaching us." And he says, "The reason for a slave's remembering his evil deeds is that he should recognize the grace of his Lord upon him and verify His bounty and generosity because he does not find himself performing any good action, yet he is healthy, blessed, and swimming in the sea of grace and blessing. And those robes were granted to him by the Real due to His sheer generosity and grace."

If anyone speaks to him with that which indicates he is making a claim or praising himself, he directs him towards the opposite. He begins to speak about the defects of the soul and its intrigues. And he manifests to him its tricks, subtleties, and the defects, shortcomings, and vices that it comprises.

---

61   Al-Mu'jam al-Awsat (Hadith no. 5541).

And he shows that they are its essence and attribute. And that the soul only wishes to attribute to itself the attributes of lordship, such as greatness and veneration, even though its defects cannot be counted and its deficiencies are equal to the perfections of Allah. In other words, there is no end to its deficiencies. And if Allah does not intervene between a man and his soul, the man will perish. And if He were to leave the path clear for it, it would deny Allah just as it denies His blessings. And he [the Shaykh ﷺ] says, "If Allah wills the destruction of a slave, He entrusts him to his soul. And He will increase him in anything. But if He wills mercy for him, He shows him His blessing, inspires him to be thankful, and saves him from its disbelief. And that is the essence of all good."

No one comes to him displaying hope while being forgetful about the Divine control, except that he instills fear in him of the Divine power and coercion, and the swiftness by which His decree and command are carried out, until he leaves fearful and alarmed. And no one comes to him displaying fear or regret, except that he diverts him from that and instills hope in him. And he causes him to recognize the grace of his Lord until he leaves happy and contented. What he wishes to accomplish by that is gathering the slave in both states towards his Lord, and that he should not stop at anything apart from Him. And if anyone claims to love in front of him, he says to him, "Among the signs of love is striving to please the Beloved, performing what He has commanded, and stopping at His prohibitions."

And he recites the following couplets:

> You disobey Allah while you claim to love Him,
> That is a very impossible situation,
>
> If your love were true, you would obey Him,
> Indeed, the lover is obedient to the Beloved.

If anyone mentions any good deed that he has done, he reproaches him for mentioning it. Or he informs him of part of his situation of which he is ignorant. Thus, he brings out the meanness of that action and its defects, until he makes it clear to him that he is sick and diseased. He does not let anyone depend on anything, trust in any action, become accustomed to any state or rely on anything except the grace and mercy of Allah and the intercession of His Messenger ﷺ. And he says, "We have nothing except the grace of Allah and His mercy."

He guides to (approaching) Allah through keeping the company of the People of Allah, who guide to Allah, gather people to Him, and cause people to reach Him. And he mentions His words ﷺ:

❰*And keep yourself patient with those who call upon their Lord in the morning and the evening, seeking His countenance. And let not your eyes pass beyond them, desiring adornments of the worldly life, and do not obey one whose heart We have made heedless of Our remembrance and who follows his desire and whose affair is ever neglectful.*❱ [62]

And he also mentions the Hadith, "A man is in the religion of his good friend."[63] And he says, "The source of all good is with whom you associate and what you eat. Eat whatever you wish, and your works will resemble it. Associate with whom you wish, and you will act just like them."

I complained to him one day about my bad state, and he said to me, "Do not speak to me right now about any of that. Do what I command you to." And he signaled to me so I sat with him ﷺ. And I asked him, "O, my Master! What is better between voluntary prayers, remembrance, other voluntary works, or sitting with the Shaykhs?" He responded, "Sitting with the Shaykhs is better. Nothing equals it. And your sitting before a Saint is better than the world and what it contains, due to what has been related, 'Your sitting before a Saint is like a nursing sheep before its mother.'"

And there is no doubt that sitting with him ﷺ is a tried and tested remedy for the maladies of the heart and the defects of the soul. How many times spiritual maladies have affected us and others, or destructive darkness gathered on our heart, only to be removed due to sitting with him? And all praise is due to Allah in a way that befits His deserving of praise and His Majesty. I am unable to praise Him properly. It has been said, "Seeing a God-conscious person is rectitude. And looking at the Elect is an ennoblement." And it has also been said, "From the mercy of Allah on His slave, and from His assistance, is that He should subjugate to him the heart of one of the Elect from the Saints." And, "All people love the Elect person. But the point is that the Elect should love you." And, "If someone does not meet a person with insight, insight is not granted to him." And, "Your Shaykh is not the one who makes a pact between you and himself, and you believe in his Shaykhhood inwardly. Rather, your Shaykh is the one who enraptures your heart, seizes your entire being, benefits you by his glance, and encompasses you with his spiritual aspiration."

He addresses everyone according to his understanding, knowledge, what benefits his state, and what is necessary for him. Thus, he addresses the ignorant with talk of study, the scholar with acting upon his knowledge, the sinful with repentance, the obedient with not witnessing his obedience

---

62 al-Kahf, 28
63 Musnad Ahmad (Hadith nos. 8028; 8417).

and with hoping for the mercy of Allah on him. But the one who is concerned about his disobedience impresses him. He sympathizes with him and pities him.

And he guides towards Allah with every spiritual state and in every state. And in every act of obedience or disobedience is a guidance toward Allah. In the case of obedience, he guides towards being grateful to Allah. In disobedience, (he guides) towards taking refuge in Allah and repenting to Him. And in the case of blessings and tests, it is the same. And one causes you to be happy with your Lord while the other raises your complaints towards Him. And he mentions the famous saying of the People of the Path ﷺ, "If one does not turn to Allah through His abundant blessings, he will be driven towards Him in the chains of tests and trials." And he speaks very copiously in this manner.

He uses many different ways and points of view in guiding to Allah. And he clarifies the ways of the different paths and their hidden realities. Thus, sometimes he will speak from the worldly point of view. At other times, he will speak from the heavenly point of view. And he makes clear, for the people of the two paths of rapture and wayfaring, their duties. At times, he does this extensively, sometimes succinctly, and sometimes by way of allusion. Examples of this in his speech are such that intellects cannot grasp them. Nor can they be encompassed completely in writing. His gatherings, with what they contain of that, are fragrant gardens. Each gathering, and what occurs therein, conforms to the requirements of the time. And what Allah reveals to him and upon his hand is provision for those who are present.

And perhaps in one gathering, he will mention various categories from all of that. And realizations, secrets, reminders, lessons, encouraging gratitude and patience and tranquility throughout the enactment of the Divine decrees, encouraging action and leaving false hopes, incitement towards good actions and warning against evil acts, seeking closeness, seeking love, giving glad tidings, and warning are all touched on in one gathering. Thus, each person who is present takes his portion of it and benefits according to the capacity of his spiritual state. Or, speaking on one of these categories may dominate an entire gathering. And you will find that when he speaks on any of the categories of guidance towards Allah, he goes very deep into the subject and speaks on it at great length. And he heals by that the breasts of the people with clear explanations and beautiful allusions in the most amazing way.

And he speaks to people with expressions familiar to them. And he explains to them in their language. Thus, (he reaches) both the scholar and the illiterate, the intelligent person and the ignorant one. And he explains to them the degrees of the religion and the stations of certainty. And he shows them the way to obtain them, as well as their beginning and their result. He makes them clear through aphorisms and sprinkles them in the hearts as spiritual states. Thus, he explains repentance, how to go about it, and that which causes one to attain it. And he also explains asceticism and its cause, thankfulness, patience, satisfaction, love, and their methodologies. Then, he explains leaving self-direction and choosing alongside it the choice of Allah. And these last two are the main content of his words and the axis of his desire.

And he draws proofs for all of that, of which no one can be ignorant. And he explains the proper place of all of it with things that everyone knows, until they know it all theoretically, then gain experiential knowledge of it, and finally, the hearts purse – in a state of certainty and firm resolve..

This is his practice, his distinguishing mark, his habit, and his way. He sincerely counsels the slaves and is eager to give them guidance and direction. He turns the faces of the negligent through orientation towards Allah. And he arouses in them a desire for repentance. He revives hearts that have been killed by desires with the spiritual assistance of belief and the light of love. And he relates to them those verses of the Qur'an and Prophetic Hadiths that have come down regarding all of this.

3.3.2 His Guiding to Repentance and Avoiding Sin and Sinful Company

How many have repented on his hand and returned from their evil actions after they had been engrossed in their disobedience and drowned in negligence at all times, being completely uninterested in repentance? Then, when they come to him, he turns his whole being towards them. And he takes pity on them and sympathizes with them. And he mentions to him the Hadith, "Allah is more joyous by the repentance of one of you than a person who finds his lost animal."[64]

Then he says:

> And look how He has emphasized it, showing concern for its importance. He mentioned it twice in one place when He said ﷻ:
>
> ❮Allah wants to make clear to you and guide you to the practices of those before you and to accept your repentance. And Allah is Knowing and Wise. Allah wants to accept your repentance, but those who follow passions want you to digress a great deviation❯[65]

---

64 Sahih al-Bukhari (Hadith no. 6309); Sahih Muslim (Hadith no. 7061).
65 al-Nisa, 26-27

SECTION THREE

So look at the mercy He has ﷻ for His slave such that He does not want to punish him for his disobedience. Rather, He only wants to accept his repentance and have mercy on him. How great is this grace, and how abundant this favor, from the Generous and Exalted One.

And he often warns of associating with evil companions and others. He warns the negligent of that out of fear that he may be increased thereby in negligence. And he warns the cautious of that out of fear that he may be swayed from his strong position. And in all of that, he refers back to the Sovereign Judge. And he often gives as proof his words ﷺ, "A man is upon the religion of his close friend. So let each of you beware of whom he befriends."[66] And he also says, "Choose for your companion one who is obedient. Indeed, the character of one person impresses upon the character of another."

And he warns from having the love of the world. And he flees from it due to its cutting one off from Allah and preventing one from turning towards Him. Turning towards Him is not complete as long as any portion of the love of the world remains with a person. And he has been made completely alone with his Lord and isolated from all apart from Him. No attachment remains that can dissuade him, nor any wish that accompanies him. Nothing impeded people or veiled them from Allah, except illusion and compound ignorance about the perfect faith in Allah. If they had realized that they were not upon anything and that they had not attained the truly perfect faith, they would have sought help with Allah due to their complete incapacity, weakness, and their realization of that; He would respond to them due to the neediness that they display. This is due to His words ﷻ:

❰*He is who responds to the desperate one when he calls upon Him...*❱ [67]

And anytime such a person seeks an increase in gnosis, he will be given it due to his desperate request due to his witnessing deficiency in himself in all things. And one's neediness of the Omnipotent, Omniscient One is strengthened according to the measure of his witnessing of his deficiency. And from his wondrous manner of address is that when he directs someone to his Lord and makes him aware of his delusion and passionate desires, he directs him with gentleness and softness. And he treats him mercifully with a clear address. And Allah guides whomever He wills to the Straight Path.

---

66   Musnad Ahmad (Hadith nos. 8028; 8417).
67   al-Naml, 62

And he warns people of the sins of the heart, such as arrogance, pride, dissimulation, seeking reputation, and others, more than he warns of outward sins. He says, "They are hidden while the others cannot be hidden." And he goes to great lengths in showing the evil of pride and arrogance. He says:

> "Their possessor is loathsome. And they are of the greatest sins that cut one off from Allah (Honored and Exalted). The greatest proof of this is the story of Adam (peace be upon him) and the disobedience of Iblis when he was commanded to prostrate. He refused and became arrogant. Adam was pardoned by his Lord and guided. But He cast Iblis out from His mercy and caused him to perish."

And he often warns of false claims. He says:

> "We fear for the one who makes false claims. And may Allah grant us refuge from an evil ending. May Allah free us from that by His blessing and generosity. If a man realizes his deficient attributes, he knows that the attributes of perfection belong only to Allah ﷻ. So when he realizes his inability, he realizes that the attribute of power belongs to his Lord. And he knows that He is the Most Powerful in His subjugation of everything else."

And he explains the Real's instruction ﷻ to His slave within the slave's self. He recites His words ﷻ:

> ❮And in yourselves. Then will you not see?❯[68]

And he says:

> "Indeed, in every state that the slave experiences is a guidance to his Lord. And Allah ﷻ created the slave and surrounded him with incapacity in his movements, moments of rest, and all of his states and orientations. If he sits, his sitting tires him. And if he stands, his standing tires him. If he sleeps for a long time, he becomes restless. But if he remains awake for a long time, he becomes desperate for sleep. And if he reclines, his reclining tires him out. If he eats, his fullness slows him down. But if he does not eat, he becomes hungry. One should use these examples to compare to other situations so that he may try to be dependent upon his Lord in every state, recognize the power of his Lord and His freedom of need of anything else, and refuse to have anything to do with

---

[68] al-Dhariyat, 21

anything other than Him, as a disclosure from Him and a gathering of his being towards Him, if he only realized. And blessed is the All-Knowing and Wise whose knowledge encompasses all things and whose command and decree is enacted on all things."

3.3.3 His Guidance Regarding Hardships and Acceptance of the Divine Decree

And the Shaykh explains how He ﷻ discloses matters that happen successively to people, such as difficulty, comfort, well-being, trials, fear, safety, sickness, health, and the turning of the state of the heart from contraction to expansion, from firm resolution to lethargy. And he recites His words ﷻ:

> ﴾We will show them Our signs in the horizons and within themselves until it becomes clear to them that He is the Real﴿[69]

And he says,

> Indeed, that people's states of difficulty are better for them than their states of ease, if only they knew. That is because, if the blessing is increased for them, they are negligent, forgetful and inattentive. But if difficulty befalls them, it forces them to call upon their Lord in desperation. And it is not possible for them to be negligent in that state, opposite to the case of their state of being blessed. So their state at that time is better for them due to their standing at the door of their Lord and asking Him to remove their difficulty.

And he mentions His words ﷻ:

> ﴾And when We bestow favor upon man, he turns away and distances himself; but when evil touches him, then he is full of extensive supplication﴿[70]

And he teaches people about certainty. And he shows them how to recognize it and how to obtain it. He says:

> ﴾Is not Allah Sufficient for His slave?﴿[71]

---

[69] Fussilat, 53
[70] Fussilat, 51
[71] al-Zumar, 36

"Is Allah not merciful to the slaves? Has He not been generous to us throughout all of our lives? So what is wrong with us that we become suspicious of Him? If you were to swear by Allah ﷻ, with His Greatest Name, that He would not give you something that He has apportioned to you, He would still give it to you. And if you were to seek what He has not apportioned for you, you would never attain it. The pen has dried regarding that which you will obtain."

And he says, "Indeed, Allah tests His slave with neediness and ease of obtaining something that is not purely lawful. But if he is patient, He will grant him such an opening that he will not experience poverty afterward." He also says, "When anything is designated by Allah for a person, and He subjugates it to him, it remains perpetually and is never cut off." And he makes this easy to understand through similitudes. He guides to Allah by the mercy of Allah. And he discloses this to people. And he makes it easy to understand through [the similitude of] the mercy of a father for his son, which is something that is not hidden from anyone. Is his gentleness for him greater than Allah's gentleness and mercy for His slaves? And he mentions the Hadith, "*Allah is more merciful to His slaves than this woman with her child.*"[72]

3.3.4 His Reminding of the Blessings of Allah and Guiding to Gratitude

And he reminds people of the blessing of their Lord and that with which He had favored them and granted them. By that, He guides them to the love of Allah ﷻ and restraint from sinning before Him due to His gifts to His slaves and His continuous blessings and generosity towards them. And he recites:

﴿*And amply bestowed upon you His favors, [both] apparent and unapparent?*﴾ [73]

And he speaks a lot about this most of the time. He explains the physical, spiritual, apparent, and hidden blessings of benefit and warding off harm that perpetually falls upon the human being. And he explains that in great detail. And brings forth a clear and evident explanation. For example, he explains that the belief in Allah and His Messengers [(peace be upon them all]) is among the hidden, perpetual, remaining blessings upon the slave. And that Allah assists him with it at every single moment. And He ﷻ

---

72 Sahih al-Bukhari (Hadith no. 5653) and Sahih Muslim (Hadith no. 4947).
73 Luqman, 20

wards off from it every dangerous thought. Nor does He give any unruly devil power to corrupt it. Nor does He allow any rebellious tyrant to take away that which He has given him, as a special concern, mercy, grace, and blessing from Him ﷻ.

And if He had allowed the Shaytan to corrupt it as he corrupts people's actions, most people would disbelieve after they had believed. And they would return to loss after having profited. However, Allah blessed people by protecting it [belief in Allah and His Messengers], just as He blessed them with being among His Elect in His pre-eternal grace and generosity. And for what reason did the slave deserve this blessing, since he was given it on the day on which the decrees were decided and the portions were allotted, whereas he did not even exist at that time? Nor did there exist any action by which he could approach its Giver. Nor was there anything for him to cling to or rely on. Rather, it was pure openhandedness, blessing, grace, and generosity.

If people were to be aware of this great blessing and recognize it, they would be drowned in contentment with Allah. And they would be overpowered by the authority of love and passion for this generous Giver and great Lord, who created and guided, showed generosity and granted gifts, and chose and elected in pre-eternity. And he ﷺ never ceases to enumerate the blessings of Allah upon His slave, continuous and sporadic, which are dispatched to him in His Earth and His Heaven. Then he recites:

❴*And if you should count the favors of Allah, you could not enumerate them*❵ [74]

And people are immersed in the sea of grace. However, they do not give thanks.

❴*And few of My slaves are grateful*❵ [75]

And if Allah wants good for a slave and to make him one of His elect slaves, He makes him recognize the blessing that is on him and inspires him to be thankful for it. And there is nothing else that he could do by which he would become elect. That is because all people are blessed. But the Elect is the one who witnesses that he is blessed. And he says, "Gratitude is the greatest door to Allah and the straightest path. For that reason, Shaytan sits in its path and prevents the believers from (traveling) it." And he mentions as a proof of this His words ﷻ quoting the Accursed:

---

74   al-Nahl, 18
75   al-A'raf, 16

❮I will surely sit in wait for them on Your straight path❯ [76]

And he says:

> "The closest door to Allah is the door of gratitude. And if anyone at this time does not enter through this door, he will not enter. This is because the souls have become thick. In other words, they are unaffected by spiritual exercises and acts of obedience. Nor are they restrained by self-appraisal and argumentation. But when they are immersed in contentment with the Granter of blessings, they become absent from all of that. And the distance they must travel is shortened. And you will find that every promise in the words of Allah is conditioned by the Divine will, except gratitude. For He said ﷻ:

❮If you are grateful, I will surely increase you❯ [77]

And He emphasized it using the "lam that indicates an oath" and the "nun of emphasis."

And he says to us, whenever he recites this verse:

> At this place, the "lam" indicates an oath. It is as if He is questioning us and we are responding to Him, "Yes." Look at how Allah gave precedence to gratitude over faith, out of concern for its importance. He said:

❮What would Allah do with your punishment if you are grateful and believe?❯ [78]

And many times, he even explains and interprets thankfulness as faith itself, just as the comparison in the previous verse indicates. So he will say, "Faith is contentment with the Granter of blessings."

Thus, he equates contentment, which is the gratitude of the heart, with faith itself. And there is no doubt that faith cannot be true without gratitude because it is its substance and essence. And the conjunction in the verse could have come for the purpose of interpretation, by which one can understand the verse to mean exactly what he ﷺ said:

---

76   Ibrahim, 7

77   Saba', 13

78   al-Nisa, 147

"Faith is gratitude. And if a person were to know the reality of gratitude, his heart would be filled, and his intellect would become loving, happy, content, and joyous with Allah. The nature of hearts is to love the one who is generous to you. And in reality, no one has been generous to you except your Lord. And it is He who has subjugated the hearts of His slaves to you. And if He had willed, it would be the opposite. Thus, they have not really benefitted you with anything."

He guides by all of that towards witnessing the blessing from Allah and rising from witnessing the intermediary to witnessing the Granter of blessings ﷻ, saying:

"And there is no one who grants blessings other than Him. Nor is there any generous person or benefactor apart from Him. And all apart from Him do not even control the benefit or harm that they receive, or attract benefit or ward off harm, much less others. And anyone who treats you well and takes you by the hand is only doing that for some motive. Even the Knower of Allah, when he takes you by the hand and has mercy on you, is only treating you that way for the sake of your Lord. And he only cares for you for the sake of His countenance. And that is a motive. However, Allah (Blessed and Exalted is He) only treats you well and has mercy on you out of grace, generosity, openhandedness, and blessing. He does not do it for any past or future reason. It is only pure generosity from the Necessary Being. So it is not fitting for a slave to recognize anything other than his Master. Nor is it fitting that he should recognize anyone's generosity and mercy except His. For it is (only) He who has been generous with him and caused His blessings to reach him."

By this, he causes every slave to love his Master. And he guides them to seek none other than Him, and not to let his heart incline towards other than Him, and to make all of his requests to his Lord alone, and not to attach his aspiration to anything else.

3.3.5 His Guiding People to Rely on Allah Alone

He guides to Allah alone, to actualizing His pure Divine unity, and to the unadulterated love of Him. He says:

> "It is not fitting for the slave to seek anything apart from his Lord. And he should do so for His sake exclusively and not for the sake of any immediate or delayed pleasure. And if he seeks Him in this manner, he will also obtain this world and the Hereafter. And there is a difference between someone who seeks you for your sake and someone who seeks you for some ulterior motive. Indeed, someone who seeks you and then says, "I want you to give me such-and-such a thing" is not like someone else who seeks you only out of love for you and hope to see you, and nothing else. And how deep the divide is between them both!"

Thus, he ﷺ diverts people from pleasures, desires, and all that is experienced through the feelings of the soul. And he recites His words ﷻ:

> ❴And they were not commanded except to worship Allah, [being] sincere to Him in religion, inclining to truth❵ [79]

And he considers acts done for the sake of obtaining some pleasure a kind of polytheism. And he recites the following verse as a subtle indication of that:

> ❴And most of them believe not in Allah except while they associate others with Him❵ [80]

3.3.6 His Guidance on Loving Allah and Abandoning Self-Direction

He speaks a lot about this and directs people towards love. He says:

> Love is the origin and foundation of everything. And that is indicated in His words ﷻ in the Hadith Qudsi:
>
> "I become his hearing…"
>
> And witnessing the beauty and favor of the loved one is the

---

79   Al-Bayyinah, 5
80   Yuusf, 106

origin and cause of love. And by that one ascends to the degree of faith.

And he ﷺ does not speak about any of the disciplines of the path, except that he gives a subtle indication of how to obtain it and guides towards it by his spiritual state and words. And he leads one towards drawing near to the Beloved, ardently loving Him, dependence on Him, humbling oneself before Him, and lowering oneself and submitting to Him. He often cites the following couplets:

> Lower yourself to the One for whom you long. For longing is not half-hearted,
>> Only when your Beloved is satisfied is communion allowed for you,
>
> Lower yourself to Him, being contented to behold His beauty,
>> And for the sake of the One you long for, obligatory and voluntary actions (are performed).

And He guides to leaving off choosing alongside the choice of Allah ﷻ. He always spends a lot of time speaking about it. As evidence, he recites the following verses:

> ❴But no, by your Lord, they will not [truly] believe until they make you judge concerning that over which they dispute among themselves and then find within themselves no discomfort from what you have judged and submit fully❵ [81]

> ❴It is not for a believing man or a believing woman when Allah and His Messenger have decided a matter, that they should [thereafter] have any choice❵ [82]

> ❴The only statement of the believers when they are called to Allah and His Messenger to judge between them is that they say, "We hear and we obey"❵ [83]

---

81 al-Nisa', 65
82 al-Ahzab, 36
83 al-Nur, 51

❮And your Lord creates what He wills and chooses; not for them was the choice❯ [84]

He says:

"Only the one who knows the outcomes of all situations should direct things. How can someone who does not know the outcomes direct? What can he direct at all? It has been said in a Hadith Qudsi, "The son of Adam wishes. And I will. And only that which I will, will be. So if you submit to Me in what I will, I will give you what you wish. But if you oppose Me in what I will, I will weary you with regards to what you wish. And in the end, only that which I will, will be."[85]

And he considers trying to direct oneself alongside the direction of Allah to be a kind of polytheism. That is because He is alone in creation and control.

❮Unquestionably, His is the creation and the command❯ [86]

Thus, whoever tries to control anything in His dominion has transgressed and opposed the Divine command. And whoever tries to control himself, he will suffer the evil consequences of his deed.

And he guides to satisfaction with the work of Allah and submitting to the decrees of Allah, because He is ﷻ the All-Wise and the Very Merciful. So if you mention to him any suffering or any affliction that befalls you, he will say:

"Among His Names ﷻ is "The All-Wise." And the All-Wise is the one who only acts out of wisdom. And His acts never lack wisdom. If the secrets of the Divine decree were to be revealed to the slave, he would see that that act, which appears to be severe affliction, is, in reality, wise and perfect. And he will see that, in reality, it is as it should be. And he would not impose anything else if he had the choice. Sometimes, something befalls the slave and appears

---

84   al-Qasas, 68

85   We did not find this Hadith attributed to the Prophet ﷺ. Rather, it was mentioned by al-Ghazali in his "Ihya'" and al-Hakim al-Tirmidhi in "Nawadir al-Usul," with the wording, "It has been narrated that Allah (Exalted is He) inspired Dawud (peace be upon him), saying, 'O, Dawud! You desire and I will...'" The rest of the narration is the same.

86   al-A'raf, 54

outwardly to be affliction. However, inwardly it is a mercy. And by it, Allah wards off something that is more severe. Or by it, He pushes away a religious trial. By Allah, Allah has not decreed any matter for His believing slave except that it is what is best for him."

And He guides to Allah by His names and witnessing His attributes. And he affirms this in ways that someone like me cannot understand, that dazzle minds, and words cannot describe. He says, "Realization of one of His attributes is a cause and means of realization of them all."

And he explains things in such a way that it clarifies and illuminates minds. Then, he goes beyond this to a higher degree: witnessing the exalted Essence and the Divine solitude. He says, "Witnessing the Divine attributes is a veil to witnessing the Divine Essence."

He speaks a lot on this subject. And he speaks on perpetuity after annihilation and the erasure of the attributes of the slave through the manifestation of the Divine attributes within him. And he brings as evidence for this the Hadith that was narrated by al-Bukhari:

> If anyone shows enmity to Me through My friend, I declare war on him. And My slave does not draw near to Me with anything more beloved to Me than what I have made obligatory upon him. And my slave continues to draw near to Me with voluntary acts until I love him. And when I love him, I become the hearing by which he hears, the sight by which he sees, the hand by which he strikes, and the leg by which he walks.[87]

And in another version of the same Hadith are the words, "And I become him."

And that version is clearer as an evidence of the Shaykh's words. And Allah knows best. He also says, "Stopping at any of the spiritual stations causes one to be cut off from the goal." Then he recites His words ﷻ:

❮ And that to your Lord is the finality ❯ [88]

And may Allah bless the person who said:

> And if you see all of the degrees revealed to you all at once,
> Turn away from them, for we also turned away from them,

---

87 Sahih al-Bukhari (Hadith no. 6137).
88 al-Najm, 42

And say, "I have no goal other than Your Essence,
    Not for any form to be revealed, nor to receive any honor."

And many times, when he speaks of annihilation to all apart from Allah ﷻ, he recites the following couplet:

Leave the sciences. Retain not any understanding,
    Nor preserve for yourself any choice, nor any affair.

This is all that was possible for us to gather in this section. And we only gathered a small portion of what has been repeated in daily and nightly gatherings and affirmed in people's minds time after time until whatever was understood was understood and whatever could be written was written; of what I was blessed to hear and wanted to compile and include here, so that the purpose of this book may be fulfilled. And it is only the purest and most essential portion. May Allah grant us benefit and make us of the people of love and emulation. Amin.

Section Four

On His Litanies and Their Arrangement, His Path, and His Followers. On the Benefit of His Litany and the Description and the Condition of the True Disciple. On the True Shaykh and the Method of the Spiritual Concert and Its People. On His Daily and Nightly Recitations and the Different Supplications That Allah Caused to Flow Upon His Tongue (It has three subsections.)

4.1 On His Litanies and Their Arrangement, His Path, and His Followers

4.1.1 Introduction

OU SHOULD KNOW THAT I have placed a brief exhortation in which I explain that there is no disagreement among the Sscholars of Law and Reality. And I say, and from Allah is facilitation:

An Honorable Exhortation
You should know that whereas the scholars of Law and the Spiritual Path knew that existence had descended, by manifestation, from Divine unity to the lowest point of descent, where it became multiplicity, and that the most important and most perfect matter is the ascension to the beginning so that the manifestation of the perfect Divine names may be completed, they busied themselves with explaining what was most important, such as the way to complete the ascension- either faster or slower, as well as its conditions consisting of the utmost purity, outwardly and inwardly. So they composed writings about it. And they did not take into account the modality of the descent into the different degrees, sufficing themselves with the fact that the knowledge that is obtained through the ascent. Allah ﷻ said:

❰ *Man will be informed that Day of what he sent ahead and kept back* ❱ [89]

The ignorant assumed that they did not know the description of Reality, nor its secrets. As for the scholars of Reality, whereas they knew the modality of ascension and its secrets, by ascending towards Divine unity through unveiling and witnessing, they busied themselves with explaining

---

89   al-Qiyamah, 13

the overpowering intoxication of the state, according to the situation of their state and station. So they composed writings about it. And the incomplete assumed that that was the Law and the Path, according to their understanding and intellect. And they considered their souls as accomplished and complete, due to their fantasy that their souls were in the degree of reality, based solely on academic knowledge and intellectual thought, without unveiling or witnessing. So they abandoned acting according to the Law and the Spiritual Path. This is a repugnant error.

But it is not hidden to the one who understands that there is no difference between matters of Law and Reality. So the scholars of Law had penetrated deeply into explaining the requirements of multiplicity and how to cultivate them, to raise the multiplicity so that oneness should manifest. That is going from the end to the beginning. The scholars of Reality, on the other hand, occupied themselves with explaining the secrets of one all-encompassing Existence and the diffusion of His light in the different degrees. And each one of them has their area.

Thus, what is necessary for the sincere disciple is to drown himself inwardly in the lights of Reality, and act upon the Sacred Law outwardly, upholding the requirements of the different degrees. And that is the Straight Path of following the Messenger ﷺ.

4.1.2 His Litanies and Their Arrangement

As for his litanies ﷺ, they are among the greatest litanies. And in them is good that is not hidden to the people who discharge their duties. And they are among the most beautiful of those with which the People of Allah have decorated their Zawiyahs, seeking to gather those people who mix with them and ally themselves with them to Allah, so that their time may be properly arranged, and their states rectified. He ﷺ revived by them the Spiritual Path after its traces had been obliterated and erected its lamp after its lights had been extinguished. He traveled thereby ﷺ the road of the honored nobles, the perfect scholarly gnostics, the Imams of the Muhammadan creed (may the blessings and peace of Allah be upon them all), until the Path became clear through His manifestation.

They came, and Allah be praised, in accordance with the Sacred Law and Reality. And his litanies ﷺ are beautiful to the ears, some parts being mixed with others in a way that is pleasant to the hearing. What had been hidden was revealed in them, and he accomplished and attained in it the highest desire of the aspirant. So they manifested to the worlds as bridegrooms, attracted many souls by their beauty, and gave them to drink from the sweetest cups.

And when Allah willed for the bliss of his contemporaries and willed to provide his neighbors with a gift that no one else had been given, He cast into his heart the light of realization regarding his beautiful affirmation and confirmation. So it was not appropriate for him to hide what was hidden within him when it had appeared upon his tongue. So he manifested to people marvels and opened the door for the seekers. And he arranged litanies, which they take as an increase for the Hereafter. Thus, they have come, and Allah be praised, with pure meanings, sweet to the taste, and with easy returns. And you will come upon, if Allah so wills, their reality and foundation. And you will witness the secret of their beauty and appearance. And you will know their origin and the hidden secrets with which they have been endowed. All of this will indicate to you, if Allah so wills, his complete inheritance from the Messenger of Allah ﷺ and his state, so that you may know that Allah has blessed him with His all-encompassing generosity. It is said:

> Who is like you, or resembles you, o father of good,
>   You have attained the secret and beautiful conduct and character,
>
> By Allah! Eyes have not seen the like of you,
>   In all of time, o splendor of the Scholars

Shaykh Zarruq has said ﷺ, at the end of his explanation of the litanies:

> "The prayers of the Shaykhs (may Allah be pleased with them) are an attribute of their state, the adornment of their speech, and the inheritance of their knowledge and action. Through them, they engaged in all of their affairs, not through desires before their completion. Perhaps some of them were approached by those who desired to attempt that by themselves for themselves and received the opposite of what they intended. However, this is only the example of the story of the bee that taught the hornet the art of weaving a home. So it weaved according to that example and built a home that resembled the home of the bee. Then it claimed that it had the same honor as that of the bee. But the bee said to him, "This is a house, but where is the honey?" The secret is in the inhabitant, not the home."

Then he [Zarruq] said, "The prayers of the People of Perfection are wedded to their states, built upon their knowledge, strengthened by their inspiration, and accompanied by their miracles."

The litanies of our Master 🌺 have, since they manifested to the eyes, not ceased to manifest numerous blessings, such as facilitating the obtainment of aspirations and attainment of desires. And they brought, and Allah be praised, a number of original writings into existence, and their prestige has been spread to the farthest parts of the land by the permission of the Master of Existence 🌺.

Thus, they continue to be famous among the worshippers, and their secrets are manifest and widespread. And they are among the greatest treasures and most sublime honors. And innumerable secrets, from the good of the world and the Hereafter, have been seen in them. So I ask Allah that He never remove them from His existence and that He perpetually encompass their lights with His witnessing, by the honor of the Master of Prophets, the Imam of the God-conscious, our Master Muhammad (may Allah bless him and his family, give them peace, honor them, be generous with them, extol them, and esteem them).

And with that, we begin. So I say, and by Him is the assistance, facilitation, and guidance, by His grace and generosity, to the Straight Path:

As for his litany 🌺, which he transmits to all people, and which the Master of Existence and Standard of Witnessing 🌺 arranged for him, they are (to say):

1. "I seek forgiveness of Allah"[90] 100 times
2. Prayers upon the Messenger of Allah 🌺, in any formula 100 times
3. And the declaration "There is no God but Allah"[91] 100 times

These remembrances are the exact arrangement which the Messenger of Allah 🌺 arranged for him and commanded him to transmit to whatever Muslim should request it, in whatever condition he may be, whether he is old or young, male or female, righteous or sinful; and to not refuse it to anyone who seeks it from him.

It is better and more preferred that the prayer upon the Messenger of Allah 🌺 be *Salat al-Fatihi*, due to what it has of grand superiority and great reward- whose worth cannot be measured, except by the One who gave it as a blessing from the outpouring of His all-encompassing grace. Its superiority will be mentioned in detail in its proper place if Allah so wills.

---

90 *Astaghfirullah*
91 *La ilaha illAllah*

Salat al-Fatihi [92] is:

$$\text{اَللَّهُمَّ صَلِّ عَلَى سَيِّدِنَا مُحَمَّدٍ الفَاتِحِ لِمَا أُغْلِقَ وَالخَاتِمِ لِمَا سَبَقَ نَاصِرِ الحَقِّ بِالحَقِّ وَالهَادِي إِلَى صِرَاطِكَ المُسْتَقِيمِ وَعَلَى آلِهِ حَقَّ قَدْرِهِ وَمِقْدَارِهِ العَظِيمِ}$$

O, Allah! Bless our Master Muhammad, the Opener of what had been locked, the Seal of what came before, the Helper of the Truth by the Truth, and the Guide to Your Straight Path, as well as his family according to his grandeur and immense worth.

Next in superiority is the "Spirit of Prayers upon the Prophet":

$$\text{اَللَّهُمَّ صَلِّ عَلَى سَيِّدِنَا مُحَمَّدٍ عَبْدِكَ وَنَبِيِّكَ وَرَسُولِكَ النَّبِيِّ الأُمِّيِّ وَعَلَى آلِهِ وَصَحْبِهِ وَسَلَّمَ تَسْلِيمًا}$$

O, Allah! Bless our Master Muhammad, Your slave, Prophet, and Messenger- the Unlettered Prophet- his family, and companions, and salute them with a worthy salutation.

Next in superiority after that is:

$$\text{اَللَّهُمَّ صَلِّ وَسَلِّمْ عَلَى سَيِّدِنَا مُحَمَّدٍ وَعَلَى آلِهِ}$$

O, Allah! Bless and grant peace to our Master Muhammad and his family

One has the choice. And it also depends on the reasoning of the one who transmits the litany. He should inspect the one who is taking the litany as to whether he is a religious and upright person, and whether he is worthy and connected. If this is the case, then he transmits to him *Salat al-Fatihi* and gives him permission only in its outward degree. If not, then if he is somewhat religious, he transmits to him the "Spirit of Prayers upon the

---

92 *Salat al-Fatihi* was not mentioned here in the text. However, due to our intention to give the Arabic of the litanies and supplications of the Shaykh in this chapter, we have placed it here.

Prophet." If he is not religious, then he transmits to him "O, Allah! Bless our Master Muhammad and his family." And whichever one he does is sufficient- with whichever formula of prayer upon the Prophet ﷺ.

The time for its performance is after the Dawn Prayer [Salat al-Subh] until the sun rises and shines bright [al-Duha], and after the 'Asr prayer until the Night Prayer [al-'Isha]. If one misses it during these two times because of an excuse, then all of the day is a time for the morning litany and all of the night is a time for the night litany.

If anyone misses a litany, he should make it up, even if it takes him his whole life. Whoever takes this litany and abandons it completely, or out of negligence, is in danger of being punished and destroyed. That is according to what the Master of Existence informed our Shaykh ﷺ. His exact words ﷺ were:

> "Say to whomever takes an invocation from you, as an advice, "Our invocation is great. So beware of missing it and beware of abandoning it. That is because the prayer upon the Prophet is great. It is the door to completion. And it is the greatest entrance. Whoever abandons it will not find any door to enter other than it."

Its conditions are observing the (obligatory) prayers at their proper times, and in congregation if possible, purity of body, clothes and place of invocation, facing the direction of prayer [qiblah] and not speaking without necessity. Its special condition, for the one who is capable, is to imagine that the Shaykh [qudwah][93] is before him, that he is sitting in front of him, from the beginning of the remembrance until the end, and that he is seeking spiritual aid from him. But even greater than that, higher and more perfect and beneficial, is that he should imagine the image of the Chosen One [al-Mustafa] ﷺ and that he is sitting before him ﷺ with awe, dignity, reverence and exaltation, and that he is seeking his spiritual assistance by the grandeur of his state and station. He should bring to mind the meanings of the words of the remembrance if he is able to understand them. If not, he should listen to the remembrance upon his tongue, so that his thoughts should be too engaged to drift away from his objective. That will help him with having presence (in the remembrance).

The litany that we have mentioned here is the obligatory litany of the Path. So no one should desist from it. As for the other litanies that we will mention, one has the option of performing them or leaving them. And you should know that this litany cannot be transmitted to anyone who has a

---

93   The word used in the text is qudwah, which literally means his exemplar and support in the path. As it obviously means one's Shaykh, I have translated it as such.

litany from any Shaykh (may Allah be pleased them all), unless he leaves it, distances himself and does not return to it ever. He must take a covenant with Allah to that effect. At that point, the one who has special permission from the Shaykh 🕊 may transmit the litany to him. If not, then he should not transmit it to him if he does not distance himself from the litany that he already has. So he should leave him to his litany and the path he is on. That is because the litanies of the Shaykhs (may Allah be pleased with them) are all upon guidance and evidence from Allah. All of them transport one on the Path and cause him to reach Allah 🕊.

This (the condition) should not be seen as arrogance from us, or exalting ourselves above the Shaykhs. Nay! Allah forbid that and protect us! Rather, this is only a condition that has been stipulated in our Path. So whoever wishes to enter our Path must comply with this condition. And he has no reason to fear any retaliation from his companion, nor anyone else from among the Saints- be they living or dead, neither in this world nor the Hereafter. And he will be safe from any harm reaching him in this world or in the Hereafter, either from his Shaykh or others, from Allah or His Messenger 🕊, by a true promise that will not be broken.

But whoever refuses to leave the litany that he already has from his Shaykh, then there is no blame on him. And he should leave alone our litany and remain with his litany and Path, because, as we have already said, the litanies of our Masters (may Allah be pleased with them) are all upon guidance from Allah. And whoever you should give permission and command him to transmit our litanies and give our Path to others, he must comply with the condition that he not transmit it to anyone who already has a litany or Path from a Shaykh [until they relinquish the previous Path, its Shaykh (as a guide, not as a rebuke) and its litany]. If he does not comply, and he transmits it without this condition, then he will benefit neither himself nor the one to whom he transmits it. So he should stipulate this condition and act upon it. Peace.

Likewise, the one who takes our litany and enters our Path should not visit anyone at all from among the living saints. As for those who have passed away, if he visits them believing that he is connecting himself to them for Allah alone, not for any other reason, it is permitted[94]. That is because they

---

94   The allowance of visiting the Saints who have passed away was abrogated by Sidna Shaykh 🕊. Since Sidi 'Ali Harazim 🕊 passed away during the lifetime of the Shaykh, some of the positions that he narrates on *fiqh* of the Path are different to what is relied upon. This is no different. In "Bughyah al-Mustafid," Sidi al-'Arabi b. Sa'ih first explains that the murid may visit any of the Prophets (peace be upon them all), the Companions of the Prophet 🕊 or the adherents to the Tijani Path that he wishes. And he makes clear that visiting any other Saint, alive or dead, is forbid-

are the doors of Allah, so he connects himself to them for Allah and seeks from Allah, while connecting himself with them, the pleasure of Allah, the pleasure of His Messenger ﷺ and the pleasure of his Shaykh, and nothing else. Peace.

As for the litany of the *Zawiyah*[95], it is:

---

den for the disciple. And he addresses what Sidi 'Ali Harazim wrote here, saying:

What was stated in "Jawahir al-Ma'ani," that the disciple may visit the Saints that have passed on with the condition that he seek to have a relationship with them for the sake of Allah alone- and that in their presence he seeks only the pleasure of Allah, His Messenger and his Shaykh alone- is correct and valid because the kind of visitation that is forbidden is one by which one seeks to benefit. And such a person is exempt from that situation, only visiting in order to establish a relationship for the sake of Allah (Exalted is He).

However, the allowance [for visting the Saints who have passed on] is only valid for someone who has become realized in the station of complete sincerity, reaching purity and purification of the soul until it does not seek to confuse him, scheme against him or seek to deceive him in any way. As for someone who is trapped in the grasp of his passions and locked away in the prison of his desires and negligence, he does not know what it means to have a relationship for the sake of Allah. And if his ego claims such, then it is only from its schemes and deceptions. Our master ﷺ used to say, "The ordinary folk don't know what it means to work for the sake of Allah."

And all good has been gathered for us, o, party of the weak and of the veiled people, in incriminating our souls and never being delueded by anything that they claim, or any action that it is pleased or avarice to perform. It is for that reason that, at the end of his life, our Master ﷺ was moved to close that door completely. And after him, the consummate practice of those of his Companions whose opinions are weighty, has been upon this [the forbiddance of visiting the Saints who have passed on].

95   The *Wazifah* that is mentioned here is slightly different from the famous *Wazifah* as performed by Tijanis worldwide. The reason is that *Jawahir al-Ma'ani* was composed in 1213 AH. And the Shaykh lived for another 17 years, during which time the *Wazifah* reached its final form. In the Kitab al-Jami', the author lists the pillars of the *Wazifah* as follows:

- *Astaghfiru 'Llaha 'lladhi la ilaha illa Huwa 'l-Hayyu 'l-Qayyum* (30 times);
- *Salat al-Fatihi* (50 times)
- *La ilaha ill Allah* (100 times)
- *Jawharat al-Kamal* (12 times)

Al-'Arabi b. Sa'ih says, in "Bughyah al-Mustafid," when commenting on the pillars of the *Wazifah*:

The summary of what the author [of Munyah al-Murid] (may Allah (Exalted is

SECTION FOUR

1. Seeking the forgiveness of Allah (Astaghfiru 'Llah) 100 times;
2. *Salat al-Fatihi* 100 or 50 times;
3. The declaration "There is no God but Allah" 100 or 200 times;
4. And the prayer *Jawharat al-Kamal* 11 times.

Jawharat al-Kamal[96]

اَللَّهُمَّ صَلِّ وَسَلِّمْ عَلَى عَيْنِ الرَّحْمَةِ الرَّبَّانِيَّةِ وَالْيَاقُوتَةِ الْمُتَحَقِّقَةِ الْحَائِطَةِ بِمَرْكَزِ الْفُهُومِ وَالْمَعَانِي وَنُورِ الْأَكْوَانِ الْمُتَكَوِّنَةِ الْآدَمِيِّ صَاحِبِ الْحَقِّ الرَّبَّانِي الْبَرْقِ الْأَسْطَعِ بِمُزُونِ الْأَرْبَاحِ الْمَالِئَةِ لِكُلِّ مُتَعَرِّضٍ مِنَ الْبُحُورِ وَالْأَوَانِي وَنُورِكَ اللَّامِعِ الَّذِي مَلَأْتَ بِهِ كَوْنَكَ الْحَائِطَ بِأَمْكِنَةِ الْمَكَانِي،

اَللَّهُمَّ صَلِّ وَسَلِّمْ عَلَى عَيْنِ الْحَقِّ الَّتِي تَتَجَلَّى مِنْهَا عُرُوشُ الْحَقَائِقِ عَيْنِ الْمَعَارِفِ الْأَقْوَمِ صِرَاطِكَ التَّامِّ الْأَسْقَمِ،

اَللَّهُمَّ صَلِّ وَسَلِّمْ عَلَى طَلْعَةِ الْحَقِّ بِالْحَقِّ الْكَنْزِ الْأَعْظَمِ إِفَاضَتِكَ مِنْكَ إِلَيْكَ إِحَاطَةِ النُّورِ الْمُطَلْسَمِ صَلَّى اللهُ عَلَيْهِ وَعَلَى آلِهِ صَلَاةً تُعَرِّفُنَا بِهَا إِيَّاهُ

He) have mercy on him) has indicated is what has been reliably transmitted form the Shaykh ﷺ on the matter, as mentioned in "Jawahir al-Ma'ani" and elsewhere, that the pillars of the *Wazifah*, from which it is constructed are Seeking forgiveness with the same formula as the *Wird* one hundred times, then *Salat al-Fatihi* one hundred times, then *La ilaha ill Allah* one hundred, or two hundred times, then *Jawharat al-Kamal* twelve times. However, this practice was not continued by the Companions, except in the eastern parts of the lands of Sahara'. I have heard that they continue to practice the *Wazifa* in this manner. However, the established practice in the majority of the lands of the east and the west, and in the big cities, is the following... [and he mentioned the pillars as mentioned in "Kitab al-Jami".

96   *Jawharat al-Kamal* does not appear at this point in the text. However, we have placed it here for the same reason that we placed *Salat al-Fatihi* above.

O, Allah! Bless and send peace upon the source of Divine mercy; the real ruby that comprises all of the stations of understandings and meanings; the Light of all creation being Adamic; the owner of the Divine right; the most radiant flash of lighting in the beneficial rainclouds that fill every receptacle, be they oceans or containers; and Your shining light with which You have filled Your creation, which encompasses all possible places.

O, Allah! Bless and send peace upon the source of the Truth from which manifest royal Realities; the source of the most upright gnosis; and Your straightest path.

O, Allah! Bless and send peace upon the manifestation of the Truth; the greatest treasure; Your effulgence from Yourself to Yourself; the enclosure of the mysterious light. May Allah bless him and his family with a prayer that will acquaint us with him.

This is the obligatory *Wazifah* in the Path. It is sufficient to recite it once- either in the morning or the night. But if it is easy for him to do it twice, that is better. This is different from the known litany, which is obligatory for the one who takes it to recite it in the morning and the evening. Reciting the *Wazifah* does not replace the recitation of the litany. So the one who recites the *Wazifah* must necessarily recite the litany. In the same way that the one who misses the litany must make it up, the one who misses the *Wazifah* must also make it up. In this way, it is similar to the litany. So if one is alone, for example, in his city, without other Tijanis with him, he would recite the *Wazifah* alone. But if there are Tijanis with him, they should gather and recite it as a congregation. That is a condition for the *Wazifah*.

If he is traveling, he should recite it alone. But if he does not recite it while traveling, there is no blame on him. *Jawharat al-Kamal* can only be recited with *wudu*. It cannot be recited upon *tayammum* since the Prophet ﷺ is present during its recitation, as will be mentioned in its proper place, if Allah so wills.

Among the litanies that are obligatory in his Path is the remembrance "There is no God but Allah" after the 'Asr prayer on Friday, in congregation. If there are Tijanis in his city, then he must gather them and perform the remembrance in congregation. That is a condition in our Path without a fixed limit or number, according to the foundation of the Khalwati Path, and if not, then according to the custom of the land where he lives. If he is alone, with no Tijanis near, he should perform the remembrance by himself.

That is a stipulated condition in our Path perpetually and eternally.

Among his litanies of great grandeur is "The Jewel of Realities in Recognizing the Reality of the Master of Creation." It is the litany that begins, "Allah! Allah! Allah! O, Allah! You are Allah other than whom there is no God…" You will be informed fully of it, if Allah so wills, in its proper place, along with its benefit, its explanation, and the aforementioned prayer upon the Prophet (*Jawharat al-Kamal*) and its explanation also in the epilogue, if Allah so wills.

Likewise, (among his litanies) is *al-Hirz al-Yamani*, which is the "Supplication of the Sword" [*Du'a al*-Sayfi]. And it has a great benefit and a grand reward. Among its benefits is that the one who recites it once has the worship of one year written for him; and the one who recites it two times, two years, etc. Also, whoever carries it with him is written among those who remember Allah a lot, even if he does not recite it, etc. Whoever wants to read its benefits in detail should read *al-Jawahir al-Khams* by Sidi Muhammad al-Ghawth ﷺ.

Also among his litanies is "The Invocation of the Sea." It has extremely special properties, and it is only transmitted to his special companions, due to the exaltedness of its degree. He took it, and the aforementioned *Sayfi* and other litanies, from the Prophet ﷺ.

Similarly, among his great litanies is the "Idrisi Names," which begins:

$$سُبْحَانَكَ لاَ إِلَهَ إِلاَّ أَنْتَ يَا رَبَّ كُلِّ شَيْءٍ وَوَارِثَهُ وَرَازِقَهُ وَرَاحِمَهُ$$

> Blessed are You. There is no God other than You. O, Lord of everything, their Inheritor, their Provider and their Benefactor.

They are forty-one names in total. The last of them is:

$$يَا غِيَاثِي عِنْدَ كُلِّ كُرْبَةٍ وَمُجِيبِي عِنْدَ كُلِّ دَعْوَةٍ وَمَعَاذِي عِنْدَ كُلِّ شِدَّةٍ وَيَا رَجَائِي حِينَ تَنْقَطِعُ حِيلَتِي$$

> O, my Succor in every affliction, the One who answers all of my supplications, my Refuge in every difficulty and my Hope when my ability has been cut off.

This name is free of any condition. So one only needs an authorization from the Shaykh. And it has a great benefit.

Also among his great litanies, incomparable is the *Surah al-Fatihah* [*Fatihat al-Kitab*] with its known specialty, and which is from among the greatest secrets and the mysterious treasures- that not one of the elite, righteous men, apart from our Master and Shaykh, obtained. The Chosen Prophet ﷺ preferred him for it. And its benefit and method will come later.

And among his litanies is the prayer upon the Prophet that raises works [*Salat Raf' al-A'mal*]. It is:

اَللَّهُمَّ صَلِّ عَلَى سَيِّدِنَا مُحَمَّدٍ النَّبِيِّ عَدَدَ مَنْ صَلَّى عَلَيْهِ مِنْ خَلْقِكَ وَصَلَّى عَلَى سَيِّدِنَا مُحَمَّدٍ النَّبِيِّ كَمَا يَنْبَغِي لَنَا أَنْ نُصَلِّيَ عَلَيْهِ وَصَلَّى عَلَى سَيِّدِنَا مُحَمَّدٍ النَّبِيِّ كَمَا أَمَرْتَنَا أَنْ نُصَلِّيَ عَلَيْهِ

O, Allah! Bless our Master Muhammad, the Prophet! According to the number of creation that send prayers upon the Prophet and bless our Master Muhammad, the Prophet, just as it is incumbent upon us to send prayers upon the Prophet, and send blessings upon our Master Muhammad, the Prophet, just as you have commanded us to send prayers upon the Prophet."

Also among his litanies ﷺ is:

اللَّهُمَّ مَغْفِرَتُكَ أَوْسَعُ مِنْ ذُنُوبِي وَرَحْمَتُكَ أَرْجَى عِنْدِي مِنْ عَمَلِي

O Allah! Your forgiveness is greater than my sins, and I have more hope in Your mercy than in my actions.

It is recited three times in the morning and three times in the evening.

Also among his litanies are these invocations in the day and the night, three times:

لَا إِلَهَ إِلَّا اللهُ أَكْبَرُ، لَا إِلَهَ إِلَّا اللهُ وَحْدَهُ، لَا إِلَهَ إِلَّا اللهُ وَلَا شَرِيكَ لَهُ، لَا إِلَهَ إِلَّا اللهُ لَهُ الْمُلْكُ وَلَهُ الْحَمْدُ، لَا إِلَهَ إِلَّا

SECTION FOUR

اللهُ وَلاَ حَوْلَ وَلاَ قُوَّةَ إِلاَّ بِاللهِ العَلِيِّ العَظِيمِ.

There is no God but Allah. Allah is the Greatest. There is no God but Allah. He is One. There is no God but Allah. He has no partner. There is no God but Allah. To Him belongs the dominion and the praise. There is no God but Allah. And there is no might nor power except in Allah, the Exalted, the Great.

Also among his litanies ﷺ is the "Exalted Pearl" [*al-Dawr al-Aʿla*] of Shaykh al-Akbar and the "Red Sulfur" of Ibn al-ʿArabi al-Hatimi ﷺ.

Among them is the "Petition of Forgiveness" [*Istighfar*] of our Master Khidr (upon him and our Prophet blessings and peace). It is:

اَللَّهُمَّ إِنِّي أَسْتَغْفِرُكَ مِنْ كُلِّ ذَنْبٍ تُبْتُ إِلَيْكَ مِنْهُ ثُمَّ عُدْتُ فِيهِ، وَأَسْتَغْفِرُكَ مُنْ كُلِّ مَا وَعَدْتُكَ بِهِ مِنْ نَفْسِي ثُمَّ لَمْ أُوفِ لَكَ بِهِ، وَأَسْتَغْفِرُكَ مِنْ كُلِّ عَمَلٍ أَرَدْتُ بِهِ وَجْهَكَ فَخَالَطَنِي فِيهِ غَيْرُكَ، وَأَسْتَغْفِرُكَ مِنْ كُلِّ نِعْمَةٍ أَنْعَمْتَ بِهَا عَلَيَّ فَاسْتَعَنْتُ بِهَا عَلَى مَعْصِيَتِكَ، وَأَسْتَغْفِرُكَ يَا عَالِمَ الغَيْبِ وَالشَّهَادَةِ مِنْ كُلِّ ذَنْبٍ أَذْنَبْتُهُ فِي ضِيَاءِ النَّهَارِ أَوْ سَوَادِ اللَّيْلِ فِي مَلَإٍ أَوْ خَلَاءٍ أَوْ سِرٍّ أَوْ عَلَانِيَةٍ يَا حَلِيمُ

O, Allah! I seek Your forgiveness for every sin from which I repented to You, then returned to it. I seek Your forgiveness from whatever I had promised You from myself, then did not fulfill it for You. I seek forgiveness from You for every work in which I intended for You alone, but something other than You was intended with it. I seek forgiveness from You for every blessing that You have blessed me with that I used to disobey You. And I seek forgiveness from You, o, Knower of the hidden and apparent! From every sin that I have committed by light of day or in the darkness of night, in a group or alone, secretly or openly, o, Forbearing One!

It is recited in the morning and the evening when one is able.

Among his great litanies is the *Musabbaʿat al-ʿAshr*, which is famous among the elite and the masses. It is:

1. *Al-Fatihah* with the invocation of Allah's Name (basmalah). (7 times);

2. *Surah al-Falaq* and *al-Nas* with the basmalah. (7 times each);

3. *Surah al-Ikhlas* with basmalah. (7 times);

4. *Surah al-Kafirun* with basmalah. (7 times);

5. *Ayah al-Kursi*. (7 times);

6. The following prayer:

سُبْحَانَ اللهِ وَالْحَمْدُ لِلَّهِ وَلاَ إِلَهَ إِلاَّ اللهُ وَاللهُ أَكْبَرُ وَلاَ حَوْلَ وَلاَ قُوَّةَ إِلاَّ بِاللهِ الْعَلِيِّ الْعَظِيمِ

Glorified be Allah! Praise be to Allah! There is no God but Allah! Allah is the Greatest! There is no might nor power except in Allah, the Knower, the Great! (7 times);

7. The following prayer:

اَللَّهُمَّ صَلِّ عَلَى سَيِّدِنَا مُحَمَّدٍ عَبْدِكَ وَنَبِيِّكَ وَرَسُولِكَ النَّبِيِّ الْأُمِّيِّ وَعَلَى آلِهِ وَصَحْبِهِ وَسَلِّمْ تَسْلِيمًا

O, Allah! Bless our Master Muhammad, Your slave, Prophet and Messenger, the Unlettered Prophet, and his family and companions; and salute them. (7 times);

8. The following prayer:

اَللَّهُمَّ اغْفِرْ لِي وَلِوَالِدَيَّ

O, Allah! Forgive my parents and me. (7 times);

9. The following prayer:

اَللَّهُمَّ اغْفِرْ لِلْمُؤْمِنِينَ وَالْمُؤْمِنَاتِ وَالْمُسْلِمِينَ وَالْمُسْلِمَاتِ الأَحْيَاءِ مِنْهُمْ وَالأَمْوَاتِ

O, Allah! Forgive the believing men and women and the Muslim men and women, those who are living among them and those who have passed away. (7 times);

10. The following prayer:

اَللَّهُمَّ افْعَلْ بِي وَبِهِمْ عَاجِلاً وَآجِلاً فِي الدِّينِ وَالدُّنْيَا وَالآخِرَةِ مَا أَنْتَ أَهْلٌ لَهُ وَلاَ تَفْعَلْ بِنَا وَبِهِمْ يَا مَوْلاَنَا مَا نَحْنُ لَهُ أَهْلٌ، إِنَّكَ غَفُورٌ حَلِيمٌ جَوَادٌ كَرِيمٌ رَؤُوفٌ رَحِيمٌ

O, Allah! Treat me, and them, swiftly and not delayed, in the religion, the world and the Hereafter, as You are capable of treating me. And do not treat me, or them, o, my Lord! According to what we deserve. Verily You are Forgiving, Forbearing, Magnanimous, Generous, Gentle, and Merciful. (7 times).

Among his litanies ﷺ is this invocation related in Sahih Bukhari:[97]

أَشْهَدُ أَنْ لاَ إِلَهَ إِلاَّ اللهُ وَحْدَهُ لاَ شَرِيكَ لَهُ وَأَنَّ مُحَمَّدًا عَبْدُهُ وَرَسُولُهُ وَأَنَّ عِيسَى عَبْدُ اللهِ وَرَسُولُهُ وَابْنُ أَمَتِهِ وَكَلِمَتُهُ أَلْقَاهَا إِلَى مَرْيَمَ وَرُوحٌ مِنْهُ وَأَنَّ الجَنَّةَ حَقٌّ وَأَنَّ النَّارَ حَقٌّ

I bear witness that there is no God but Allah, that He is One, that He has no partner, that Muhammad is His slave and Messenger, that Jesus is His slave and Messenger, the son of His female slave, His Word that He cast into Mary and a spirit from Him, that Paradise is real and that the Fire is real.

---

97   Sahih al-Bukhari (Hadith no. 3435).

One should recite it as much as one is able. And our Master ﷺ ordered us to recite it when one goes to sleep.

Among the litanies are some that he recited after every prayer and some in the morning and the night. As for those recited after every prayer, they are *al-Fatihah* four times after every prayer, and then *Ayah al-Kursi* once. Then:

اَللَّهُمَّ إِنِّي أُقَدِّمُ إِلَيْكَ بَيْنَ يَدَيْ كُلِّ نَفَسٍ وَلَمْحَةٍ وَلَحْظَةٍ وَطَرْفَةٍ يَطْرِفُ بِهَا أَهْلُ السَّمَاوَاتِ وَأَهْلُ الأَرْضِ وَكُلِّ شَيْءٍ هُوَ فِي عِلْمِكَ كَائِنٌ أَوْ قَدْ كَانَ، أُقَدِّمُ إِلَيْكَ بَيْنَ يَدَيْ كُلِّ ذَلِكَ

> O, Allah! Indeed, I give offer to You, before every breath, every glance, every moment and every blinking of the eye by the People of the Heavens and the People of the earth, and before everything that exists or could possibly exist in Your knowledge. I offer to You before all of that.

Then, he recites, "Allah! There is no God but He, the Living, the Eternal…" until the end of the verse. Next (he would recite) *Surah al-Ikhlas* once, placing his hand upon his eyes or chest as he recites it.

Then he recites:

أَعُوذُ بِكَلِمَاتِ اللهِ التَّامَّاتِ مِنْ شَرِّ مَا خَلَقَ، بِاسْمِ اللهِ الَّذِي لاَ يَضُرُّ مَعَ اسْمِهِ شَيْءٌ فِي الأَرْضِ وَلاَ فِي السَّمَاءِ وَهُوَ السَّمِيعُ العَلِيمُ

> I seek refuge in the perfect words of Allah from the evil of what He created. In the name of Allah, whom nothing in the Earth or the Heavens can harm with His Name. And He is the Hearing, the Knowing.

He recites this thrice after each prayer.

Then he recites:

SECTION FOUR

تَبَارَكْتَ إِلَهِي مِنَ الدَّهْرِ إِلَى الدَّهْرِ، وَتَعَالَيْتَ إِلَهِي مِنَ الدَّهْرِ إِلَى الدَّهْرِ، وَتَقَدَّسْتَ إِلَهِي مِنَ الدَّهْرِ إِلَى الدَّهْرِ، وَأَنْتَ رَبِّي وَرَبَّ كُلِّ شَيْءٍ لاَ إِلَهَ إِلاَّ أَنْتَ يَا أَكْرَمَ الأَكْرَمِينَ وَالفَتَّاحَ بِالخَيْرَاتِ، اغْفِرْ لِي وَلِعِبَادِكَ الَّذِينَ آمَنُوا بِمَا أَنْزَلْتَ عَلَى رُسُلِكَ

Blessed are You, my God, throughout all time. And Exalted are You, my God, throughout all time. And Holy are You, my God, throughout all time. You are my Lord and the Lord of everything. There is no God but You. O, Most Generous of the Generous! And Grantor of all blessings! Forgive me and all of Your slaves who believe in what You have revealed to Your Messengers.

He recites this after every prayer.

Then he recites:

سُبْحَانَ مَنْ تَعَزَّزَ بِالعَظَمَةِ، سُبْحَانَ مَنْ تَرَدَّى بِالكِبْرِيَاءِ، سُبْحَانَ مَنْ تَفَرَّدَ بِالوَحْدَانِيَةِ، سُبْحَانَ مَنِ احْتَجَبَ بِالنُّورِ، سُبْحَانَ مَنْ قَهَرَ العِبَادِ بِالـمَوْتِ، صَلَّى اللهُ عَلَى سَيِّدِنَا مُحَمَّدٍ النَّبِيِّ الكَرِيمِ وَعَلَى آلِهِ وَصَحْبِهِ وَسَلَّمَ تَسْلِيمًا

Blessed is He who is honored with greatness. Blessed is He who is clothed in grandeur. Blessed is He who is unique in unity. Blessed is He who veiled Himself with light. Blessed is He who overpowered His slaves with death. May Allah bless our Master Muhammad, the Honored Prophet, his family, and companions, and extend them a worthy salutation.

He recites this after every prayer.

The benefit of always reciting this after every prayer is that Allah will revive one as a king, and it will suffice him for all of his missed prayers- meaning the obligatory prayers that have accumulated in his debt. However, he should not depend on that. Rather, if prayers have accumulated in his debt, he should make them up. And the grace of Allah is grand.

Among his litanies done in the morning and at night are *Ayah al-Kursi* seven times, the last two verses of *Surah al-Tawbah*, "I seek refuge in the perfect words of Allah from the evil of what He created. In the name of Allah, whom nothing in the Earth or the Heavens can harm with His name. And He is the Hearing, the Knowing" three times, *Hizb al-Bahr,* and *al-Musabba'at al-'Ashr.*

Then:

يَا مَنْ أَظْهَرَ الْجَمِيلَ وَسَتَرَ الْقَبِيحَ وَلَمْ يُؤَاخِذْ بِالْجَرِيرَةِ وَلَمْ يَهْتِكِ السِّتْرَ، وَيَا عَظِيمَ الْعَفْوِ وَيَا حَسَنَ التَّجَاوُزِ وَيَا وَاسِعَ الْمَغْفِرَةِ وَيَا بَاسِطَ الْيَدَيْنِ بِالرَّحْمَةِ، وَيَا سَامِعَ كُلِّ نَجْوَى وَيَا مُنْتَهَى كُلِّ شَكْوَى، وَيَا كَرِيمَ الصَّفْحِ وَيَا عَظِيمَ الْمَنِّ، وَيَا مُبْتَدِئًا بِالنِّعَمِ قَبْلَ اسْتِحْقَاقِهَا، يَا رَبِّ وَيَا سَيِّدِي وَيَا مَوْلاَيَ وَيَا غَايَةَ رَغْبَتِي، أَسْأَلُكَ أَنْ لاَ تُشَوِّهَ خِلْقَتِي بِبَلاَءِ الدُّنْيَا وَلاَ بِعَذَابِ النَّارِ

> O, You who manifests beauty, and covers over ugliness, who does not seize me for my crimes, who does not remove the veil, o, Grand in pardon, who beautifully overlooks, o, You whose forgiveness is vast, whose hands are outspread in mercy. O, You Hearer of all secret speech! O, You to whom all complaints are raised! O, Generous in forgiveness! O, You who are Great in grace! O, You who initiates a blessing before one deserves it! O, my Lord! O, my Chief! O, my Master! O, You who are the extent of my hope! I ask You not to disgrace my being with the afflictions of the world, or with the punishment of the fire.

Likewise, he would recite the *Idrisi Names, Surah al-Ikhlas* eleven times for protection, *Ayah al-Kursi* seven times for protection, the last two verses of *Surah al-Tawbah* seven times for protection, *al-Sayfi* for protection, and *Hizb al-Bahr* three times, and:

$$\text{لاَ إِلَهَ إِلاَّ اللهُ يَا دَافِعُ يَا مَانِعُ يَا حَفِيظُ يَا حَكِيمُ}$$

There is no God but Allah. O, Averter! O, Preventer! O, Guardian! O, Wise One!

This is recited one hundred times, all in the morning and at night.

Also among his litanies is a supplication that Abu Talib mentioned in *Qut al-Qulub*. He mentioned a great benefit for it, which you will find in the section on benefits if Allah so wills. It is:

أَنْتَ اللهُ لاَ إِلَهَ إِلاَّ أَنْتَ رَبُّ العَالَمِينَ، أَنْتَ اللهُ لاَ إِلَهَ إِلاَّ أَنْتَ الحَيُّ القَيُّومُ، أَنْتَ اللهُ لاَ إِلَهَ إِلاَّ أَنْتَ العَلِيُّ العَظِيمُ، أَنْتَ اللهُ لاَ إِلَهَ إِلاَّ أَنْتَ العَفُوُّ الغَفُورُ، أَنْتَ اللهُ لاَ إِلَهَ إِلاَّ أَنْتَ مُبْدِئُ كُلِّ شَيْءٍ وَإِلَيْكَ يَعُودُ، أَنْتَ اللهُ لاَ إِلَهَ إِلاَّ أَنْتَ لَمْ تَلِدْ وَلَمْ تُولَدْ، أَنْتَ اللهُ لاَ إِلَهَ إِلاَّ أَنْتَ العَزِيزُ الحَكِيمُ، أَنْتَ اللهُ لاَ إِلَهَ إِلاَّ أَنْتَ الرَّحْمَانُ الرَّحِيمُ، أَنْتَ اللهُ لاَ إِلَهَ إِلاَّ أَنْتَ مَلِكُ يَوْمِ الدِّينِ، أَنْتَ اللهُ لاَ إِلَهَ إِلاَّ أَنْتَ خَالِقُ الخَيْرِ والشَّرِّ، أَنْتَ اللهُ لاَ إِلَهَ إِلاَّ أَنْتَ خَالِقُ الجَنَّةِ والنَّارِ، أَنْتَ اللهُ لاَ إِلَهَ إِلاَّ أَنْتَ الوَاحِدُ الأَحَدُ الفَرْدُ الصَّمَدُ الَّذِي لَمْ يَتَّخِذْ صَاحِبَةً وَلاَ وَلَدًا، أَنْتَ اللهُ لاَ إِلَهَ إِلاَّ أَنْتَ الفَرْدُ الوَتْرُ، أَنْتَ اللهُ لاَ إِلَهَ إِلاَّ أَنْتَ عَالِمُ الغَيْبِ والشَّهَادَةِ، أَنْتَ اللهُ لاَ إِلَهَ إِلاَّ أَنْتَ المَلِكُ القُدُّوسُ، أَنْتَ اللهُ لاَ إِلَهَ إِلاَّ أَنْتَ السَّلاَمُ المُؤْمِنُ المُهَيْمِنُ، أَنْتَ اللهُ لاَ إِلَهَ إِلاَّ أَنْتَ العَزِيزُ الجَبَّارُ المُتَكَبِّرُ، أَنْتَ اللهُ لاَ إِلَهَ إِلاَّ أَنْتَ الخَالِقُ البَارِئُ، أَنْتَ اللهُ لاَ إِلَهَ إِلاَّ أَنْتَ الأَحَدُ

PRECIOUS MEANINGS AND ATTAINMENT OF HOPES

الْمُصَوِّرُ، أَنْتَ اللهُ لاَ إِلَهَ إِلاَّ أَنْتَ الكَبِيرُ المُتَعَالِ، أَنْتَ اللهُ لاَ إِلَهَ إِلاَّ أَنْتَ المُقْتَدِرُ القَهَّارُ، أَنْتَ اللهُ لاَ إِلَهَ إِلاَّ أَنْتَ الـحَلِيمُ الكَرِيمُ، أَنْتَ اللهُ لاَ إِلَهَ إِلاَّ أَنْتَ القَادِرُ الرَّزَّاقُ، أَنْتَ اللهُ لاَ إِلَهَ إِلاَّ أَنْتَ أَهْلُ الثَّنَاءِ وَالمَجْدِ، أَنْتَ اللهُ لاَ إِلَهَ إِلاَّ أَنْتَ تَعْلَمُ السِّرَّ وَأَخْفَى، أَنْتَ اللهُ لاَ إِلَهَ إِلاَّ أَنْتَ فَوْقَ الخَلْقِ وَالـخَلِيقَةِ، أَنْتَ اللهُ لاَ إِلَهَ إِلاَّ أَنْتَ الـجَبَّارُ المُتَكَبِّرُ

You are Allah. There is no God but You, the Lord of the Worlds. You are Allah. There is no God but You, the Living, the Eternal. You are Allah. There is no God but You, the Exalted, the Great. You are Allah. There is no God but You, the Pardoning, the Forgiving. You are Allah. There is no God but You, the Originator of all things and to You they return. You are Allah. There is no God but You. You did not beget nor are You begotten. You are Allah. There is no God but You, the Honored, the Wise. You are Allah. There is no God but You, the Beneficent, the Merciful. You are Allah. There is no God but You, the Sovereign of the Day of Judgment. You are Allah. There is no God but You, the Creator of good and evil. You are Allah. There is no God but You, the Creator of Paradise and Hell. You are Allah. There is no God but You, the Unified, the One, the Unique, the Absolute, who did not take any wife or child. You are Allah. There is no God but You, the Unified, the One, the Unique, the Odd-numbered. You are Allah. There is no God but You, the Knower of the hidden and the apparent. You are Allah. There is no God but You, the Holy King. You are Allah. There is no God but You, the Guardian of peace and belief, the Protector. You are Allah. There is no God but You, the Honored, the Compelling, the Glorified. You are Allah. There is no God but You, the Creator, the Maker. You are Allah. There is no God but You, the One, the Fashioner. You are Allah. There is no God but You, the Great, the Exalted. You are Allah. There is no God but You, Owner of Destiny, the Overpowering. You are Allah. There is no God but You, the Forbearing, the Generous. You are Allah. There is no God but You, the Determiner, the Provider. You are Allah.

There is no God but You, Worthy of all Praise and Majesty. You are Allah. There is no God but You. You know the secret and the more hidden. You are Allah. There is no God but You, over the creation and creating. You are Allah. There is no God but You, the Overpowering, the Glorified.

It is recited either once in the morning and once in the evening, or once after every prayer.
Also among his litanies is this glorification:

$$سُبْحَانَ اللهِ وَالْحَمْدُ لِلَّهِ لاَ إِلَهَ إِلاَّ اللهُ وَاللهُ أَكْبَرُ وَلاَ حَوْلَ وَلاَ قُوَّةَ إِلاَّ بِاللهِ مِلْءَ مَا عَلِمَ وَعَدَدَ مَا عَلِمَ وَزِنَةَ مَا عَلِمَ$$

Blessed be Allah! Praise be to Allah! There is no God but Allah! Allah is the Greatest! There is no Might or Power except in Allah! According to the quantity of what He knows, in the number of what He knows, and according to the weight of what He knows.

It is recited at any time without any limit, specified number, or time. And its benefit will come if Allah so wills.

4.1.3 The Chain of Transmission of His Path

As for the chain of transmission of his Muhammadan Path, he informed us:

"We took from a number of Shaykhs (may Allah be pleased with them). But Allah did not decree that I would obtain my goal through them. And our transmission and means of support in this Path is only by way of the Master of Existence ﷺ. Allah had decreed that we would be granted our illumination and arrive upon his [the Prophet's ﷺ] hand. No one other than him among the Shaykhs has any authority over us. And that is sufficient."

4.1.4 The Benefit of Being Among His Followers

As for the benefit of being among his followers ﷺ, the Master of Existence ﷺ informed him that everyone who loves him is beloved to the Prophet ﷺ, and that not one of them would die until he attains sainthood. And in that is sufficient worth.

4.2 On the Benefit of His Litany and the Description and Condition of the True Disciple

4.2.1 On the Guarantee for His Disciples and Lovers

I say, and success is through Allah, and by Him, is assistance and the guide to the Straight Path. He said ﷺ:

> "The Master of Existence ﷻ informed me, in a wakeful vision and not in a dream, "You are from those who are safe. And anyone who sees you is of those who are safe if he dies upon faith. And whoever is generous to you through service or anything else, and whoever feeds you, will all enter Paradise without any reckoning or punishment.""

Then he said ﷺ:

> "When I saw the love that he ﷻ directed towards me, and singled me out for, I remembered my beloveds, those who had been kind to me and those who connected themselves with me through some service- while I heard most of them saying to me, "We will hold you accountable before Allah if we enter the Fire while you are watching," and I was responding to them, "I am not able to do anything for you,"- when I saw that love from him ﷻ, I asked him that everyone who loved me and did not show enmity to me afterward, who were kind to me in the weight of a mustard seed or greater, and did not show enmity to me afterward, or the most important of that, who gave me to eat from his food, that every one of them should enter Paradise without reckoning or punishment."

Then he said ﷺ:

> "I asked him ﷺ for everyone who takes any invocation from me that all of their sins, past and future, be forgiven them, and that their followers be rewarded from the treasures of Allah's grace, not from their deeds, and that the assessment of Allah be lifted from them, and that they should be among those who are safe from the punishment of Allah from the time of their death until they enter Paradise, and that they enter Paradise, without any reckoning or punishment, in the very first group, and that all of them will be in the *'Illiyyun* among the neighbors of the Prophet ﷺ."

He replied ﷺ, "*I have guaranteed all of that for them with a guarantee that will not be cut off until they neighbor me in the 'Illiyyun.*"

Then you should know that after I had written what is above from what we heard and what he related to us ﷺ from his memory and in his words, I came to what was written in his handwriting. The text is as follows:

> I ask, from the grace of our Master, the Messenger of Allah ﷺ, that he guarantee for me entrance into Paradise, without any reckoning or punishment, in the very first group; for me and all of my forefathers in Islam, from both my mother's and father's sides, as well as all of the children of my male and female ancestors until my eleventh grandfather and eleventh grandmother, and all of those who descend from them from their time until the death of our Master 'Isa b. Maryam, from among all of the males and females, the young and the old; and for all of those who have been generous with me with any physical or spiritual favor the weight of a mustard seed or more, and whoever has benefitted me with any physical or spiritual benefit the weight of a mustard seed or more, from the time that I exited the womb of my mother until my death; and also all of those who have been my Shaykhs in knowledge, the Qur'an, remembrance or secrets; and whoever did not show me enmity from among all of those. As for those who show me enmity or hate me, then no. And I also ask this for all of those who love me and do not show me any enmity, and whoever befriends me or takes me as a Shaykh or takes any invocation from me, and anyone who visits me, everyone who renders me any service, or fulfilled any need of mine, or supplicated for me. I ask all of this for all of the aforementioned from the time that I exited the womb of my mother until my death; as well as for their fathers, mothers, children, wives and their wives' parents, as well as those who nursed

me, their children, parents, and the parents of their spouses. I ask that our Master, the Messenger of Allah ﷺ, guarantee for me and for all of those whom I have mentioned that we should die while I and everyone living among them are upon faith and Islam, and that Allah should safeguard us and all of them from all of His punishments, retributions, threats, intimidations, frightening, and every evil from death until we are settled in Paradise and that all of our past and future sins and theirs be forgiven us; and that all of our wrongs and their wrongs, and that of our followers and theirs, be repaid from the treasures of the grace of Allah, and not from our good deeds; and that Allah (Honored and Exalted) should keep me safe from all of His assessments, interrogations, and questions- small or large- on the Day of Judgment; and that Allah should shade me and all of them in the shade of His Throne on the Day of Judgment; and that my Lord should reward me and every one of those who I mentioned in a manner quicker than the blinking of an eye on the wings of the angels; and that Allah should give me to drink, and all of them, from the pool of our Master Muhammad ﷺ on the Day of Judgment; and that my Lord cause all of them as well as me to enter Paradise without any reckoning or punishment. And that my Lord should cause me and all of them to be settled in Paradise in the 'Illiyyun of the Garden of Paradise in the Garden of Eden. And I ask our Master, the Messenger of Allah ﷺ, by Allah, that he guarantee me and all of those whom I have mentioned in this letter all of that which I have sought from Allah for them and me in this letter, by His generosity, all of it being with a guarantee that will cause all of that which I sought from Allah in this letter to reach me and all those whom I have mentioned here in this letter.

He responded ﷺ with his honored words, "*I have guaranteed for you everything that is in this letter with a guarantee that will never deviate from you or them until you and all those you mention come to be my neighbors in the highest part of the 'Illiyyun. And I have guaranteed for you all of what you sought from us with a guarantee that will not be broken upon you. Peace*"

One should not assume that the "*'Illiyun*" is a general term for all of Paradise. Rather, their comparison is that if a grape seed- or that of any other fruit that is in the first Garden- should fall to the earth, this is not to mention the maidens, it would put out the light of the sun. And if a grape seed from the second Garden were to fall to the first Garden, it would put out all of their lights and would entice them. And if a grape seed, or any other seed, from the third Garden were to fall to the second Garden, it would put out all of their light. And if a grape seed, or any other seed, from the fourth Garden were to fall to the third Garden, it would put out all of their light.

And if a grape seed, or any other seed, from the fifth Garden were to fall to the fourth Garden, it would put out all of their light. And if a grape seed, or any other seed, from the sixth Garden were to fall to the fifth Garden, it would put out all of their light. And if a grape seed, or any other seed, from the seventh Garden were to fall to the sixth Garden, it would put out all of their light. And the seventh is the Garden of Paradise. And the *'Illiyyun* is over Paradise. And if a grape seed, or any other seed, were to fall from it to Paradise, it would put out all of their lights and would distract all of them from what they have.

'Illiyun is the station of the Prophets and the Great Saints from this Community, and all those who were guided among the previous communities without being Prophets; not anyone else. So recognize the relationship between the *'Illiyun* and the Gardens. And contrast it with everything Allah created in Paradise of maidens and castles, etc. If you consider that, you will know the worth of the Garden of *'Illiyun* and the other Gardens and the relationship between them. And he ﷺ had preferred me to the point that he guaranteed that all those whom I mentioned would enter therein without any reckoning or retribution, as well as their being settled therein. And (he also promised me) that whoever only saw me, that the majority of them will enter Paradise without any reckoning, retribution, or punishment. But no one has a share of the *'Illiyun* except those whom I had mentioned: those who love us, are kind to us, and take an invocation from us. All of them will be settled in the *'Illiyun* with us. And that has been guaranteed to us by a true promise that will not be broken. However, I removed those who showed me enmity after having loved me or showed me kindness. They have no share in that. And I also sought from him that they would all die upon Islam. So if you do adhere to our love, then rejoice by what I have informed you of because it will occur to all of those who love us without exception.

4.2.2 On the Benefit of His Litany

Then he said ﷺ:

> And whoever takes from me the well-known litany, which is mandatory in the Path, or from anyone whom I have authorized to give it, will enter Paradise- him, his parents, his wives, and his children, but not his descendants- without reckoning or retribution, on the condition that no abuse, hatred or enmity should issue forth from

them, and on the condition that they continuously love the Shaykh without interruption until death. Likewise, it is on the condition that they perpetuate in performing the litany until death.

Then he said ﷺ:

I said to the Messenger of Allah ﷺ, "Is this grace specific to those who take the remembrance from me directly, or is it for everyone who takes it, even through one of my intermediaries?" He replied, *"If you authorize someone, and they give it to someone else, then it is as if they have taken it directly from you. And I am their guarantor."* And this grace includes whoever recites this litany, whether or not he sees me.

And he informed him ﷺ:

By the might of my Lord, on Monday and Friday, I will not part from you from Fajr until Maghrib. And with me are seven Angels. Whoever sees you on those two days, the Angels will write his name on a cloth made of gold. And they will write him as among the People of Paradise. And I am a witness to that. So increase your blessings upon me on those two days. For every blessing you send upon me, I hear you, and I return them upon you. And all of your deeds are likewise conveyed to me. Peace.

I say: This- the entrance into Paradise without reckoning or retribution to whoever takes his litany, as well as the entering of his parents, his wives, and his offspring- is the miracle of the greatest caliber. And no report has reached us from our Masters the Saints (may Allah be pleased with them all), such as Shaykh 'Abd al-Qadir al-Jilani, Sidi 'Abd al-Rahman al-Tha'labi and Mawlay al-Tuham (may Allah be pleased with them all), that it had occurred to them, that whoever saw those who saw them would enter Paradise. It has not been narrated from any one of them that their companions would not be reckoned with or punished, nor those who saw them, as it occurred to our Shaykh ﷺ. Even though all over those had mentioned that their followers would enter Paradise, as we have mentioned, this was a special benefit for our Master ﷺ and his companions.

Nevertheless, he said ﷺ, warning his companions and guiding them to what would rectify them:

I say to you: Indeed, the Master of Existence ﷺ guaranteed for us that whoever abuses us and perpetuates on that without repenting will only die a disbeliever. And I say to the brethren: Indeed, whoever takes our litany and hears what it contains, in that its reciter enters into Paradise without reckoning or retribution, and his sins will not harm him; whoever hears that and casts himself into disobedience of Allah due to what he has heard, and takes that as a guarantee of safety from the retribution of Allah for his disobedience, Allah will clothe his heart with hatred until he abuses us. And if he abuses us, Allah will cause him to die as a disbeliever. So beware of disobeying Allah and His retribution. And for whomever among you that Allah has decreed sin- and the slave is never free from sin- then let him not approach it, except that his heart is crying out of fear of the retribution of Allah. Peace.'

We will mention here a couplet on the benefit of the litany by one writer. He said:

> The abode of our Tijani is inhabited by remembrance,
> And has been inundated with prayer and goodness,
>
> Fixed in it is the remembrance of Allah while the sun,
> rises and when it sets. That is well known,
>
> He revived the Path of the People of Allah, so by him,
> It encompasses them completely and the restoration of their foundation,
>
> Shaykh of all Shaykhs, under whose scarf,
> Is a heart that gathers all lights and secrets,
>
> The one whose abode is the Garden of Paradise, and he is in it,
> The distributer of its treasures and its oft-remembered maidens,
>
> There overflows from the river of remembrance its pool,
> So drink from its outlets and you will be rewarded,
>
> His litanies from the Messenger of Allah were transmitted,
> And likewise his actions and the secret that was passed down,
>
> Then perform it and your redemption has been put forth on its vestiges,
> Because if you perform it, that performance is stored away,
>
> So be ardent that you should one day depend upon him,
> For the attainment of the one who depends upon him is plentiful,

And adhere to his litanies alone or in a group,
> For one who remembers Allah is remembered in the presence of Allah.

Then be satisfied with it, o, disciple! And know that it is one of the most confirmed matters in your favor. So remain devout to it, morning and evening, because it is one of the greatest intermediaries for obtaining objectives and requests. So beautify your life by it, and arrange your time around its performance. Perhaps Allah will place your salvation in it. For the slave only obtains from this world that which he consumes in the obedience of his Lord. So let him cast whatever is beyond that behind him. In that is sufficient esteem for the one for whom the assistance of Allah has been decreed. What we have mentioned is the benefit of the litany, which is obligatory in the Path, which our Master ؓ received from our Master, the Messenger of Allah ﷺ. And he ordered him to give it to all people.

As for the benefits of the remembrances individually, I say, and with Allah is success:

4.2.3 On the Benefit of Seeking Forgiveness of Allah

Our Lord (How Sublime a Speaker) said:

> ﴿And suffice yourself with those who call upon their Lord in the morning and the evening﴾[98]

It is reported that Qatadah ؓ said, "The Qur'an indicates to you your illness and your medicine. As for your illness, it is your sins. And your medicine is seeking forgiveness of Allah."

And al-Tirmidhi reported, on the authority of Abu Musa al-Ash'ari ؓ, that the Messenger of Allah ﷺ said:

Allah revealed two securities for my Community:

> ﴿Allah would not punish them while you are among them. And Allah would not punish them while they seek forgiveness﴾ [99]

So when I go forth, I will leave with them the seeking of forgiveness [al-Istighfar] until the Day of Judgment.[100]

---

98   al-Kahf, 28
99   al-Anfal, 33
100   Sunan al-Tirmidhi (Hadith no. 3336).

Ahmad reported on the authority of Fadalah b. 'Ubayd ؓ that the Prophet ﷺ said, "*The slave is safe from the punishment of Allah as long as he seeks forgiveness*[101]." And Ibn Abi Shaybah reported on the authority of Abi Sa'id al-Khudri ؓ that the Messenger of Allah ﷺ said, "*Whoever says, 'I seek forgiveness in Allah, than whom there is no other God, the Living, the Eternal, and I return to Him in repentance,' five times, he will be forgiven what is against him the likes of the foam of the sea.*"[102]
And He said ﷻ:

﴾ *Whoever does an evil deed, or wrongs himself, then seeks Allah's forgiveness, he will find Allah Forgiving, Merciful* ﴿ [103]

4.2.4 On the Benefit of *Salat al-Fatihi*

As for the benefit of *Salat al-Fatihi*, I have heard our Shaykh ؓ say:

I had been busying myself with reciting *Salat al-Fatihi* when I returned from Hajj to Tilimsan due to the benefit that I recognized in it; that one recitation of it is worth six hundred thousand of any other prayer upon the Prophet ﷺ, as was mentioned in "Wardat al-Juyub." And the author of the "Wardah" mentioned that its owner, Sidi Muhammad al-Bikri al-Siddiqi, the guest from Egypt who was a Qutb ؓ, said, "If anyone recites it once and does not enter Paradise, then let him accuse its owner in front of Allah."

I then kept reciting it until I traveled from Tilimsan to Abi Samghun. But when I saw the prayer upon the Prophet of which one recitation is worth seventy thousand complete recitations of *Dala'il al-Khayrat*, I left *Salat al-Fatihi* and occupied myself with its recitation, due to the immense benefit that I recognized in it. That prayer upon the Prophet is:

"O, Allah! Bless our Master Muhammad and his family with a blessing that will equal thethe blessings sent by all of the people who You love and send peace upon our Master Muhammad and his family with a salutation that will equal all of their salutations."

Then he ﷺ ordered me to return to *Salat al-Fatihi*. So when he

---

101   Musnad Ahmad b. Hanbal (Hadith no. 23953).

102   Musnad Ibn Abi Shaybah (Hadith no. 29938). However, it is a saying attributed to the Companion (*mawquf*), Abu Sa'id al-Khudri ؓ. However, when it comes to Hadiths of this nature, they are judged as implicitly attributed (*marfu'*) to the Prophet ﷺ.

103   al-Nisa, 110

ordered me to return to it, I asked him ﷺ about its benefit. And he informed me first that one recitation of it is equal to reciting the Qur'an six times. Then a second time he informed me that reciting it once is equal to all of the glorification that has taken place in the universe in every remembrance and supplication, large or small, and six thousand recitations of the Qur'an because it is a form of remembrance.

4.2.5 On the Benefit of the Supplications *al-Sayfi* and *Ya Man Azhar al-Jamil*

And among his many supplications is *Du'a al-Sayfi*. And one recitation of it contains the reward of fasting Ramadan, standing on the Night of Power and the worship of one year. And *Surah al-Qadr* is similar to it in reward, as our Master ﷺ was informed by the Master of Existence ﷺ.

Even greater than the *Sayfi* is the supplication "Ya man azhar al-jamil…." The narrator stated:

> Jibril (peace be upon him) brought it to the Prophet ﷺ and said, "I have brought you a gift." He said, "What is this gift?" And he recited this supplication. Then he said ﷺ, "What is the reward for the one who recites this supplication once?" Jibril said, "If all of the Angels of the seven Heavens were to get together in order to describe it, they would not succeed in fully describing it till the Day of Judgment. Each one of them would describe something that the others did not. So they would not be able to do it. But among its rewards is that Allah says about its reciter, 'I give him reward equal to what I have created in the seven Heavens, in Paradise, in the Fire, in the Throne and in the Footstool, as well as equal to the number of drops of rain and the amount of water in the sea, and the number of pebbles and grains of sand. Also among its rewards is that Allah ﷻ will give him the reward of all creation. And among its rewards is that Allah ﷻ will give him the reward of seventy Prophets, all of whom had reached Messengerhood. And there are more rewards.'"

This narration is authentic and established in the Book of 'Amru b. Shu'ayb on the authority of his father, on the authority of his grandfather, who narrated it from the Prophet ﷺ. His grandfather is 'Abd Allah b. 'Amru b. Al-'As, one of the senior companions ﷺ. And al-Hakim authenticated it and said, "All of its narrators are from Madinah."

4.2.6 On the Benefit of *Salat al-Fatihi*

Then he said 🌹:

As for *Salat al-Fatihi*, I asked him 🌹 about it, and he responded at first that it was worth six hundred thousand of any other prayer upon the Prophet. So I asked him, "Is each one of those (six hundred thousand) prayers upon the Prophet worth the reward of one who sends a single prayer upon the Prophet?" He 🌹 said (what means), "*Yes. He will receive for every recitation of Salat al-Fatihi the reward of one who recites six hundred thousand of any other prayer upon the Prophet.*"

Then I asked him 🌹, "Is one bird created from it, according to the Hadith that one is created for every prayer upon the Prophet?" I meant the bird that is created with seventy thousand wings as in the Hadith. "Or would there be created six hundred thousand birds with that description, with the reward for their glorification going to the one who recited the prayer upon the Prophet 🌹?" He replied 🌹, "*Indeed, for every recitation, six hundred thousand birds will be created with that description.*"

Then he said 🌹:

So I asked him 🌹 whether or not the following Hadith is authentic: "*Indeed one prayer upon the Prophet 🌹 is worth the reward of four hundred battles, with each battle being worth four hundred Pilgrimages.*" He replied 🌹, "*Indeed, it is authentic.*"

So I asked him 🌹 about the number of battles: "Would one recitation of *Salat al-Fatihi* be rewarded the equivalent of four hundred battles, or would four hundred battles be rewarded for each of the six hundred thousand prayers upon the Prophet (that *Salat al-Fatihi* equals)?" He said 🌹 [what means], "*Indeed Salat al-Fatihi is worth six hundred thousand prayers upon the Prophet. And each of those six hundred thousand prayers upon the Prophet is worth four hundred battles.*"

Then he said thereafter 🌹:

Whoever sends prayers upon the Prophet by it- meaning Salat al-Fatihi- once, he will receive the reward for every prayer upon the Prophet that has taken place in the universe, from every man, jinn and Angel, six hundred thousand times over, from the beginning of the universe until the time that its reciter had uttered it. In other words, it is as if he had sent prayers upon the Prophet six hundred thousand times for the prayer upon the Prophet of everyone who sends prayers upon the Prophet, whether they are Angel, jinn or human being. And each one of those prayers upon the Prophet is worth four hundred battles. And for each one of them, he will receive a wife from among the maidens of Paradise, ten good deeds, erasure of ten evil deeds, and he will be raised ten degrees. And also, for each one of those prayers upon the Prophet, Allah and His Angels will send ten prayers upon the Prophet.

The Shaykh ﷺ said:

When I had understood all of that in my heart, I knew that no worship could match even one recitation of this prayer upon the Prophet ﷺ. So how about a person who recites it many times over? What a reward he would have with Allah if he attains all of that with one recitation of it!

Then the Shaykh ﷺ said:

He ﷺ informed me that it- meaning *Salat al-Fatihi*- was not written by al-Bakri. Rather, he turned towards Allah for a long time, asking Him to bless him with a prayer upon the Prophet ﷺ that includes the rewards and secrets of all prayers upon the Prophet. And he sought that from Him for a long time. Then Allah answered his supplication, and an Angel came with this prayer upon the Prophet written on a page of light.

Then the Shaykh ﷺ said, "So when I had understood this prayer upon the Prophet ﷺ, I found that the worship of all of jinn, human beings, and Angels could not equal its weight."

He said ﷺ:

He ﷺ used to inform me about the reward of the Greatest Name. So I asked him, "Is it (*Salat al-Fatihi*) greater than it?" He replied ﷺ, "No. Rather, it (the Greatest Name) is greater. And no worship can equal it."

He ﷺ said, "One recitation of the Greatest Name is worth six thousand recitations of *Salat al-Fatihi*."

And one recitation of *Salat al-Fatihi* equals six thousand of all of the remembrances, be they glorifications, petitions of forgiveness, or of every supplication in the universe, small or large, as was mentioned before. And the Shaykh 🕮 said:

> For the person who recites *Salat al-Fatihi* once [is a reward equal to] six thousand of the invocations of every animate and inanimate being. The invocations of each inanimate being are invoking the name that has been manifested in it since every atom in existence has a particular name manifested in it. As for animate beings, their invocations are varied.

This is the benefit of *Salat al-Fatihi* of which the Master of Existence 🕮 informed our Master and Means of Connection 🕮.

Then he said 🕮, "As for the weight of *Salat al-Fatihi*, for those who are engrossed in it, meaning that they recite *Salat al-Fatihi* at least ten thousand times, one recitation of it equals one hundred twenty years of worship."

I asked, "Is that with consideration of those who recite it with you?" He replied, "Yes." That is because he informed us that whenever he does any invocation, seventy thousand Angels recite it with him, each one of their recitations being worth seventy thousand recitations. And all of that reward goes to our Master as an ennoblement and gift from Allah to him. And our Shaykh, our Master and Teacher, has conferred this benefit upon his companions, so that any one of them that recites any invocation, seventy thousand Angels recite it with him, as a favor, mercy, gift and ennoblement from Allah. Peace.

Then he said 🕮:

> And among the supplications are those whose benefit is equal to the standing in worship on the Night of Power, such as one recitation of the *Sayfi*, as we have already mentioned. So if, considering that one recitation of the *Sayfi* is worth the worship of the Night of Power, you contemplate how many Nights of Power the Greatest Name is worth, you would find that one recitation of the Greatest Name is worth thirty-six million Nights of Power. That is because one recitation of the Greatest Name is worth six thousand recitations of *Salat al-Fatihi*. And one recitation of *Salat al-Fatihi* is worth six thousand recitations of the *Sayfi*. And when you multiply six thousand by six thousand, the outcome is thirty-six million. That is only regarding one recitation. As for what is more than that, no one knows its worth except Allah 🕮. Then, Glorified is He who gives His grace to whom He wills!

And congratulations are due to the one who has been given this great benefit, of which neither we, nor our beloveds, have been deprived, through His blessing, generosity, and grace. Amin.

4.2.7 On Why the Formula of *Salat al-Fatihi* Does Not Include "Salam"

I asked him ﷺ about why *Salat al-Fatihi* does not include "salam" (greeting of peace). Was it because of some necessary reason? He replied ﷺ:

> As for your question about *Salat al-Fatihi*, it was revealed from the unseen realm in that form. And if something is revealed from the unseen realm, its completeness is established without reliance upon the conventional, fundamental principles. And it is not from humanly composed formulas. Aside from that, there are some formulas for prayer upon the Prophet, which have been narrated from him ﷺ, that do not contain "salam." And they are Prophetic formulas for the purpose of worshiping Allah. So, pay no attention to what [some of] the jurists say.
>
> The special quality of *Salat al-Fatihi* is a Divine matter in which the intellect has no role. But imagine that there are one hundred thousand nations. Each nation consists of one hundred thousand tribes. Each tribe consists of one hundred thousand men. Each man lived for one hundred thousand years, reciting prayers upon the Prophet ﷺ one hundred thousand times each day with a prayer upon the Prophet ﷺ other than *Salat al-Fatihi*. If you were to gather the reward for all of those nations, in all of those years, for all of those recitations, it would not equal the reward of one recitation of *Salat al-Fatihi*. So pay attention to neither the rejection of the rejector nor the slander of the defamer, for all grace is in the hands of Allah. He gives it to whomever He wills.
>
> That is because Allah ﷻ has a grace beyond the sphere of analogy. It should suffice you that He (Blessed and Exalted is He) says:
>
> ❴*He creates what you do not know*❵ [104]
>
> Thus, no one turns towards Allah ﷻ with an action that will surpass it, be it as it may. And no one turns towards Allah with any action more beloved to Him than it. And nothing has more weight with Allah than it- except one degree. That is only if one turns to

---

104   al-Nahl, 8

Allah with the Greatest Sublime Name. Nothing else. That is the utmost of manners in which to turn to Him and the highest level of all worship. There is no level higher than it. And this prayer upon the Prophet (*Salat al-Fatihi*) follows it in degree, means of turning, reward, the amount of love from Allah that its reciter obtains and excellent returns. So whoever turns to Allah ﷻ by it, confirming all of this, he will obtain the pleasure of Allah and His reward- which cannot be surpassed by any other acts- in this world and the next. The Divine outpouring, which no aspiration can reach, has born witness to that.

But one can only achieve the aforementioned benefit by submission. So whoever wishes to argue about this matter is left alone. And it is of no benefit to ask about the proofs for what has been said. So leave off seeking proofs for the one who seeks proof for you. Because delving into that by refutation, or responding to refutation, is like a sea whose waves do not end. And the hearts are in the hands of Allah. He controls them. And it is He who accepts some and turns some away.

Thus, for whom Allah wills the bliss, success, and reward that this Unique Pearl contains, Allah will attract his heart to acceptance of what he has heard about it. And He will characterize him with submission to the fact that the grace of Allah ﷻ has neither limit nor analogy. So He will direct his aspiration towards turning to Allah ﷻ by it and accepting its place with Allah. And no soul knows what pleasurable things are hidden from it. But for whom Allah wills deprivation of its benefit, Allah will divert his heart with whispers, saying, "Where has it been narrated from?"

So busy yourself with what we have said to you and those who obey you in that. And turn away from those who dispute with you by seeking proof for that. We took it in the matter that you already know. And that is sufficient.

4.2.8 On Various Issues Related to the Transmission from the Prophet ﷺ After His Death and the Superiority of *Salat al-Fatihi*

I also asked him ﷺ whether narrations from the Chief of Existence ﷺ are the same after his death as in life. He replied ﷺ:

The matter of the general commands, which he used to give to the entire Community, came to an end with his passing away ﷺ. But the special commands that he used to convey to the Elect are perpetual, during his life and after his death, and will never end. And *Salat al-Fatihi* is greater than all methods of action and worship, all kinds of righteousness, completely and without exception, and all types of capacity for superiority, except for that of *Da'irah al-Ihatah*. That is because reciting that once is better than doing a lot of other actions. Peace.

It may be said that perhaps some incapable person with no knowledge would come to find out about this vast grace and generosity, and would say, "If it is as you say, then it would mean that occupying oneself with it is more important than any other remembrance- including the Qur'an." We would say to that person:

Rather, the recitation of the Qur'an is more important since it is required by the Sacred Law due to the benefit that has been related regarding it. And that is also due to its being the basis of the Sacred Law and the sphere of Divine interaction. And due to the severe threat that has been narrated regarding the one who leaves it, it is not permissible for its reader to abandon its recitation. However, as to the benefit of the prayer upon the Prophet ﷺ with which we are concerned, it is from the category of optional things the abandoner of which incurs no blame. Secondly, this matter is not the proper place for investigation and dispute. Rather, it is from the category of the Benefits of Works. And you are very aware that the scholars have said that there is no dispute about the Benefits of Works.

And our Master ﷺ had responded to this (apparent) contradiction, saying:

> There is no contradiction between this and what has been narrated about the benefit of the Qur'an and the Noble Word since the benefit of the Qur'an and the Noble Word is general and is meant for the entire Community, while this is special. And there is no contradiction between them since he ﷺ used to transmit the general rulings to the entire Community during his lifetime. I mean that when he would forbid something, he would forbid it for everyone; and when he would enjoin something, he would enjoin it upon everyone. And the same went for the rest of the external verdicts of the Sacred Law. But at the same time, he would ﷺ transmit the

special verdicts to the Elect. And he would choose for some matters some of his Companions apart from others. This is widespread and apparent in his reports ﷺ.

Then when he was transferred to the Abode Hereafter- and he is in that just as he was in life ﷺ- he began to transmit only to his Community the special commands to the Elect. And it is not possible to transmit general commands to the entire Community. That was cut off by his passing away ﷺ. But his outpouring of the special commands to Elect remains. Whoever assumes that all of his benefit for his Community ﷺ ended with his passing away- just like all other dead people- he is ignorant of the degree of the Prophet ﷺ and has bad conduct with him. And it is feared that he will die a disbeliever if he does not repent from that belief.

I asked our Master ﷺ if the Master of Existence ﷺ had known in his time about this grace that would come later. He replied, "Yes. He knew about it." I then asked, "If it has indescribable benefit in it, why then did he not mention it to his Companions (may Allah be pleased with them all)?"

> He replied: Two things prevented him. The first is that he knew that its time would only come later and that at that time, there was no one upon whose hand Allah could manifest it. The second is that if he had mentioned to them this great benefit through such small deeds, they would have asked him to explain it to them, due to the strength of their avidness for all that was good. But its manifestation was not possible at that time. For that reason, he did not mention it to them.
>
> Another angle is that since Allah ﷻ knew the weakness of the people of this time, and their condition of negligence and corruption, He had mercy upon them and was generous with them (by giving them) a lot of benefit in exchange for few actions. He chooses for His mercy whom He wills at the time that He wills. And it should not be said, "His traditions after his death are not the same as his traditions during his life. Rather, they are the same in everything that he related ﷺ, except in the aforementioned division of general rules to all people and the special rules for the Elect.

Then he said ﷺ:

> The aforementioned benefit is with regards to actions that are not obligatory. As for those that are obligatory, it does not apply, due

to the Hadith: "'*What action is best, o, Messenger of Allah?*' *He replied* ﷺ, '*Prayer at the beginning of its time.*'"[105]

I said to our Master ؓ:

> It can be understood from what has preceded that the reciter of the aforementioned prayers upon the Prophet has a greater benefit than all of the believing worshipers of Allah that preceded him, since *Salat al-Fatihi* is worth the multiplied reward of all of their prayers upon the Prophet ﷺ, and all of their remembrances and litanies; except for in one case, which is the recitation of *Da'irah al-Ihatah*. There is no mention of that here, and the multiplication of reward does not apply to it.

He replied ؓ:

> The multiplication of the rewards for deeds for its reciter is exactly as you have mentioned it. However, all of the Companions who transmitted the religion have had written in their book of deeds all of the works of those who came after them from their era to the last of this Community. So if you have understood that, there is no disputing the superiority of the Companions over those who came after them, even if they are from the people who received the aforementioned benefit, due to the degree of being a Companion.

Then he ؓ gave a comparison between the actions of the Companions and those after them. He said, "Our actions compared to theirs are like the walking of an ant compared to the swift flight of the sand grouse."

And he was truthful ؓ with the comparison since they (may Allah be pleased with them) had taken the lion's share by their being Companions of the Master of Existence ﷺ. He ﷺ said about them, "*Indeed, Allah chose my Companions over the entire universe, except for the Prophets and Messengers.*"[106] And he said ﷺ, "*If one of you were to spend gold equal to Uhud, he would not reach the worth of one of them, and not even half of it.*"[107]

And he ؓ mentioned another angle to explain the different levels of superiority. He said:

> Indeed, the reward whose mention preceded, which is due to the special quality of some remembrances- as we have already mentioned- is according to the custom of every actor. For example,

---

105 Sahih al-Bukhari (Hadith no. 2782); Sahih Muslim (Hadith no. 86).
106 Majma' al-Zawa'id wa Manba' al-Fawa'id (Hadith no. 16383).
107 Sahih al-Bukhari (Hadith no. 3673); Sahih Muslim (Hadith no. 2541).

if he usually receives ten good deeds, one hundred, one thousand- or more- for his remembrance, then that is the benefit that is multiplied for the one who performs a special invocation, like *Salat al-Fatihi*, etc. But that is concerning other than the people of degrees. As for them, their reward for an action is multiplied according to their degree. Thus, the degree of Messengerhood is not like the degree of Prophethood, nor *Siddiqiyyah* like Prophethood. So the ordinary scheme of multiplication [of their rewards] does not apply to them. For everyone else, when considering the multiplication [of their rewards], one must consider their degree as well.

For that reason, our Master Jibril (peace be upon him) said to the Prophet ﷺ, "*Verily 'Umar is a good deed from the good deeds of Abu Bakr.*"[108] He said this after he had first said, "*If I had spoken to you about the merits of 'Umar for the duration of the existence of the world, I would never finish.*"[109] This is the case even though they did similar deeds or almost the same. He only surpassed him due to his degree, not due to the actions themselves. For that reason, he said ﷺ, "*Abu Bakr did not surpass you through a lot of fasting, nor through a lot of prayer. He only surpassed you due to something that has settled in his heart.*"[110] May Allah be pleased with him and with all of the Companions of the Messenger of Allah ﷺ.

And I heard him ﷺ mention the differences between the Saints in action and rewards. He said:

> Among them are those whose days are like other people. And among them are those whose days are like the Night of Power. Among them are those whose days are like one thousand years. And among them are those whose days are like the Day of Ascension- fifty thousand years.

---

108 Musnad Abi Ya'la (Hadith no. 1603).

109 Musnad Abi Ya'la (Hadith no. 1603), but with the wording, "*If I had spoken to you on the excellent qualities of Umar for the length of time that Noah (peace be upon him) dwelled among his people- 950 years, the excellent qualities of Umar would not be exhausted.*"

110 Narrated by Imam al-Ghazali in "Ihya 'Ulum al-Din." Al-'Iraqi said, in "Takhrij Ahadith Ihya' 'Ulum al-Din," "There is no basis for its attribution to the Prophet ﷺ. It is only known as a statement of Bakr b. 'Abdullah al-Muzani, which was narrated by al-Hakim al-Tirmidhi in his 'Nawadir al-Usul.'" Al-Subki commented, "However, Bakr is trustworthy. He took Hadiths from Ibn 'Abbas and Ibn 'Umar. And Ibn al-Qayyim narrated it by way of Abu Bakr b. 'Iyash.

So I said to him, "Is that in the action itself or the multiplication of the reward?"
He said:

> Among them are those whose work is like the work of others. And among them are those whose work is like the work of others in the time mentioned, such as the work of a regular person in one day. And among them are those the reward of whose work in one day is like the mentioned length of time.

Then I said to him, "Does the one who has the Greatest Name receive a reward than what you have mentioned, may Allah be pleased with you, and what about the benefit that you mentioned?" He replied, "That is incomparable, since it is priceless, and since the benefit that its invoker receives is only known by Allah. May Allah provide us with what He has provided him through His pure grace and generosity. Amin."

4.2.9 A Beneficial Lesson on the Multiplication of the Rewards of *Salat al-Fatihi*

The Shaykh said:

> The number of tongues on the bird which Allah creates from the prayer upon the Prophet, which has seventy thousand wings (to the end of the Hadith), is one octillion, six hundred eighty sextillion, seven hundred quadrillion (1,000,000,680,000,700,000,000,000,000). That is the total number of tongues. And each tongue glorifies Allah in seventy thousand languages every second. And all of that reward is for the one who sent the prayer upon the Prophet. That is for prayer upon the Prophet other than the Unique Pearl, which is *Salat al-Fatihi*. As for the Unique Pearl, from each recitation is created six hundred thousand birds upon the aforementioned description, as has already been mentioned. So Glorified is the One who has preferred whom He wills from His slaves without any obligation or cause.

4.2.10 On The Meaning of *Salat al-Fatihi*

I asked him ﷺ about the meaning of *Salat al-Fatihi*, and he answered, may Allah be pleased with him:

> It means [that the Prophet ﷺ] is the Opener of what had been locked of all forms of being. That is because they had been locked behind the veil of hiddenness in the state of nonexistence. And their locks were opened by the means of his existence ﷺ. So they emerged from the state of nonexistence to the state of existence, and from the veils of hiddenness to (become) themselves in the world of manifestation, since, if it were not for him, Allah would not have created any being, nor would He have caused it to emerge from non-existence to existence. That is one of the meanings.
>
> The second is that he ﷺ opened the locks of the doors of Divine mercy. And by means of him, they were opened to the creation. And had Allah ﷻ not created our Master Muhammad ﷺ, He would not have had mercy on any created being. So mercy arrives from Allah to His creation by means of His Prophet ﷺ.
>
> The third of its meanings is that the hearts were trapped in polytheism and filled with it. And faith found no way of entering them. Then, they were opened by his call ﷺ] so that faith entered them and purified them of polytheism. So they were filled with belief and wisdom.
>
> His saying, "the Seal of what went before," refers to Prophethood and Messengerhood, since he sealed them both and locked their door ﷺ. So there is no hope for (attaining) it for anyone after him. Likewise (he is) the Seal of what went before of all kinds of Divine manifestations by which the Real ﷻ revealed Himself in the world of outward manifestation. That is because he ﷺ is the first being that Allah caused to exist, emerging from the veils of hiddenness and the state of Divine obscurity, in the universe. Then the forms of the universe continued to expand by the manifestations of different species, according to the order erected by the Divine will, species after species, until the last of what He revealed Himself in, in the world of manifestation, was the Adamic form- upon his own form ﷺ. And that is what is meant by the "Adamic form."
>
> Thus, just as the manifestation of existence was opened by him, the manifestation of the different forms of being was sealed by him ﷺ.

Expressing it another way, he said ﷺ:

> The first being that Allah ﷻ caused to exist from the Hidden Presence is the spirit of our Master Muhammad ﷺ. Then Allah caused the spirits of the universe to descend from his spirit ﷺ. The spirit, here, is the means by which life stretched forth into the bodies. And He created from his spirit ﷺ the bodies of light, such as the Angels and those who resemble them. As for the thick bodies of darkness, they were only created from a second connection belonging to his spirit ﷺ. That is because his spirit ﷺ has two connections, both of which He outpoured onto all of existence.
>
> The first connection is that of pure light. From it were created all of the spirits and the bodies of light, which contain no darkness. The second connection that belongs to his spirit ﷺ is that of darkness. And from this connection were created the bodies of darkness, like the devils, thick bodies, and Hell and its pits. Likewise, Paradise and all of its levels were created from the connection of light. Thus, that is the relationship of all of existence with his spirit ﷺ.
>
> As for the Muhammadan Reality ﷺ, it is the first thing that Allah caused to exist from the Hidden Presence. And there was not with Allah any created being before that. But this reality is not known as a "thing." Some scholars had deviated by examining this reality. They said:
>
> "This reality is singular. Nothing exists with it. But it cannot avoid being either a substance or an accident. If it were a form, it would be in need of a place to indwell. Then it would not be independent of another existent thing. That is because if it comes to exist along with its place all at one time, it has no precedence, because, in that case, they are two. If it were an accident and not a substance, then accidents are not even addressed because an accident only exists for the blinking of an eye. Then it ceases. So, where is the precedence that you speak of?"
>
> The answer to this issue is that it is a substantial reality, which has two connections: one of light and one of darkness. As for its needing a place, this limitation is not sound. That is because this limitation has been laid down by those whose intellects are firmly rooted in the Station of Forms. But what is confirmed is that Allah ﷻ is able to create these created beings without any place for them to indwell. The intellect's deeming this matter impossible is due to the impossibility that bodies should exist without a place.

That is because that is the nature upon which Allah ﷻ has created them, and in which the intellect is firmly rooted. And it was not set free in the unlimited existence of realities. If it had been set free in the unlimited existence of realities, it would have known that Allah ﷻ is capable of creating the universe without a place. This being the case, Allah created the Muhammadan Reality as a substance, without the need of a place. And there is no doubt that if the Divine Reality is unveiled to anyone, he will know certainly and unequivocally that causing the universe to exist without a place is absolutely and verifiably possible.

As for the Muhammadan Reality, it is not known or perceived in that degree. And there is no hope for anyone to reach it in that sphere. Then it was appropriated robes of Divine light and was veiled by them from the creation. And in this sphere, it is called a "spirit," after being veiled by the robes. And that is the limit of the knowledge of the Prophets, Messengers, and Aqtab. They arrive at this place and stop. Then it was appropriated more robes of Divine light and, because of them, it was called "intellect." Then it was appropriated more robes of Divine light. And because of them, it was called "heart." Then it was appropriated even more robes of Divine light. And because of them, it was called a "soul." Then, after that, his blessed body ﷺ manifested.

And the Saints differ in their knowledge of these degrees. So the highest knowledge that a group of them possesses is that of his soul ﷺ. And they have sciences, secrets, and knowledge of that. And the highest knowledge that a group of them possesses is that of his heart ﷺ. And they have different sciences, secrets, and knowledge in that. And the highest knowledge that another group of them possesses is that of his intellect. And they have differing sciences, secrets, and knowledge in that. But a group of them- the highest of them- has reached the limit of knowledge. So they gain knowledge of the Station of his Spirit ﷺ. And that is the highest form of knowledge. And there is no hope for anyone to know his reality in the original form in which it was created.

And in this regard, Abu Zayd says, "I dived into the abyss of knowledge, seeking to know the source of the reality of the Prophet ﷺ. But there were between it and me one thousand veils of light. If I had lifted the first veil, I would have disintegrated, just as a hair disintegrates when thrown into a fire."

Likewise, Shaykh Mawlana 'Abd as-Salam said, in his prayer upon the Prophet ﷺ, "Before him, intellects dwindle. And it is disclosed to neither the first nor the last among us." In the same vein, Uways al-Qarni said ﷺ, to our Master 'Umar and our Master 'Ali (may Allah be pleased with them both), "You only saw the shadow of the Messenger of Allah ﷺ." They said, "Not even Ibn Abi Quhafah (Abu Bakr as-Siddiq)?" He said, "Not even Ibn Abi Quhafah." Perhaps, he had dived into the abyss of knowledge seeking to know the source of the Muhammadan Reality, and it was said to him, "That is a matter of which the greatest Messengers and Prophets were incapable. So there is no hope in it for other than them."

Shaykh al-Akbar said in his prayer upon the Prophet, "The White Pearl from which the Red Ruby was caused to be." He meant by "the White Pearl" the Muhammadan Reality. And by "the Red Ruby" he meant the existence of the entire universe.

As for what Shaykh Mawlana 'Abdul-Qadir indicated in his poem, "Upon the 'White Pearl' was our reunion," it is the pearl that existed before the creation of the Heavens and the earth. Then He (Blessed and Exalted is He) dissolved it and made it into the water. Then the waves crashed against one another for one thousand long periods of time. Each of those periods contained one thousand ages. Each of those ages contained one thousand years. Each of those years contained one thousand days. Each of those days contained one thousand hours. And each of those hours was like the length of time of the existence of the world seventy times over. And in that time there accumulated a pile of foam. And He spread it out on the surface of the water, and it became land. And He created from it the seven layers. Then He created the Heavens thereafter. That is what the Shaykh ﷺ was referring to.

And he has said ﷺ:

> The first thing that Allah created was his noble spirit: the Muhammadan Reality ﷺ. Then after that, Allah caused the spirits of all beings to descend from his noble, honorable spirit. As for his clay, which is his noble body, Allah created from it the bodies of the Angels, the Prophets, and the Aqtab. Then he mixed his noble clay with the water of eternity for a number of years equal to the multiplication of the number of his two noble names- our Master Muhammad ﷺ and our Master Ahmad ﷺ- by seven; then the outcome of that [multiplied] by itself; then that total by one thousand. Every unit of each of those numbers was equal to one thousand

years, with each day in those years equal to one thousand years. These are the "Days of the Lord." And in each of these years is three hundred sixty thousand years. The total of all of that multiplication is three billion, thirty million, one hundred twenty-five thousand (3,030,125,000). And that outcome was multiplied by the "Days of the Lord." And the outcome is three hundred seventy trillion, eight hundred eighty-one billion (300,881,000,000,000). That is the length of time that his noble Muhammadan clay was mixed.

4.2.11 Another Beneficial Lesson: More on the Multiplication of the Reward of *Salat al-Fatihi*

He said ﷺ:

You should know that if you send prayer upon the Prophet ﷺ by *Salat al-Fatihi* one time, it would be worth six hundred thousand of any other prayer upon the Prophet that has taken place in the universe, by any jinn, human or Angel. Then, if you were to recite it a second time, it has in it all that was in the first, and the first *Salat al-Fatihi* as well would be multiplied by six hundred thousand (600,000). Then, if you were to recite it a third time, it would have what was in the first two, and six hundred thousand of *Salat al-Fatihi* would be added twice- meaning that one million two hundred thousand (1,200,000) *Salat al-Fatihi* would be added to it. And it would progress in that matter until ten, and then until one hundred one. In the first recitation after one hundred, there would be all that was in the first one hundred, plus six hundred thousand *Salat al-Fatihi* multiplied by one hundred. That would be sixty million (60,000,000) *Salat al-Fatihi*.

It would then progress in this manner until it reached one thousand one. The first recitation after one thousand would have in it six hundred thousand *Salat al-Fatihi*, multiplied by one thousand, which is six hundred million (600,000,000). And it would continue upon that established method.

But if you were to recite it at the time just before Fajr, each one of them is worth five hundred thousand (500,000) recitations. So if you recite it one thousand one times, for example, in the first recitation after one thousand would be (the reward of) three hundred billion (300,000,000,000) *Salat al-Fatihi*. And the total in the one thousand one recitations would be (the reward of) one hundred fifty trillion, one hundred fifty billion (150,150,000,000,000) recitations. This is especially for the time just before Fajr. As for other times, it is upon the aforementioned multiplication.

Our Shaykh related to me:

> The Messenger of Allah said to me, "*No one has sent a prayer upon the Prophet on me better than Salat al-Fatihi.*" And he said, "*If all of the people of the seven Heavens and what they contain, and the seven Earths and what they contain, were to unite in order to describe the reward of Salat al-Fatihi, they would not be able to do it.*"

And he said, "What you have heard regarding the benefit of *Salat al-Fatihi* is only a drop in the ocean compared to what is hidden in it."

Then Glorified be the One who chose for this great blessing this Noble Shaykh.

At this time, we will return to the benefits of the litanies. As for the benefit of the declaration that there is no God but, I say:

4.2.12 On the Benefit of the Noble Word (*la ilaha ill Allah*)

Allah has said:

> ❴ *Then know that there is no God but Allah* ❵ [111]

And the Prophet said, "*The best that the other Prophets before me and I have said is 'There is no God but Allah.'*"[112] And its benefit is well known and famous in the Muhammadan religion. So we will not go into details.

---

[111] Muhammad, 19

[112] Al-Muwatta' (Hadith no. 572 and 1270); Sunan al-Bayhaqi (Hadith no. 9473), all with the wording, "*The most beneficial [afdal] of supplications is on the Day of 'Arafah. And the most beneficial [afdal] word that I and the Prophets before me have said is, "There is no God but Allah, Alone, without partner.*" Sunan al-Tirmidhi (Hadith no 3902) with the wording: "*The best [khayr] supplication is on the Day of 'Arafah and the best [khayr] word that I and the Prophets before me have said is, "There is no God but Allah, Alone, without partner.*"

4.2.13 On the Benefit of His Other Litanies

As for the *Sayfi*, some of its benefits have already been mentioned.

As for *Hizb al-Bahr*, it is what was related from the Messenger of Allah ﷺ to the Shaykh of Tariqah and Haqiqah, Mawlana Abi al-Hasan al-Shadhili ؓ. And it is said that the Greatest Sublime Name of Allah is contained within it. And it has a special quality for protection in the land and the sea- if one has an authentic permission from those able to give it. And it has different methods of recitation and protection. Whoever desires them should seek them from those who possess them and approach the houses from their doors.

As for the *Idrisi* Names, they have immense special properties and many benefits. Whoever desires them should read the book "*al-Jawahir al-Khams*" by Sidi Muhammad al-Ghawth, along with its explanation by Sidi Muhammad al-Shannawi ؓ. In that book, he has mentioned benefits whose number cannot be counted and extremely amazing things. So whoever desires, let him read it in its place with an authentic permission from those able to give it.

4.2.14 On the Benefit of *Surah al-Fatihah* and *Surah al-Qadr*

As for the *Fatihah*, it has been narrated in a Hadith that it is greater than the Qur'an and that it is the Seven Oft-repeated and the Great Qur'an, etc. And other things have been narrated on its benefit in well-known hadiths. So whoever desires should see it in its place.

As for what our Master ؓ related to us on its benefit from the Master of Existence ﷺ, he said ؓ, "As for the *Fatihah*, the Messenger of Allah ﷺ mentioned to us that in it, for every recitation, is the reward of reciting the entire Qur'an."

So I said to him ؓ, "It has reached me in some narrations that whoever recites it once, it is as if he has glorified Allah with all of the glorification of all of His creation in all of the universe. Does he receive all of that reward?" He said to me, "*It has more reward than that. Its reciter receives for every recitation, for every letter of it and every letter of the Qur'an, seven palaces and seven maidens of Paradise.*"

I say: And it has been said that the letters of the Qur'an number three hundred twenty-one thousand seventy-five (321,075). If you multiply it by seven, which is the number of maidens for every letter, it equals one million, two hundred forty-seven thousand, five hundred twenty-five maidens.

For *Surah al-Qadr*, there are three hundred sixty thousand maidens, since, in it, is the reward of fasting Ramadan. Every day of Ramadan is rewarded with twelve thousand maidens. So if one were to add that to the first, it would be two million, six hundred seven thousand, five hundred twenty-five.

That is outside of the prayer. As for during the prayer, it is multiplied twice if he prayed sitting and four times if he prayed standing. This is if he prays alone. If he were to recite it in a congregational prayer, it would be multiplied one hundred eight times. And if you consider the number of cycles, which are twenty-seven in a twenty-four hour period, it would become one thousand, eight hundred thirty-seven, meaning how many times its aforementioned benefit of one million is multiplied. And likewise, the rewards of the glorification of the universe, the reward for standing on the Night of Power, the worship of many years and the complete recitations of the Qur'an are multiplied by the same.

The outcome is that whoever recites it in the congregational prayer is given as a reward every day four billion, seven hundred eighty-six million, sixty thousand, seven hundred (4,786,060,700) maidens, along with the aforementioned reward of the glorification of the universe, the complete recitations, etc.

Our Shaykh said, "And in a Hadith it is related that the one who prays behind the Imam, he has (the reward of) the Imam's recitation."[113] Then our Master (may Allah be pleased with him said), "That is if he does not understand its explanation. As for the one who knows its explanation, the reward is doubled, meaning that it is two hundred good deeds for every letter." Then he said, "And no evil deed is written for him in that year- meaning for the one who recites the *Fatihah* once."

Then he said, "That is for its recitation without the intention of the Name. As for reciting the *Fatihah* with the intention of the Name, only Allah encompasses its benefit. And that is not a lot compared to His generosity (Exalted is His Majesty). That is because the Allah's grace has no limit. Peace."

Then he said, "The Messenger of Allah said to me":

> The reward for one who recites it once is that he will be my neighbor in the 'Illiyyun. But whoever recites it believing that he is reciting the Greatest Name along with it, since all of the letters of the Name are in it, for every recitation he will attain the reward of reciting the Name and the reward of reciting the Fatihah. And every time he recites it, he has recited it with it. That is specific to the Fatihah alone, and not any of the litanies that contain all of the letters of the Name.

---

113 Sunan Ibn Majah (Hadith no. 850).

And you should know that whoever recites it exclusively for Allah, without realizing that he is reciting the Name along with it, then he gets the first reward. But the one who recites it believing that he is reciting the Name, because all the letters are found within it, he will have the reward for reciting the Fatihah and the reward for reciting the Name, with every recitation. However, that is only if he believes that it is the Name that was chosen for the exalted Essence, and that the exalted purified Essence has no other name.

4.2.15 On the Benefit of Various Other Litanies

As for the benefit of the prayer upon the Prophet that raises acts, it has been related in some traditions that whoever recites it ten times in the morning and ten times in the evening, actions equal to the actions of all the people of the Earth will be raised up for him.

As for the invocation "O, Allah! Your mercy is greater than my sins…," it is among the wipers of sins.

As for the benefit of the daily recitation, "There is no God but Allah! Allah is the Greatest…," whoever recites it three times in the morning, no sin is written against him during that day. And whoever recites it three times in the evening, likewise no sin will be written against him on that night.

As for the benefit of the "Exalted Pear" [al-Dur al-A'la] of Shaykh al-Akbar, we have not read anything about it except that it is a protection and preservation of its reciter.

As for the "Petition of Forgiveness" of al-Khidr [Istighfar al-Khidr] (peace be upon him), our Master ﷺ said, "Whoever recites it, all of his past and future sins are forgiven him." That is the "Petition of Forgiveness" that was attributed to our Master al-Khidr (peace be upon him).

As for the *Musabba'at al-'Ashr*, Shaykh Abdullah al-Kharrubi al-Tarabulsi has said, "It is among the great litanies, which the pious and the worshippers- past and present- made a habit of reciting, and which they added to their morning and evening programs." And the Shaykhs (may Allah be pleased with them) continue to order their brethren and companions to recite it and single them out for it. Abu Talib al-Makki relates the Hadith, in "al-Qut," that mentions [al-Musabba'at al-'Ashr] with a chain of transmission, "On the authority of Kurz b. Barah- one of the *Abdal* according to his brother among the people of the Levant- who reported it from Ibrahim al-Taymi, from al-Khidr (peace be upon him), from the Prophet ﷺ."

But we have another high chain of transmission. It is from our Shaykh and Support, from his Shaykh Sidi Mahmud al-Kurdi, from al-Khidr (peace be upon him) directly with the aforementioned transmission. And we took it from our Master, and he gave us permission in it ﷺ. And this chain of transmission is only found with us.

As for the benefit of the invocation, "I bear witness that there is no God but Allah. He is One and has no partner, and that Muhammad is His Slave and Messenger and that Jesus...," it is reported in al-Bukhari from 'Ubadah b. al-Samit, that he ﷺ said, *"Whoever recites, 'I bear witness that there is no God but Allah...,' Allah will enter him into Paradise by whichever door he chooses, regardless of his works."*[114]

As for the invocations after the prayers, the *Fatihah*'s benefit has been mentioned. Whoever recites *Ayah al-Kursi* after every prayer, nothing prevents him from entering Paradise except death. As for *Surah al-Ikhlas*, it has been related in an authentic Hadith that one recitation of it is equal to one-third of a complete recitation of the Qur'an. As for, "I seek refuge in the perfect Words of Allah..." up to "And He is Hearing, Knowing," whoever recites it three times in the morning and three times in the evening will not be affected by poison. As for the benefit of "Blessed be my God...," whoever says it after any act, it will be accepted by him. *Ayah al-Kursi*'s benefit has been mentioned. As for ❴*There has come to you a Messenger*❵ until the end of the Surah, whoever recites it seven times in the morning and the evening will not die as long as he recites it. The benefit of, "I seek refuge in the perfect Words of Allah, from the evil of what He created..." has already been mentioned.

The benefit of *Hizb al-Bahr* has already been mentioned, as well as that of "O, you who manifested beauty," the *Idrisi* Names, *Ikhlas, Ayah al-Kursi, Ayah al-Hirs*, the *Sayfi*, and "There is no God but Allah! O, You who wards off..." The benefit of the supplication that Abu Talib al-Makki mentioned- which is "O, Allah! There is no God but You..."- is that whoever recites it is written among those who humbly prostrate, who will be neighbors of our Master Muhammad ﷺ and Ibrahim and Musa in the Abode of the Gardens. And he will have the reward of the worshippers in the Heavens and the earth.

As for the benefit of the invocation, "Glorified is Allah! Praise be to Allah! There is no God but Allah! Allah is the Greatest ...," to the end, whoever recites it once will be written among those who remember Allah a lot. And he would be the best of those who invokes Allah at night or in the day. And Allah will look at him. And Allah will never punish the one at whom He looks. And his sins will be lifted from him. And he will have a place in Paradise.

---

114   Sahih al-Bukhari (Hadith no. 3435).

4.2.16 On the Disciple, His Characteristics and States

As for the description of a disciple, his state and what cuts him off from his teacher, then you should know that we asked our Master ﷺ about some issues. The summary of them is as follows:

> Our Master. May Allah be pleased with you and please you and bless the Muslims by your long life. We seek your answer to some questions. Who is a truly sincere disciple? Describe the reality of his leaving the detestable state by a sincere promise, his wayfaring and training before he meets the true Shaykh, and his remaining steadfast upon that which comes from his Lord to save him through a sincere resolve. And when Allah blesses him with the coolness of his eyes and lifts the veils so that he may see that he (the true Shaykh) is his bondsman and spiritual educator, should he submit himself and his volition completely to him and follow him in everything that he indicates, without disobeying him, in what he commands or recommends him to do, for even a moment? And should he not ask him about the wisdom in what he has indicated to him, due to doubt that arises in him about whether or not it violates the Sacred Law of his Prophet ﷺ? Or should he not investigate them and look into the evidence that he has at his disposal so that he will not fall into the snares of the deviant deviators who are around him? If we say, our Master, that he should confirm, from the start, his claim to Shaykhhood, spiritual education, spiritual elevation, insight and spiritual states, we may see, at some point in time, that which negates that. But if we say that he should investigate him and put him to the test, we fear that we should be cast out of the Presence of the Sovereign Judge. So what is a sign- meaning in his daily life- that would make clear to us the true complete Shaykh, as well as the accomplished disciple, clearly and completely? And is seeking a Shaykh a personal obligation upon every Muslim? Would it be obligatory upon every individual to seek someone who can cause him to arrive at Allah ﷻ after learning obligatory knowledge? Or is it obligatory upon some over others? If we say that it is obligatory upon every individual, make clear for us its evidence. And if we say that it is obligatory for some over others, then make clear for us the evidence of that. And continual peace and mercy of Allah be upon you.

He responded ﷺ:

> You should know, may Allah strengthen you with His Spirit, that the sincere disciple is the one who recognizes the Majesty of Lordship, as well as what rights it has upon the creation, in the degree of Divinity. And he recognizes its requirement, upon all of His slaves, that they persevere in humbling and lowering themselves to Him, in busying themselves with loving and venerating Him. And they should observe perpetual flight towards Him and busying the heart with Him by refusing to desire or love anything apart from Him. So he has neither motive nor desire other than Him, due to his knowing that everything apart from Him is ❴*like a mirage in a lowland that a thirsty one thinks is water until, when he comes to it, he finds it is nothing*❵ [115]
>
> When he recognized this, and he recognized that it is incumbent upon him to perpetually busy himself with cutting himself off towards the Divine Presence, and he also recognized his soul's vileness, evil and misfortune, and its being oriented towards any direction but the Divine Presence. And he knows that all of its pleasures and desires violate the Divine rights, and that it has encroached itself, refusing to undertake compliance with the rights of the Real and recognizing the servitude and conduct that He ﷻ had obliged him, due to the inclination towards laziness that it has become accustomed to, its busying itself with desires, its separation from the Creator of the Earth and the Heavens and because all of its pleasures circulate this sphere.
>
> And he knew that he was unable to rectify this soul that commands evil, (and unable) to return it to the Divine Presence by cutting it off from its desires and passions, and he also knew that if he continues in that state, sooner or later, it would cause the anger of Allah upon him, humiliation, extreme punishment, and continuous, eternal retribution without limit. And his heart became alarmed due to the affliction that he was in and the vile defect that he was unable to escape. And it was not possible for him to continue with his soul in the state that was mentioned before, which would require anger and humiliation from Allah. But it was not possible for him to transfer his soul from its repulsive position to taking up residence in the Divine Presence. Since he knew all of that, he began to seek, with sincerity, resolve, diligence and struggle, the doctor who would rectify for him this despicable weakness and

---

115 al-Nur, 39

direct him towards the medicine that would bring about perfect healing and health. That is the sincere disciple. As for others who do not possess the aforementioned attributes, they are only a student. He may find what he seeks, or he may not. His [the student's] soul became attached to something, and he sought it out.

Due to the sincerity of the first, the Shaykh is closer to him than his seeking. That is because the Concern of the Real is what gave him the aforementioned knowledge, then guided him to the complete Shaykh and conveyed him into the presence of an accomplished Shaykh, and turned the heart of the Shaykh towards him with love and esteem. So a union and beautiful conduct occurred between them, and the door of arrival was opened. That is because when the Concern of the Real seeks a matter, it attracts it with a strong attraction that is impossible to stop, regardless of circumstances. Then what is required of the sincere disciple in his search, along with the aforementioned knowledge in its entirety, strong concentration on what he is seeking and turning his heart away from anything else, is that he should not busy himself with anything other than his goal. That is beneficial sincerity. And it is that which will remove him from his pitiful state.

Before meeting the Shaykh, what is incumbent upon the disciple is that he should adhere to the remembrance of Allah and sending prayers upon the Prophet ﷺ with strong presence of heart, contemplating the meanings as much as he is able. This, along with his believing that he is sitting before him ﷺ, while constantly rejecting the desires and aims of his soul as much as he is able, and striving to do those voluntary prayers, which will cause Allah ﷻ to love him. Those prayers and their times are well known: post-sunrise, before al-Zuhr and after it, before al-'Asr, after Maghrib, after 'Isha', after waking from sleep and in the last part of the night. But he should only do a little of that. And he should concentrate more on the remembrance of Allah and sending prayers upon the Prophet ﷺ than he does on voluntary (ritual) prayers. That is because the remembrance of Allah and sending prayers upon the Prophet ﷺ is the key to the doors of good. He should do this while observing solitude at the time of remembrance, eating and drinking little and practicing fasting and silence at times, as well as the other recommendations documented with the People of the Path.

But take every precaution against combining too many invocations and scattering one's thoughts between all of the sayings of the Sufis. No one ever follows that path and succeeds. Rather, he should adopt for himself one invocation and objective to concentrate on and an established foundation in the Path upon which to rely. That is his wayfaring and education before meeting the Shaykh. Then he should strive to follow the Complete Shaykh as Tamtam said, "The sincere student only pays attention to his goal. The sincere student only strives for his goal. The sincere student only concentrates on his goal." That is the disciple and his states.

4.2.17 On What Cuts the Disciple Off From His Shaykh

As for what cuts him off from his teacher, there are several matters. Our Master 🙠 said:

> The matters which can be a reason for the disciple being cast out of the presence of his Shaykh are ulterior motives, rejecting him with his heart or his tongue, the aversion of the disciple to the manifestation of the humanity of the Shaykh, due to a matter that does not befit one with Knowledge of Allah, or the removal of his respect for him from his heart.
>
> As for ulterior motives, they may be worldly or otherworldly. That is because one only keeps the company of the Shaykh and knows him for Allah (Honored and Exalted), and nothing else. And companionship is for two reasons. It is either so that Allah 🙠 should take him as a friend because of his saying, "He is a friend of Allah, and so I befriend him for the sake of Allah." The secret in that is his words 🙠: "*If anyone shows enmity to Me through My friend, I declare war on him.*"[116]
>
> Its opposite would be, "Whoever befriends My friend because he is My friend, I have chosen him and taken him as a friend." This is the greatest secret that attracts the disciple towards the Presence of Allah 🙠. Or he knows that the Shaykh is one of the slaves of the Presence, and he knows the conduct required for the Presence and the desires and objectives that corrupt a man in it. And since he knows that, he keeps his company so that he will direct him towards Allah and to what will draw him near to Him. Companionship is for one of these two reasons and nothing else. If someone keeps their company for anything else, he will lose this world and the next.
>
> If you have understood this, then you should recognize that the Lord 🙠 is not worshipped for any ulterior motive. Rather, He is

---

116   Sahih al-Bukhari (6137).

worshiped for His being a deity deserving of Divinity and worship because of His Essence and the praiseworthy, exalted attributes and sublime names that it possesses. That is the highest form of worship.

Likewise, the Shaykh's company is not kept for any ulterior motive. Rather, his company is kept so that his being a friend of Allah will pull the disciple to friendship with Allah, and that he may inform him of the conduct that pleases Allah and what would shame the slave in the Presence of Allah. And everything that falls under the description of following one's desires- even if it is a praiseworthy desire- is shameful for the slave in the Presence of Allah ﷻ.

For that reason, the Shaykhs were commanded to suppress the disciples and prevent them from following their desires, even to the smallest degree. That is because, at the time of following his desires, the disciple is a disbeliever in Allah- literally, not figuratively- due to the fact that he has raised himself to the status of the Divine and has contravened the command of Allah and disobeyed Him. So he is truly worshipping other than Allah. And he has nothing at all to do with Allah. And if he says, "There is no God but Allah," in that state, the tongue of Truth will say, "You have lied. Rather, you are a polytheist." And from this point of view did he say ﷺ: "*There is not under the canopy of the Heavens anything worshiped, other than Allah, greater than the desire that is followed.*"[117]

If the disciple has understood this, he should not become angry with the Shaykh nor should his attitude be altered if he does not agree to satisfy his desires in his worldly objectives. That is because the Shaykh is more knowledgeable of the rectification of souls and more acquainted with the different ways of harming oneself. And the disciple is ignorant of that. So when he seeks from him some worldly objective, whatever it may be, and the Shaykh does not satisfy him in that, he should know that the Shaykh refused it from him for the purpose of rectifying him and preventing his corruption. But if his soul becomes accustomed to changing its attitude with regards to the Shaykh in these situations, he will be cast out from the Presence of Allah ﷻ and cut off from the Shaykh. And if the disciple should become angry with the Shaykh after that alteration, he will be cut off completely without being able to return at all.

---

117   al-Mu'jam al-Kabir (Hadith 7502).

As for rejecting him in his heart or with the tongue, it is a sharp sword that cuts the cord between the Shaykh and the disciple. So he should not reject any matter with regards to the Shaykh. If any situation does not coincide with the exterior or interior knowledge that the disciple possesses, he should know that there are subtle matters between the Shaykh and his Lord of which the student is unaware. And the Shaykh adheres to the requirements of those subtle matters between him and his Lord. So if he apparently violates the exterior purport of the Sacred Law, he should know that in the inner reality of the matter, he is adhering to the requirements of the Sacred Law from a point of view of which people are unaware.

As for the disciple's aversion to the manifestation of the humanity of the Shaykh, it is because of his ignorance of Allah ﷻ and of His degrees of manifestation in His creation. That is that Allah ﷻ revealed Himself in every degree in a situation and according to a decree, in which He had not revealed Himself in other degrees. At times, that manifestation may be complete in relation to the Divine wisdom. And at times, it may be in the form of deficiency in relation to the Divine wisdom. Furthermore, if the form of a particular manifestation is that of deficiency in relation to the Divine wisdom, it is unavoidable that, in that degree, it should reveal that deficiency. That is because that is the result of the Divine will. And it is impossible for anything that is connected to the Divine will to digress from that to which it is connected.

Thus, it is unavoidable for the Knower of Allah to manifest deficiency in his essence. Furthermore, at times he disguises this deficiency in the form of completeness, due to the subtle matters between him and his Lord. And at times, he manifests it intentionally as a deficiency. But in that disguise, he is only acting according to a Divine command whose result is overpowering and forced in such a way that the slave is unable to avoid it. So if the disciple should witness the humanity of his Shaykh, which indicates deficiency- either in his following of the Sacred Law, or in terms of something not befitting a chivalrous person- he should bear in mind the meaning of what we have mentioned. And he should know that that does not remove the Shaykh from the Presence of his Lord, nor does it move him from his place of nearness to Him, nor decrease his perfect conduct.

If he has understood that, he should not reject his Shaykh due to the manifestation of his humanity. And any disciple who seeks a degree of the Real which is connected to His nearness and communion, but not wanting any deficiency to manifest therein, the tongue of his state will be calling out: "There is no way for you to enter the Presence of Allah ﷻ, since it is imperative for every degree to have a deficiency."

And completion does not manifest, in form, meaning, or perception, free from deficiency from every point of view and in every manner, except in three degrees alone. They are "Messengerhood" for the one who enters its presence; "Prophethood" for the one who enters its presence; and *Qutbaniyyah* for the one who enters its presence. There is no form of deficiency in these three. But deficiency manifests in the remainder of the degrees in most cases, though it is possible for it not to manifest. But if the form of deficiency should manifest in the person who is in one of those three degrees, it is the utmost perfection. And people only attribute deficiency to them out of ignorance. This is what he ﷺ indicated with his words: "*What is wrong with people who abstain from doing something that I, myself, do? By Allah! I am indeed more knowledgeable than them of Allah and have more fear of Him than them.*"[118]

As for the removal of his respect, it is the greatest of those things that cut one off from Allah. And removal of respect is that he never manifests any concern for what he has commanded or prohibited. And among the greatest conditions of the union between the Shaykh and the disciple is that he should not cause anyone else to share his love and esteem for him, his seeking spiritual aid from him, or his isolating his heart towards him. This is exemplified in the Sacred Law of his Prophet ﷺ. For if he considers the degree of his Prophet ﷺ the same as the degrees of the other Prophets and Messengers, in terms of love, esteem, seeking spiritual aid, isolating his heart for him, and legislation, it is a sign that he will die a disbeliever unless a Divine concern reaches him due to a preceding Divine love. So if you have understood that, the disciple should be with his Shaykh just as he would be with his Prophet ﷺ in terms of esteem, love, seeking spiritual aid and isolating his heart for him. And he should not hold anyone on par with him in these matters, nor allow anyone to have a share in them along with him.

And among the greatest of those things that cut one off from Allah is that he should attribute his illuminations and secrets to someone other than his Shaykh, since those are Divine lights, which cause to arrive to the slave secrets, states, sciences, knowledge

---

118   Sahih al-Bukhari (Hadith no. 6101); Sahih Muslim (Hadith no. 2356).

and ascension into the different stations. And each of these lights longs for its station, which is the Divine Presence from which it appeared and in which it originated. And each Shaykh among the People of Allah has a presence that he does not share with anyone else. And when a light emits therefrom, due to one of the matters that we have mentioned, but it is attributed to a Divine Presence other than the Presence from which it originated, it becomes angry, flies and returns to its place. And the form of that in the Divine wisdom is that Allah decreed in His Book that every child should be attributed to his father. He said ﷻ:

❰ *Call them by their fathers' names. That is fairer with Allah* ❱ [119]

Thus, whoever attributes a light to other than its proper place in the Divine Presence, he has had bad conduct with the Presence of the Real and lied upon Allah. And the Presence does not support lies. For that reason, he is cast out and deprived. And we seek refuge in Allah ﷻ from that.

And it has occurred to us, here, to mention some "Ra'iyyah" couplets written by Imam al-Sharishi ؓ related to the conditions that our Master ؓ mentioned. The text of the couplets is as follows:

Do not advance before you believe that he,
    Is an educator unmatched by anyone in his time,

Because constant observation of indifference to others,
    Convinces the departing lover not to leave,

And if your soul should raise the question of poverty, cast away,
    Its desires and flee from it as you flee from evil,

And place it in the lap of the Shaykh like an infant, and do not,
    Let it leave without being weaned from his protection and home,

And whoever does not have the attribute of suppressing desires,
    Has no hope of smelling the fragrance of poverty,

And he should not for any moment reject him, because that,
    Guarantees the dispersal of the disciple in abandonment,

---

[119]   al-Ahzab, 5

And whoever rejects while knowledge is detached from him,
    Will see deficiency in pure perfection, while he is unaware,

If one's beliefs do not conform to his Shaykh,
    He will persevere in denial in a smoldering fire,

So the intelligent one is not satisfied with anyone else, even if [the Shaykh should diverge,
    From the Truth, a distance equal to that between the night from the True Dawn,

And do not recognize anyone else in the presence of the Shaykh,
    Nor fill your eyes by glancing sideways at someone else,

Do not ever speak in front of him, but if he is requested,
    Let him not incline towards frivolous speech,

And do not raise your voice over his voice,
    And do not speak loudly as if he was in an empty space,

And do not ever sit in front of him cross-legged,
    Nor pointing his feet towards him; and (if it should happen) promptly excuse yourself,

Nor spreading one's prayer mat in his presence,
    Because the dutiful servant has no goal except giving effort,

And the prayer mat of the Sufi is his place of rest,
    And there is no rest unless he rushes towards the nest,

And flee to him for every important matter,
    For you will meet with assistance in that flight,

And do not be of those who act beautifully in his presence,
    And thereby is corrupted unless he rushes to repent,

And whoever makes his home sincere repentance,
    Will see the defects in his actions, even though he be fully healed.

4.3 On the True Shaykh and the Method of the Spiritual Concert and Its People. On His Daily and Nightly Recitations and the Different Supplications That Allah Caused to Flow Upon His Tongue

4.3.1 On the Importance of Keeping the Company of a Living Shaykh

He said ﷺ:

You should know that Allah ﷻ decreed, in His pre-eternal will, that the support that reaches His creation, from the outpouring of His mercy- in every era- should circulate among the Elect Exalted people among His creation, from among the Prophets and the *Siddiqun*. So whoever takes refuge with the living Elect Exalted people of his era, keeps their company, follows them and seeks assistance from them, will succeed at attaining the support that outpours from Allah. But whoever rejects the People of his era, sufficing himself with the words of those who preceded him among the saints who had passed on, he is stamped with the stamp of deprivation. His likeness is that of those who rejected the Prophet of their time and his legislation, sufficing themselves with the legislations of the Prophets who came before him, so they were recorded with the stamp of disbelief. We seek refuge in Allah from that.

    The proof that companionship is only to the living is his saying ﷺ to Abu Juhayfah, "*Ask the scholars (ulama'), mix with the wise (hukama') and keep the company of the Great Saints (kubara').*"[120] The guidance of the scholar (al-'alim) is in general matters, commanding and prohibiting, according to what brings about

---

120   al-Mu'jam al-Kabir (Hadith no. 17779).

praise from Allah and prevents the suffering of the slave. The end of that is Paradise. The guidance of the wise person (al-hakim) is towards drawing near to Allah ﷻ by purifying oneself from the passions of the ego and from following one's desires. The end of that is the different levels of nearness. The guidance of the Great Saint is to Allah ﷻ by way of erasure of the ego and becoming free from self-direction in all that brings about its [the ego's] rectification in this world and the next, and all that distances from it harm in this world and the next. The end of that is Allah. What is taken from this is that companionship is only to the living since the dead do not keep company, do not speak, and do not mix with others.

He also said ☙:

You should know that the Prophet ﷺ, during his life, used to transmit general verdicts to all, meaning if he prohibited something, he prohibited it to everyone. And if he made something obligatory, he made it obligatory on everyone. The same applies to all of the verdicts of the outward law. However, he ﷺ used to transmit the special commands to the special ones. And he used to choose some matters for some of his companions apart from others. This is widespread and well known in his traditional reports ﷺ.

Then, when he had been transported to the abode of the Hereafter- and he is, there, alive just as he was in the world- he began to transmit to his Community the special matters to the special ones. But there is no entrance to the general matters here, since that was cut off by his death ﷺ. However, his outpouring of the special matters to the special ones remains. Whoever assumes that all of his support for his Community ﷺ was cut off, just as is the case with all other dead people, is ignorant of his station ﷺ and has bad manners towards him. And it is feared for him that he will have a bad ending. We ask Allah for safety, sufficiency and to die with the best of endings.

4.3.2 On the True Accomplished Shaykh

You should know that our Master ﷺ was asked about the true accomplished Shaykh, "Who is he?" He responded ﷺ:

Regarding the true, accomplished Shaykh, he is the one for whom the veils to perfect beholding- visually, experientially and with certainty- of the Divine Presence had been lifted. For the beginning of the matter is "presence," which is to view the realities from behind a thick curtain. Then comes "unveiling," which is to view the realities from behind a thin curtain. Next is "witnessing," which is the manifestation of the realities without a veil, but in a particular manner. Then, there is "manifestation," which is to see the realities without a veil or a particularity, without another, or otherness, remaining- either in what one sees or what one experiences. That is the station of pulverization, obliteration, destruction and annihilation of annihilation so that there is nothing but the manifestation of the Real in the Real to the Real by the Real.

So nothing remains except Allah. There is nothing other than Him,
And there is no arrival and there is no one who arrives.

Finally, there is "life," which is distinguishing all the degrees [of existence] with intimate knowledge of all of their specifications, their requirements, their prerequisites, what they [the degrees] require of all things, which Presence each level proceed from, why it came into being, what is desired of it, what its matter returns to, as well as intimate knowledge of what the Divine Presence is, its greatness, exaltedness and its exalted attributes and perfection- with a manifest, certain experiential knowledge. The person at this level is one whom lives are spent in search of him. However, things being as they are, in him is the complete permission of the Real (Blessed and Exalted is He)- a special permission to guide His slaves and to turn to them for the purpose of guiding them to the Divine Presence. That is the one who deserves to be sought out. And he is what is meant by his saying ﷺ, "*Ask the scholars, mix with the wise and keep the company of the great Saints.*"[121]

---

121   al-Mu'jam al-Kabir (Hadith no. 17779).

The one at this level is who is indicated by "great Saint." When the disciple has discovered someone whose description is what preceded, then what is required of him is that he cast himself down in front of him, like the dead body in the hands of its washer. It has no choice, no will; it gives nothing and does not benefit. And his desire from him, should be that he should deliver him from the affliction in which he is immersed unto complete purity in entering the Divine Presence by rejecting all aside from Him. And he should free himself from all desires and aspirations apart from this. And when he indicates to him an action or a command, he should beware of questioning, "Why?" or "How?" or "For what purpose?" or "For what exactly?" for that is the door to aversion and rejection. Instead, he should believe that the Shaykh is more aware of what will rectify him than himself. And whatever course he sets him on, he conducts him, in all of it, to what is for Allah and by Allah, by taking him away from the darkness of his ego and its desires.

4.3.3 How to Meet a Shaykh with This Description and How He Is Recognized

(Our Master ﷺ continued:)

The Shaykhs fitting this description are many. The majority of them are in the large cities because that is where they live. As for recognizing and meeting them, that is a difficult matter to achieve, rarer than the Red Sulfur, for they have taken on the appearance and the states of the normal folk. And whoever asks them about that state, they turn him away and reject him and give him the impression that they do not possess any of that. The defect that obliges them to that is that the general order of the universe has been corrupted by the will of the Real ﷻ from which there is no escape. So all human beings are completely immersed in their worldly pursuits and desires, rejecting the Divine Presence, and the rights and moral conduct it is due.

In this time, the common folk do not rush to the Saints except desiring to fulfill corrupt aims such as the enjoyment of this world, its delights and passions, or to be saved from the afflictions and ruins of this abode, along with their entering into and persistence in highly disastrous and destructive habits from the greatest abominations which leave no end for their perpetrator except the abode of perdition. And they have no way out of this state of affairs, nor have they any means of entry into the sphere of returning to the Divine Presence.

So when the Knowers of Allah recognized that this was the affair of the common folk, they veiled themselves to the common folk and warded them off in every circumstance and from every point of view. What that required was for them to live in desolate and uncultivated regions. However, the Real wanted from them that they should remain in the midst of the common folk and live amongst them for some matters that the Real wanted from them (Blessed and Exalted is He) which He had decreed for them. And they have no escape from His decree. So they did not see any way out of that, nor did they see any way to rectify the common folk and return them to the Divine Presence. So they are in the same position as the person who has been placed among a foolish mob that is stoning him, but has been tasked with being patient and remaining among them. He is in torment.

For that reason, they have veiled themselves from the common folk and repelled them in every circumstance. But it is possible that the common folk sense the breeze of their arrival from behind a veil and pounce at (the opportunity) to connect themselves with them seeking what they desire of worldly pursuits. So the Knowers of Allah commingled with them in several different ways, covering themselves from the common folk by manifesting serious matters such as fornication, excessive lying, consuming alcohol, murder and other such destructive habits by which it is judged that the one who does them is in the displeasure of Allah and His punishment.

But the matters in which the Knowers of Allah involve themselves in this sphere are only forms that manifest from the unseen, having no reality for the most part. They are only imaginary forms that others see as a reality. And they do, in these forms, things that are blameworthy according to the Sacred Law. But they, in reality, have not done a thing. So they veiled themselves with this from the common folk, guarding their station and avoiding their conduct. Knowing this, the fact is that the truthful and the liars have been commingled in this sphere. And one is not known from the other. And there is no power for anyone to recognize the accomplished gnostic completely or partially, except for a rare, most exceptional case. That is that some of the complete Saints had manifested in the spheres of following the Sacred Law completely. So whoever manifests in this sphere and claims Shaykhhood, then he is recognized by his calling to Allah ﷻ, to returning to Him, to abstaining from the world and its people and not being concerned with it or its existence, along with the manifestation of the illumination in others upon his hand. If he should manifest himself to the seeker in this description, he should give himself over to him in the first meeting. What is required of the disciple, however, in this regard is that he should not give himself over to him until he has investigated the widespread stories about him from his trustworthy followers and his neighbors. And if the aforementioned description manifests from him, he should keep his company. If not, then no.

Whoever desires to connect himself to a Shaykh in this time, yet does not find himself able to recognize one, and fears that he may be caught in the snares of the liars, should turn to Allah with absolute sincerity, fleeing to Him with the heart at all times, along with constantly humbling oneself before Him and humbly supplicating to Him to reveal to him the accomplished Shaykh who can deliver him from this darkness and that He lead him to him and enable him to follow his commands until he completely drowns in the waves of his ocean. For he is not capable of more than that. But greater and more important than that and more beneficial and more effective for obtaining his goal, and more exalted for the one who does not have the capability of discovering a complete Shaykh, is that he should consume whatever time he has in sending a lot of blessings on the Prophet ﷺ with proper décor and presence of the heart, and the conviction of the heart that he is sitting before him ﷺ. And he should persist in that.

For whoever persists in that, and his earnestness to arrive before Allah is like the earnestness of one dying of thirst to find water, Allah will take him by the hand and pull him towards Himself either by assigning a complete, accomplished Shaykh to take him by the hand, or He will assign His Prophet ﷺ to train him, or yet He may open a door to arrival and the lifting of the veils by reason of his adhering to sending blessings upon His Beloved ﷺ since that is the greatest means to Allah ﷻ and to arrival before Him. And no one adheres to it, whatsoever, seeking arrival before Allah and ever fails.

4.3.4 Testing the Shaykh

(Our Master ﷺ continued:)

As for your question about putting the Shaykh to the test and evaluating his actions and states, that is not proper, and no one follows that path and succeeds at all since that is a cause for the closing of the doors of Allah ﷻ. And whoever desires that and follows that with all people, Allah ﷻ will show him the attribute of deficiency of all people, so that he will not trust anyone. As for belief in the Shaykh, it is a Divine matter which Allah places in the heart so that the one who possesses it is not capable of separating from him, even if he should see from him one thousand acts of disobedience. However, if he is a sincere disciple, the reward for his sincerity is that he will not see from the Shaykh anything except what causes his heart to be at ease regarding him. And that only happens with a true Shaykh. But whoever's inner being is impure, and seeks defects, he will only see what causes him to deny him and attribute deficiency to him, and what causes him to turn away from him and show him enmity.

4.3.5 The Obligation of Seeking a Shaykh

(Our Master ﷺ continued:)

Regarding the question about whether seeking a Shaykh is obligatory on every single individual, or some people apart from others, and under what conditions:

In the Sacred Law, seeking a Shaykh is not obligatory in terms of legal obligations whose performance is rewarded and whose neglect is punished. For there is nothing in the Sacred Law that obligates that. Instead, it is obligatory from the standpoint of discernment, like the dehydrated person who, if he does not seek water, will perish. For him, it is obligatory to seek it from the standpoint of discernment.

The standpoint of discernment in this (seeking a Shaykh) is what we had already mentioned regarding humanity's being created to worship Allah and to focus on the Divine Presence by rejecting everything apart from it. The aspirant knows well the impediments and hindrances to his advancement towards the Divine Presence that exist within him. He also knows his inability to rectify himself according to what he desires: entrance into the Divine Presence and discharging its rights and the proper conduct owed to it. And he knows that he has no escape from Allah and no savior if he should agree with his ego, following its desires and turning away from Allah ﷻ. So, from this point of view, it is obligatory for him to seek a complete Shaykh.

Therefore, this recognized obligation, although it is not from a legislative text, is a natural and conventional conclusion- since there is nothing in the legislative texts except for the obligation upon every single individual among the slaves to uphold the rights of Allah, inwardly and outwardly. And there is no excuse for anyone to abandon that from the standpoint of the Sacred Law, nor is there any excuse for his desires' dominating him nor his being incapable of rectifying himself. There is nothing in the Sacred Law except that obligation and the prohibition of leaving that by obligating punishment upon the perpetrator. That is what is in the Sacred Law.

And there is no Shaykh whom it is obligatory to follow except the Shaykh of instruction who teaches the manner of legislative matters whose performance is sought by the slaves- commands, prohibitions, acting and refraining. It is obligatory for every ignorant person to seek this Shaykh. And it is not proper for anyone to abandon that. But beyond this, it is not obligatory according to the Sacred Law to seek a Shaykh. Instead, it is obligatory from the standpoint of discernment, in the same manner of the sick person who has a puzzling illness that he is unable to remedy from all angles, and his health has diminished, we say, "If he wishes to remain in that illness, he remains." But, if he wishes to become free of it and attain perfect health, we say, "It is imperative for him to seek an adept physician who is familiar with the illness and its cause, as well as the remedy required to remove it and the method of treatment, in terms of amount, method of administration, length of time and condition."

4.3.6 On the Rulings of the Spiritual Concert

(Our Master ؊ continued:)

Regarding the question about the Spiritual Concert, its ruling, its use, its method, who listens and from whom one should listen and in what state he should be and what speech constitutes it:

The answer, and Allah is the One who facilitates all things, by His blessings and grace, what is correct is:

You should know that there are differing verdicts on the Spiritual Concert among the great Shaykhs who had been established in complete gnosis of Allah by seeing and witnessing, as well as a special experience of Divine oneness, complete guidance, and freedom from all manners of following the ego and desires. There are those who say that it is permitted but encourage one to neither do it nor leave it. Others say that it is completely unlawful and have disparaged the one who performs and the one who attends. And another group has said that it is disliked but not unlawful. Still another group has recommended it and encouraged one to incline towards it. But there is no opinion that it is mandatory. However, the verdict on it has been explained in detail in the books of Sufism, so we will not explain it exhaustively.

However, there is another opinion that the verdict on it hangs between encouraging its performance and discouraging it, between prohibiting, discouraging and recommending it. Encouraging an inkling towards it depends on the demands of both time and spiritual state. And all of that has been detailed in the books of Sufism. But the confirmed verdict at this time is that whatever does not consist of pure entertainment, confuse one's senses, involve singing the praises of women, nor listening to their voices or the voices of beautiful young boys- what is beyond all of that and also free from matters prohibited in the Sacred Law, such as the mixing of women and men- its verdict is that a person should look at his spiritual state at the time of attending the Spiritual Concert. If he finds that it increases his spiritual state, or mobilizes his stagnated aspiration towards restoring his seeking of the Divine Presence, or towards distancing himself from customary habits and prohibited and reprobate matters, or towards connecting himself with Allah ؊ and stirring within his heart His love, this person should attach himself to attending them and be encouraged towards it, as long as he does not transgress into neglecting his litanies and does not neglect all of the other demands of his time. That is because if he does that, then he will be harmed more than he is benefitted (by it).

But if a person finds within it laxity in his resolve and tendency towards relaxation, and he sees that his soul has become entrenched in that- by decreasing its aspiration for the Divine Presence- then for the one in that state, it is not lawful to either attend the Spiritual Concert or discuss it.

If a person does not see either increase or decrease in the aforementioned, and only enjoys the beautiful voices and amazing melodies, then the ruling of that is permissibility. If he wishes, he may attend, or if he wishes, he may leave it.

However, the Spiritual Concert that features the voices of handsome young boys and women remains unlawful- or tantamount to it for all those who we have mentioned- even if he should notice from it an increase in his spiritual state as mentioned before. That is because the one who enjoys that, in spite of the increase one may see in his spiritual state, is like the man who consumes honey in which is hidden a small amount of poison. It kills him from where he does not perceive.

As to what is beyond all of that yet contains some instruments of entertainment, it befits the intelligent person to leave it, unless there is a complete accomplished Shaykh present. In that case, it is recommended for him to attend. That is because the Spiritual Concert that contains instruments of entertainment- even if he is not influenced by its harm- will cause an internal corruption, just like the clouds that people joyously expect to quench their thirst, yet a dangerous cold falls from them, and they produce lightning and damage the crops that they had hoped would be mended. That is unless a complete accomplished Shaykh is present because his presence is a protection from harm and destruction.

All of these things are about the people who are veiled. As for those who are drowned in the oceans of realities and Divine unity, they are not judged by this ruling. Rather, they are left to the ruling of their spiritual state and station. That is because the gnostic does, in his station, what corresponds to it- either through a text, an indication, a clear sign or an allusion- without paying attention to those who deny it or recommend it. Then, if his station indicates to him that he should attend the Spiritual Concert and encourages him to do it, he is left to his spiritual state, and he is not denied, because he is more knowing of his strengths and weaknesses. But, if his station indicates to him to leave it and to flee from it, no one can recommend it to him, nor encourage him to attend. For the states of gnosis differ. And each taste is distinct. And benefits, levels, outpourings, and illuminations are not equal, nor do they resemble each other.

How many a person in one station is harmed by his attending the Spiritual Concert for the smallest amount of time. And that is worse for him than a small amount of poison that kills the body. Yet how many a gnostic- while attending the Spiritual Concert- receives influxes of spiritual states and gnosis from the Holy Presence that propel him to stations that he would not have attained in a thousand years by worship. Then, that is the explanation of the matter regarding the Knowers of Allah (may Allah be pleased with them). Each one of them has a taste, a station, and a state. And natural dispositions differ. All structures are not in harmony. That is because for every station is a different speech. For each taste and rapture is a different person. For each period of time, there is a specific ruling. And for each spiritual state, there is a time when it will spread.

The upshot of that is that the Knower of Allah is judged in his attending the Spiritual Concert by his time, his station, his state, his taste, and his rapture. So he is not rejected for either attending or leaving it. As for the people who are veiled, the explanation of their ruling has already been mentioned.

4.3.7 On the Supplications That Allah Caused to Flow from His Tongue

They are:

بِسْمِ اللهِ الرَّحْمَنِ الرَّحِيمِ

اَللَّهُمَّ إِنِّي أَسْأَلُكَ أَنْ تُصَلِّيَ وَتُسَلِّمَ عَلَى سَيِّدِنَا مُحَمَّدٍ وَعَلَى آلِهِ عَدَدَ مَا فِي عِلْمِكَ، وَأَنْ تُعْطِيَنِي وَتُعْطِيَ فُلاَنًا كَذَا وَكَذَا جَمْعًا أَوْ إِفْرَادًا مِنْ كُلِّ مَا شِئْتَ مِنَ ابْتِدَاءِ خَلْقِكَ إِلَى انْتِهَاءِ

يَوْمِ الْقِيَامَةِ فِي كُلِّ مِقْدَارِ طَرْفَةِ عَيْنٍ لِكُلِّ وَاحِدٍ عَلَى انْفِرَادِهِ عِشْرِينَ فَيْضَةٍ مِنْ بَحْرِ رِضَاكَ،

وَأَنْ تُعْطِيَ كُلَّ وَاحِدٍ فِي كُلِّ فَيْضَةٍ أَوْفَرَ حَظٍّ وَنَصِيبٍ مِنْ كُلِّ خَيْرٍ سَأَلَكَ مِنْهُ سَيِّدُنَا مُحَمَّدٌ نَبِيُّكَ وَرَسُولُكَ صَلَّى اللهُ عَلَيْهِ وَسَلَّمَ، مَا عَلِمْتُ مِنْ ذَلِكَ وَمَا لَمْ أَعْلَمْ مِنْ خَيْرَاتِ الدُّنْيَا وَالْآخِرَةِ، وَالنَّجَاةِ مِنْ كُلِّ شَرٍّ اسْتَعَاذَكَ مِنْهُ سَيِّدُنَا مُحَمَّدٌ نَبِيُّكَ وَرَسُولُكَ صَلَّى اللهُ عَلَيْهِ وَسَلَّمَ، مَا عَلِمْتُ مِنْ ذَلِكَ وَمَا لَمْ أَعْلَمْ مِنْ شُرُورِ الدُّنْيَا وَالْآخِرَةِ، وَمَغْفِرَةِ جَمِيعِ ذُنُوبِنَا مَا تَقَدَّمَ مِنْهَا وَمَا تَأَخَّرَ فِي الدُّنْيَا وَالْآخِرَةِ،

وَأَدَاءِ جَمِيعِ تَبِعَاتِنَا مِنْ خَزَائِنِ فَضْلِكَ وَكَرَمِكَ، لَا مِنْ حَسَنَاتِنَا، وَالَّذِي فِي كُلِّ فَيْضَةٍ غَيْرُ الَّذِي فِي الْأُخْرَى، وَهَذَا كُلُّهُ غَيْرُ الَّذِي تَقَدَّمَ، وَأَسْأَلُكَ أَنْ تُعْطِيَنِي وَكُلَّ وَاحِدٍ مِنْهُمْ جَمِيعَ ذَا وَذَاكَ، وَأَنْ تُجِيبَنِي وَكُلَّ وَاحِدٍ مِنْهُمْ فِي جَمِيعِ ذَا وَذَاكَ، بِمَحْضِ فَضْلِكَ وَكَرَمِكَ

In the Name of Allah, the Beneficent, the Merciful.

O, Allah! Verily I ask You that You send blessings and salutations upon our Master Muhammad, and upon his family in the number of those things that You know, and that You give me and so-and-so such-and-such thing, collectively or individually, from whatever You have willed from the beginning of Your creation until the end of the Day of Judgment, with every blinking of an eye, each one among us receiving twenty outpourings from the sea of Your satisfaction;

And that You give each one of us, in each outpouring, an abundant portion and share of every good which our Master Muhammad, Your Prophet and Messenger ﷺ, requested from You- whatever I know therefrom and what I do not know, from the good of this world and the Hereafter; as well as salvation from every evil from which our Master Muhammad, Your Prophet and Messenger ﷺ, sought refuge in You- from those evils of this world and the Hereafter that I know, and those that I do not know; and forgiveness of all of our sins- past and future, in this world and the Hereafter;

And payment of all of our debts from the treasures of Your grace and generosity, and not from our good deeds; and make what is in each outpouring unique to that which is in the others, and each one of them different from what I have mentioned. And I ask You to give each one of them all of this and that; and to grant me for each one of them all of this and that, out of Your pure generosity and grace.

Not all of this supplication is for the ordinary people of Islam. For them, one arrives at "the good of this world and the Hereafter..." and does not add the part beginning with "salvation..." He then skips to the part of the supplication that starts "and make what is in each outpouring unique to that which is in the others..." That is because supplicating the rest for the general people of Islam is to supplicate for that which it is known that Allah will not do. So it is like the one who supplicates asking Allah for Prophethood or Messengerhood after our Prophet ﷺ. If that does not imply disbelief, it is not far off from it, because the decree of Allah (Honored and Exalted) regarding that has already gone forth, as He has informed us. And if someone asks for something that invalidates that which His decree had already sent forth, he comes close to disbelieving in Him. That is because he has asked of Allah an injustice, while He is purified above injustice. So he wants that Allah should not be Holy, because His decree is the essence of justice, and whatever invalidates it is the essence of injustice. Peace.

And this supplication has three degrees. One degree is for the entire body of monotheists. Another degree is for the supplicant and whomever he chooses. And a final degree for all those who have been kind to him, or between him and them is love, or who have a right upon him. So whoever wishes to recite this supplication, upon one of these three degrees, should request whatever is appropriate for each group of people. Understand. I heard such from our Shaykh ﷺ.

Among his supplications 🌺, which he related to us from his memory and in his exact words is the following:

اَللَّهُمَّ اجْذِبْنِي إِلَيْكَ بِحَقِّ قَلْبًا وَقَالِبًا بِجَوَاذِبِ عِنَايَتِكَ، وَأَلْبِسْنِي خِلْعَةَ اسْتِغْرَاقِ أَوْقَاتِي فِي الِاشْتِغَالِ بِكَ، وَامْلَأْ قَلْبِي وَجَوَارِحِي بِذِكْرِكَ وَحُبِّكَ وَالشَّوْقِ إِلَيْكَ امْتِلَاءً لَا يُبْقِي فِي مُتَّسِعًا لِغَيْرِكَ، وَاسْقِنِي كَأْسَ انْقِطَاعِي إِلَيْكَ بِتَكْمِيلِ الْبَرَائَةِ مِنْ غَيْرِكَ وَعَدَمِ الْتِفَاتِ قَلْبِي لِسِوَاكَ،

وَاجْعَلْنِي بِكَ لَكَ قَائِمًا وَعِنْدَكَ آخِذًا وَمِنْكَ مُسْتَمِعًا وَإِلَيْكَ نَاظِرًا وَرَاجِعًا وَعَلَيْكَ مُعَوِّلاً، وَفِيكَ مُتَحَرِّكًا وَسَاكِنًا مُطَهَّرًا بِفُيُوضِ تَجَلِّيَاتِكَ مِنْ جَمِيعِ الْحُظُوظِ وَالْبَقَايَا وَمِنْ جَمِيعِ الْمُسَاكِنَاتِ وَالْمُلَاحَظَاتِ لِغَيْرِكَ،

وَحُلَّ بَيْنِي وَبَيْنَ النَّفْسِ وَهَوَاهَا وَالشَّيْطَانِ بِسُرَادِقَاتِ عِصْمَتِكَ لِي مِنْهُمْ، وَأَدِمْ لِي صَفَاءَ الْوُقُوفِ بَيْنَ يَدَيْكَ بِكَ لَكَ مِنْ حَيْثُ تَرْضَى بِمَا تَرْضَى كَمَا تَرْضَى، مِثْلَ أَكَابِرِ الصِّدِّيقِينَ بَيْنَ يَدَيْكَ، وَحُفَّنِي بِجُنُودِ نَصْرِكَ لِي وَتَأْيِيدِكَ لِي وَعَوْنِكَ لِي بِكَمَالِ تَوَلِّيكَ لِي بِعِنَايَتِكَ بِي وَمَحَبَّتِكَ لِي وَاصْطِفَائِكَ لِي،

وَحُلَّ بَيْنِي وَبَيْنَ غَيْرِكَ مِنْ أَوَّلِ الْأَمْرِ إِلَى آخِرِهِ، حَتَّى تُمِيتَنِي عَلَى ذَلِكَ، وَاجْعَلْنِي فِي الدُّنْيَا وَالْآخِرَةِ مِنْ أَهْلِ وِلَايَتِكَ الْخَاصَّةِ الْكَامِلَةِ الصِّرْفَةِ الَّتِي لَا شَائِبَةَ فِيهَا لِغَيْرِكَ، إِنَّكَ عَلَى كُلِّ شَيْءٍ قَدِيرٌ، وَصَلَّى اللهُ عَلَى سَيِّدِنَا مُحَمَّدٍ وَآلِهِ وَصَحْبِهِ

SECTION FOUR

وَسَلَّمَ تَسْلِيمًا

O, Allah! Attract me towards You with the Truth inwardly and outwardly and with the attraction of Your concern, clothe me with the robe of honor of consuming all of my time with You, fill my heart and my limbs with Your remembrance, love and longing for You, with a filling up such that no room for anything other than You remains with me, give me to drink from the cup of total isolation with You by complete freedom from, and my heart's never inclining to, anything other than You,

Make me to stand for You by You, taking from You, listening to You, returning and looking towards You, relying upon You, moving and resting in You, purified by the outpouring of Your manifestations from all pleasures and remnants, from all movements and observations of anything other than You,

Separate between me and my soul, its desires and Shaytan, through the sanctuary of Your protection from them, perpetuate the purity of my standing before You, with You, for You- where You are satisfied, by what satisfies You and however You are satisfied, in the same way as [You are satisfied with] the great *Siddiqun* [standing] before You, and encompass me with the armies of Your helping, strengthening and assisting me by Your complete protection, concern, love and choosing me;

And separate between me and anything other than You from the beginning of the matter to the end of the matter until You cause me to die upon that. And make me in this world and the Hereafter among the people of Your complete, special, unadulterated friendship, in which nothing besides You has a share. Indeed, You have power over all things. May Allah bless our Master Muhammad, his family, and companions, and extend them a worthy salutation.

Whoever wishes to recite this supplication should recite one thousand prayers upon the Messenger of Allah ﷺ in the morning and one thousand in the evening. Then he should recite this supplication after each one thousand. And he should gift the reward for the prayers upon the Prophet to the Messenger of Allah ﷺ, exalting and esteeming Allah and His Messenger ﷺ. He should do all of that in measured tones with as much presence of heart as he is able to muster. He should persist upon this while adhering to seclusion, silence, and reduced eating and drinking, without excess or negligence. And he should guard his heart against being engrossed in worldly matters, women or desires, from being upset with decreed matters, and from anxiety over whatever contradicts one's desires at any time. Whoever does this will see innumerable secrets and lights. And success is by Allah.

And among his supplications ﷺ for all objectives is the following:

اَللَّهُمَّ إِنِّي أَسْأَلُكَ بِمَا وَارَتْهُ حُجُبُ جَلاَلِكَ مِنْ سُبُحَاتِ وَجْهِكَ الَّتِي لَوْ أَظْهَرَتْ لِلْوُجُودِ لَتَدَكْدَكَ الوُجُودُ وَانْحَرَقَ وَصَارَ مَحْضَ العَدَمِ، نَسْأَلُكَ بِتِلْكَ السُّبُحَاتِ وَجَلاَلَتِهَا وَعَظَمَتِهَا أَنْ تُصَلِّي وتُسَلِّمَ عَلَى سَيِّدِنَا مُحَمَّدٍ وَعَلَى آلِ سَيِّدِنَا مُحَمَّدٍ، وَأَسْأَلُكَ أَنْ تُعْطِيَنِي كَذَا وَكَذَا، وَيُسَمَّى حَاجَتَهُ

> O, Allah! I ask You by the sublime splendor of Your countenance, which the veils of Your majesty hide, which if it were to be revealed to the universe, it would be pulverized and burned and become pure nothingness. We ask You by that sublime splendor, and its majesty and greatness, that You send blessings and peace upon our Master Muhammad and upon the family of our Master Muhammad. And I ask You that You give me such-and-such (he should name his need).

What follows is one of his supplications ﷺ, with which he supplicated Allah, and which encompasses all of the stations, levels, positions, presences, ascensions, states and degrees which the Complete Knowers of Allah, *Aqtab*, *Afrad* attained. And I beckon you to pay attention from the beginning of it so that you may recognize and confirm the vastness of the gnosis of this noble man, his vastness, his worth before Allah and what Allah had promised him out of His generosity and openhandedness. It is:[122]

---

122   We did not include the Arabic of this supplication because it is one of his personal supplications and was not transmitted to be recited by his students.

SECTION FOUR

> My Lord! I request from Your grace by Your grace, Your generosity by Your generosity, Your beneficence by Your beneficence, that You do not cause me to die until You cause me to reach the highest limit of the Qutbaniyyah of Sidi "so-and-so" and the highest limit of Sidi "so-and-so."

And he continued that until he had numbered more than fifty of the greatest of the Predecessors ﷺ. Then he said:

> And the Khilafah of all of them, their *Ghawthiyah*, *Fardiyyah* and the gathering of all of what they gathered in their *Qutbaniyyah*, *Khilafah* and all of the necessary sciences- investigative and transmitted, through unveiling and direct spiritual knowledge- and all of their gnosis of Your Essence, attributes, all of Your names and actions, and all of their secrets and lights, their actions and states, their stations and levels, their unveilings and illuminations, their certainty and unification, their witnessing and love, their reservation and good conduct in front of You, their understanding from You, their deep understanding of Your religion and the appearances of Your manifestations at the moment of their appearance, their upholding the Lordly rights, their being consumed in the witnessing of Your greatness and grandeur, their perpetual wilting and melting from Your reverence and the might of Your majesty, their tranquility during the stormy winds of Your decrees, their perfect standing with You for You, in submission, faith and excellence, knowledge, action and states, levels and stations, being convicted and perfumed. The upshot is that You not cause me to die until You have given me everything that You gave to them in all of their Qutbaniyyah, in their life and their death, from everything that I mentioned and everything I did not mention and everything that Your knowledge encompasses; and that You give me along with that, the *Qutbaniyyah* of every *Qutb* from the time of his being dispatched ﷺ until the blowing of the trumpet, however it may be, the *Khilafah* of each *Khalifah*, the *Ghawthiyah* of every *Ghawth*, and the all-encompassing nature of every all-encompassing Qutb and the Fardiyyah of every *Fard*, from the time of his being dispatched ﷺ until the blowing of the trumpet.

He continued in that manner until he said, "And that You give me, with all of that, in that Qutbaniyyah, everything that You gave to our Master Talhah, our Master al-Zubayr..."

And he continued in that manner until he had listed seventy of the greatest Companions, the Followers and the Followers of the Followers, except that in the first list he only mentioned those who are famous for their Qutbaniyyah among the Companions and the others. Then he said in the second list, "In that, You make me an inheritor of all of those in all of the sciences, gnosis, secrets, lights, actions, and states."

And he continued in that way until he mentioned many matters. Then he said:

> And that You make my station in this *Qutbaniyyah*[123], *Fardiyyah*[124], *Ghawthiyyah*[125], *Khilafah*, and all-Encompassing Sainthood so large to the point that the stations of all of the *Aqtab*, *Afrad*, *Ghawths*, *Khalifahs* and All-encompassing Saints, as well as that of the Knowers of Allah, Lovers, Beloveds, Wayfarers and Attracted ones, dwindle and fade before it; and that You make my illumination in that, at every blinking of an eye and moment, in the same proportion of the Night of Power to other nights. Rather, increase it a nonillion times.

And he continued upon that until he had mentioned more times than that, until he reached an unfathomable number. Then he said:

> And that You make me in that *Qutbaniyyah* the unique, all-Encompassing, *Ghawth* and Qutb, the greatest *Khalifah*, whose spiritual assistance is from the Messenger of Allah ﷺ without any intermediary, Your representative and his, Your *Khalifah* in all of the worlds, who has complete, unrestricted authority to dispose of affairs in all of the worlds, who relies upon our Master Muhammad ﷺ, Abu Bakr, 'Umar, 'Uthman, 'Ali, Israfil, Jibril, Mika'il, 'Izra'il and the Spirit; and the authority in all of the worlds and all of creation, whose comparison to all of the Saints of his time is like the sun compared to all of the stars.

And he continued upon that until he had listed many requests. Then he said after all of that, "I ask You, o, my Lord! That You cause to reach gnosis upon my hand such-and-such a number of men and jinn."

---

123   The state of being a *Qutb*.
124   The state of being a *Fard*.
125   The state of being a *Ghawth*.

And he mentioned a large number that no one among the Saints of Allah had sought, as far as we have heard.

As far as what he sought ﷺ in Paradise- of dominion, servants, maidens and palaces, and from all of the different types of things in Paradise and all of what it encompasses- everything that was mentioned in Paradise, or was not mentioned, but is possible, he sought from that what would dazzle the intellect, and what the tongue would fail to articulate. And every type of thing that he ﷺ mentioned, he mentioned in thousands multiplied by themselves until each of the sums would be multiplied by what is over it until it reached a number so large that I do not believe anyone can enumerate it other than him ﷺ. Then he informed us that he was guaranteed to obtain all of those things that he sought in the supplication by the Master of Existence ﷺ. And to Allah belongs the praise and the gratitude. That is all that it is possible to write in this blessed collection as far as the mention of those things our Master ﷺ sought in his beginning stages. As for now, he has attained what he sought. And to Allah belongs the praise and the gratitude for that.

As for the entirety of what he sought, we will not mention it all right now due to its immensity and because it contains some things that should not be revealed. We only mentioned the upshot of it seeking blessing from it and the grandeur of our Master ﷺ, and his perfection and realization in the station of the greatest *Qubtaniyya*. Peace.

Also among his supplications, which he related to us ﷺ is the following:

اَللَّهُمَّ حَقِّقْنِي بِكَ تَحْقِيقًا يُسْقِطُ النِّسَبَ وَالرُّتَبَ وَالتَّعَيُّنَاتِ وَالتَّعَلُّقَاتِ وَالِاعْتِبَارَاتِ وَالتَّوَهُّمَاتِ وَالتَّخَيُّلَاتِ، حَيْثُ لَا أَيْنَ وَلَا كَيْفَ وَلَا رَسْمَ وَلَا عِلْمَ وَلَا وَصْفَ وَلَا مُسَاكَنَةَ وَلَا مُلَاحَظَةَ وَ، مُسْتَغْرِقًا فِيكَ بِمَحْقِ الْغَيْرِ وَالْغَيْرِيَّةِ بِتَحْقِيقِي بِكَ مِنْ حَيْثُ أَنْتَ كَمَا أَنْتَ، وَكَيْفَ أَنْتَ حَيْثُ لَا حِسَّ وض لَا اعْتِبَارَ إِلَّا أَنْتَ بِكَ لَكَ عَنْكَ مِنْكَ، لِأَكُونَ لَكَ خَالِصًا وَبِكَ قَائِمًا وَإِلَيْكَ آئِبًا وَفِيكَ ذَاهِبًا، بِإِسْقَاطِ الضَّمَائِرِ وَالْإِضَافَاتِ، وَاجْعَلْنِي فِي جَمِيعِ ذَلِكَ مَصُونًا بِعِنَايَتِكَ بِي وَتَوَلِّيكَ لِي وَاصْطِفَائِكَ لِي وَنَصْرِكَ لِي آمِّينَ

O, Allah! Cause me to realize, by You, a realization that will remove all connections, degrees, visualizations, contemplations, reflections, assumptions and imaginations, to the point that there will be no place, modality, subject, knowledge, description, rest, perception; being consumed with You by the destruction of duality and otherness, by my realization in You from the point of view that You are as You are and how You are, whereas there is no number and no expression except You, by You, for You, on behalf of You and from You, that I may be exclusively for You, standing for You, returning to You, going in You by removing all indications and associations. And make me in all of that preserved by Your concern for me, Your taking me as a friend, Your choosing me and Your helping me. Amin.

It is recited forty times consecutively or divided between the times of the obligatory prayers. This supplication is for those who are isolated to Allah ﷻ.

And among his supplications ﷺ is "The Recital of Humble Entreaty, Prayer, and Knocking on the Door of the Exalted King." He said ﷺ:

Recite first the *Fatihah* after invoking the name of Allah and seeking refuge in Him once, and then *Salat al-Fatihi* once. Then say:

إِلَهِي وَسَيِّدِي وَمَوْلاَيَ، هَذَا مَقَامُ الْمُعْتَرِفِ بِكَثْرَةِ ذُنُوبِهِ وَعِصْيَانِهِ وَسُوءِ فِعْلِهِ وَعَدَمِ مُرَاعَاتِ أَدَبِهِ، حَالِي لاَ يَخْفَى عَلَيْكَ، وَهَذَا ذُلِّي ظَاهِرٌ بَيْنَ يَدَيْكَ، وَلاَ عُذْرَ لِي فَأُبْدِيهِ لَدَيْكَ، وَلاَ حُجَّةَ لِي فِي دَفْعِ مَا ارْتَكَبْتُهُ مِنْ مَنَاهِيكَ وَعَدَمِ طَاعَتِكَ،

وَقَدِ ارْتَكَبْتُ مَا ارْتَكَبْتُهُ غَيْرَ جَاهِلٍ بِعَظَمَتِكَ وَجَلاَلِكَ وَسَطْوَةِ كِبْرِيَائِكَ، وَلاَ غَافِلٍ عَنْ شِدَّةِ عِقَابِكَ وَعَذَابِكَ، وَلَقَدْ عَلِمْتُ أَنِّي مُعْتَرِضٌ بِذَلِكَ لِسَخَطِكَ وَغَضَبِكَ، وَلَسْتُ فِي ذَلِكَ مُضَادًّا لَكَ وَلاَ مُعَانِدًا وَلاَ مُتَصَاغِرًا بِعَظَمَتِكَ وَجَلاَلِكَ وَلاَ مُتَهَاوِنًا بِعِزِّكَ وَكِبْرِيَائِكَ وَلَكِنْ غَلَبَتْ عَلَيَّ شَقْوَتِي وَأَحْدَقَتْ بِي شَهَوَتِي فَارْتَكَبْتُ مَا ارْتَكَبْتُهُ عَجْزًا

عَنْ مُدَافَعَةِ شَهَوَاتِي، فَحُجَّتُكَ عَلَيَّ ظَاهِرَةٌ وَحُكْمُكَ فِي نَافِذٌ، وَلَيْسَ لِضَعْفِي مَنْ يَنْصُرُنِي مِنْكَ غَيْرُكَ، وَأَنْتَ العَفُوُّ الكَرِيمُ وَالبَرُّ الرَّحِيمُ الَّذِي لاَ تُخَيِّبُ سَائِلاً وَ لاَ تَرُدُّ قَاصِدًا، وَأَنَا مُتَذَلِّلٌ لَكَ مُتَضَرِّعٌ لِجَلاَلِكَ مُسْتَمْطِرٌ جُودَكَ وَنَوَالَكَ، مُسْتَعْطِفًا لِعَفْوِكَ وَرَحْمَتِكَ،

فَأَسْأَلُكَ بِمَا أَحَاطَ بِهِ عِلْمُكَ مِنْ عَظَمَتِكَ وَجَلاَلِكَ وَكَرَمِكَ وَمَجْدِكَ، وَبِمَرْتَبَةِ أُلُوهِيَتِكَ الجَامِعَةِ لِجَمِيعِ صَفَاتِكَ وَأَسْمَائِكَ، أَنْ تَرْحَمَ ذُلِّي وَفَقْرِي وَتَبْسُطَ رِدَاءَ عَفْوِكَ وَحِلْمِكَ وَكَرَمِكَ وَمَجْدِكَ عَلَى كُلِّ مَا أَحَاطَ بِهِ عِلْمُكَ مِمَّا أَنَا مُتَّصِفٌ بِهِ مِنَ المَسَاوِي وَالمُخَالَفَاتِ، وَعَلَى كُلِّ مَا فَرَّطْتُ فِيهِ مِنْ حُقُوقِكَ، فَإِنَّكَ أَكْرَمُ مَنْ وَقَفَ بِبَابِهِ السَّائِلُونَ، وَأَنْتَ أَوْسَعُ مَجْدًا وَفَضْلاً مِنْ جَمِيعِ مَنْ مُدَّتْ إِلَيْهِ أَيْدِي الفُقَرَاءِ المُحْتَاجِينَ، وَكَرَمُكَ أَوْسَعُ وَمَجْدُكَ أَكْبَرُ وَأَعْظَمُ مِنْ أَنْ يَمُدَّ إِلَيْكَ فَقِيرٌ يَدَهُ يَسْتَمْطِرُ عَفْوَكَ وَحِلْمَكَ عَنْ ذُنُوبِهِ وَمَعَاصِيهِ فَتَرُدَّهُ خَائِبًا،

فَاغْفِرْ لِي، وَارْحَمْنِي، وَاعْفُ عَنِّي، فَإِنَّمَا سَأَلْتُكَ مِنْ حَيْثُ أَنْتَ لِاتِّصَافِكَ بِعُلُوِّ الكَرَمِ وَالمَجْدِ وَعُلُوِّ عَفْوٍ وَالحِلْمِ وَالحَمْدِ، إِلَهِي لَوْ كَانَ سُؤَالِي مِنْ حَيْثُ أَنَا لَمْ أَتَوَجَّهْ إِلَيْكَ وَلَمْ أَقِفْ بِبَابِكَ لِعِلْمِي بِمَا أَنَا عَلَيْهِ مِنْ كَثْرَةِ المَسَاوِي وَالمُخَالَفَاتِ، فَلَمْ يَكُنْ جَزَائِي فِي ذَلِكَ إِلاَّ الطَّرْدُ وَاللَّعْنُ وَالبُعْدُ، وَلَكِنِّي سَأَلْتُكَ مِنْ حَيْثُ أَنْتَ، مُعْتَمِدًا عَلَى مَا أَنْتَ

عَلَيْهِ مِنْ صِفَةِ الـمَجْدِ وَالكَرَمِ وَالعَفْوِ وَالـحِلْمِ، وَلَمَّا وَسَمْتَ بِهِ نَفْسَكَ مِنَ الـحَيَاءِ عَلَى لِسَانِ رَسُولِكَ صَلَّى اللهُ عَلَيْهِ وَسَلَّمَ أَنْ تُمَدَّ إِلَيْكَ يَدُ فَقِيرٍ فَتَرُدَّهَا صَفْرَاءَ،

وَإِنَّ ذُنُوبِي وَإِنْ عَظُمَتْ وَأَرْبَتْ عَلَى الـحَصْرِ وَالعَدَدِ فَلاَ نِسْبَةَ لَهَا فِي سَعَةِ كَرَمِكَ وَعَفْوِكَ، وَلاَ تَكُونُ نِسْبَتُهَا فِي كَرَمِكَ مِقْدَارَ مَا تَبْلُغُ هَبَاءَةٌ مِنْ عَظَمَةِ كَوْرَةِ العَالَمِ، فَبِحَقِّ كَرَمِكَ وَمَجْدِكَ وَعَفْوِكَ وَحِلْمِكَ اللَّوَاتِي جَعَلْتُهُنَّ وَسِيلَةً فِي اسْتِمْطَارِي لِعَفْوِكَ وَغُفْرَانِكَ اعْفُ عَنِّي وَاغْفِرْ لِي بِفَضْلِكَ وَعَفْوِكَ، وَإِنْ كُنْتُ لَسْتُ أَهْلاً لِذَلِكَ فَإِنَّكَ أَهْلُ أَنْ تَعْفُوَ عَمَّنْ لَيْسَ أَهْلاً لِعَفْوِكَ وَكَرَمِكَ، فَأَنْتَ أَهْلُ أَنْ تَمْحُوَ فِي كُلِّ طَرَفَةِ عَيْنٍ جَمِيعَ مَا لِـمَخْلُوقَاتِكَ مِنْ جَمِيعِ الـمَعَاصِي وَالذُّنُوبِ، يَا مَجِيدُ يَا كَرِيمُ يَا عَفُوُّ يَا رَحِيمُ، يَا ذَا الفَضْلِ العَظِيمِ وَالطَّوْلِ الجَسِيمِ

My God, my Master, my Director, this is the standing before You of one who recognizes the numerousness of his sins, his disobedience, and evil deeds, as well as his never observing proper conduct. My state is not hidden from You. And this weakness is manifest in front of You. And I have no excuse to put forth to You, nor any evidence that can ward off what I have committed of those things You have prohibited And my consummate disobedience to You.

I committed what I committed without being ignorant of Your greatness and majesty, nor being ignorant of the power of Your grandeur, nor being unaware of Your calling to account and punishment. And I knew that I would be cast by that into Your anger and wrath. But I was not opposing You, nor being rebellious, nor belittling Your greatness and majesty, nor being indifferent to Your honor and grandeur. Rather, my wretchedness overtook me and my desires spoiled me, so I committed what I committed, being unable to push back my desires. Thus, Your evidence is manifest upon me, and Your decree has been affected upon me. And there is no one to assist me against my weakness except You. And You are the One who Pardons, the Generous, the Kind, the Merciful, who does not reject any request, nor frustrate any objective, while I am lowering myself to You, humbling myself before Your majesty, requesting Your generosity and favor, and attaching myself to Your pardon and mercy.

And I ask You by what Your knowledge encompasses of Your greatness, majesty, generosity and illustriousness, and by the degree of Your divinity, which gathers all of Your attributes and names, that You have mercy upon my lowliness and neediness and that You extend the robe of your pardon, forbearance, and illustriousness upon all of what Your knowledge encompasses of my attributes of disobedience and defiance, and upon all of my violations of Your rights.

Indeed, You are the most generous of those at whose doors the beggars stand. And You are the grandest in illustriousness and grace of those towards whom the needy, impoverished ones stretch forth their hands. And Your generosity is more encompassing, and Your Illustriousness is greater and grander than that the impoverished one should stretch forth his hand towards You, requesting Your pardon and forbearance for his sins and disobedience, and that You should reject him and frustrate him. So forgive me, have mercy on me and pardon me. I have asked You on Your behalf, due to Your being attributed with exalted generosity and illustriousness, and exalted forgiveness, forbearance, and praise.

My God! If my asking had been on my behalf, I would not have turned towards You, nor would I have stood at Your door, due to my knowledge of my numerous disobediences and transgressions. So my response in that would not be anything other than being rejected, cursed and cast out. However, I have asked You on Your behalf, depending upon Your attributes of illustriousness, generosity, pardoning, forbearance and due to the way that You have described Yourself upon the tongue of Your Messenger ﷺ, that You are too shy that any impoverished person should stretch forth his hands towards You, and that You should send it back empty.

And my sins, even though they are great and have reached the point where it is impossible to number or measure, it is not comparable to the grandness of Your generosity and pardoning. And its comparison to Your generosity would not even reach that of a speck of dust against the greatness of the universe. So by the right of Your generosity, illustriousness, pardon, and forbearance, which You have made a means of seeking Your pardon and forgiveness, pardon and forgive me by Your grace and pardon. And if I am not worthy of that, then You are certainly capable of pardoning the one who is not worthy of Your forgiveness and generosity. For You are capable of erasing, at every blinking of an eye, all of the sins and disobedience of all of the creation. O, Illustrious One! O, Generous One! O, Pardoner! O, Most Merciful! O, Possessor of Great Grace and Vast Eminence."

Then recite *Salat al-Fatihi* once.

Then he said ﷺ:

The most appropriate time to turn towards Him with this supplication is in the last third of the night. That is because it is a time in which the rejection of Allah ﷻ has been distanced. And it is also appropriate to recite it during the times when it is known that Allah accepts supplications. And he ﷺ gave authorization for its recital to all those who can recite it in an excellent manner.

And it is imperative if one supplicates with this supplication that he gather his aspirations. Our Master ﷺ said:

The aspiration of the human being is more powerful than anything else in the universe when he connects it to an objective and concentrates in seeking that objective with complete seriousness. For he will not attain his objective by showing half-heartedness, nor retreating from seeking it, nor by finding its pursuit too difficult- and he will not attain it by doubting or returning from it. Rather, if he believes completely that he will attain it or will die seeking it, he will attain his objective, even if it is above the Throne.

He has other supplications. However, we will not mention them at length, since they are many. And whoever wishes to obtain them should look for them in their place. And we ended this section with these blessed supplications, hoping from Allah that He allow us to benefit from them. Amin.

www.ingramcontent.com/pod-product-compliance
Lightning Source LLC
Chambersburg PA
CBHW031102080526
44587CB00011B/780